Changing our
Secondary Schools

NZCER PRESS
New Zealand Council for Educational Research
PO Box 3237
Wellington
New Zealand

© Bali Haque, 2014

ISBN 978-1-927231-47-0
All rights reserved
A catalogue record for this book is available from the
National Library of New Zealand

Designed by Book Design Ltd (www.bookdesign.co.nz)
Distributed by NZCER Distribution Services
PO Box 3237
Wellington
New Zealand
www.nzcer.org.nz

Cover concept: Cara Haque, Sue Plyler and Thomas Wynne

Changing our Secondary Schools

Bali Haque

NZCER PRESS

Contents

Acknowledgements ix

About the author x

Preface xi

Part 1: Looking for quality 1

Chapter 1: How good are we? 3
   Introduction 3
   Are PISA data valid? 4
   School decile and NCEA achievement data 10
   Ethnicity and NCEA achievement data 12
   Concluding comments 13

Chapter 2: More about the deciles 15
   Calculating deciles 15
   Deciles are not averages 16
   Decile and school funding 18
   School decile and school population 19
   School decile and school ethnicity 21
   Concluding comments 23

Chapter 3: Do schooling and teaching matter? 24
   Cultural capital 24
   Cultural capital and New Zealand Māori 26
   The impact of cultural capital and socioeconomic status on achievement 27
   In-school and between-school differences in achievement 29
   Socioeconomics or schools and teachers? 32
   Concluding comments 35

Chapter 4: School effectiveness 38
   The school effectiveness movement 38
   Effective school research methodologies 39
   OECD PISA effectiveness judgements 43
   The ERO perspective on quality 43
   Using proven teaching strategies: a different perspective on quality 46
   Shifting the focus to the quality of the teacher 48

Teaching as inquiry	49
Concluding comments	52

Chapter 5: Measuring quality in schools — 55
- Introduction — 55
- NCEA data — 55
- ERO and differentiated reviews — 61
- Are low-decile schools underperforming? — 66
- Problems with the ERO review process — 67
- Concluding comments — 69

PART 2: Educational reform in New Zealand: What goes wrong? — 71

Chapter 6: Tomorrow's Schools — 73
- Introduction — 73
- Background — 73
- Has the Tomorrow's Schools reform achieved its objectives? — 78
- The reform process — 82
- Concluding comments — 87

Chapter 7: NCEA — 88
- Background — 88
- Rolling out the new achievement standards — 94
- Policy and implementation issues — 99
- NCEA: The reform process — 107
- Concluding comments — 119

Chapter 8: The New Zealand Curriculum 2007 — 120
- Background — 120
- Did *NZC* achieve its purpose? — 131
- The reform process — 135
- Concluding comments — 140

Chapter 9: National Standards — 142
- Background — 142
- Have the new literacy and numeracy standards achieved the desired objectives? — 145
- The reform process — 148
- Concluding comments — 153

PART 3: Problems with the Ministry of Education, the PPTA and principals — 155

Chapter 10: The Ministry of Education — 156
Introduction — 156
Poor policy development — 157
Poor implementation — 160
Leadership issues — 165
Poor support for teaching and teachers — 170
Concluding comments — 176

Chapter 11: The Post Primary Teachers' Association — 177
Introduction — 177
Teacher competence — 177
Teacher pay and performance — 179
Teacher workload — 182
Teachers who spend too much time *not* teaching — 185
Concluding comments — 186

Chapter 12: Secondary school principals — 187
Two principals' organisations — 187
Principals are overwhelmed by their jobs — 189
Principals behave badly in a competitive environment — 192
Concluding comments — 196

PART 4: Future pathways — 197

Chapter 13: Socioeconomic status matters: Address economic and social disparities — 199

Chapter 14: Find new tools to measure school effectiveness — 202
Publishing league tables — 202
Publishing useful and valid achievement data — 204
Concluding comments — 214

Chapter 15: Focus on teacher support and professional development — 215
Introduction — 215
Attracting the top tier to teaching — 216
Concluding comments — 235

Chapter 16: Improve the selection and training of school leaders   236
    Introduction   236
    Principal appointments and performance management   238
    Principals' appointment, training and support   239
    Concluding comments   244

Chapter 17: Ensure that reform is well planned, implemented, evaluated and supported   246
    Improving the quality of policy advice   246
    The government must change the way schools are structured and reduce their number   250
    The school decile system   254
    Bulk funding of teachers' salaries and resourcing   255
    Concluding comments   257

End note   259

Index   260

References   267

Further reading   273

Acknowledgements

Thanks to…

Calum Gilmour who assessed the original manuscript, Ray Prebble who copyedited the book with such professionalism, and also David Ellis of NZCER Press who provided advice and guidance, and is the person who has been prepared to take something of a risk with a new author such as myself.

Judie Alison, who critiqued an early draft of this book and gave me feedback with tact, force and her usual thoughtful and incisive logic. I do wish to record my appreciation of her professionalism and complete dedication to the teaching profession.

Rose Hipkins and Jessica Le Bas, who also took the time to read early drafts and give me advice and encouragement.

Michael Johnston and Jim Strachan who read sections and provided detailed comments and asked pointed questions.

Neil Couch, Camilla Highfield, Al Kirk, Karl Mutch, Sheryl Ofner, Bill Shortis and Tony Turnock, all of whom had quite detailed conversations with me about different aspects of the book or who read drafts and provided critiques.

Daniel and Tobias who both took the time to look at early drafts and bring me down to earth whilst at the same time providing me with lots of encouragement.

Cara, my partner in all things who engaged with me in hours of sometimes heated conversation, read numerous drafts, and accepted by "mental" absence at weekends for a considerable period of time.

It should be made clear that the views expressed in this book are entirely my own.

About the author

Bali Haque is a career educator. He has led successful change in four secondary schools ranging in size from 650 to 2200 students. At the end of 2014 he completed a 3-year assignment leading the National College in Rarotonga. He has been an executive member of the PPTA and President of the Secondary Principals' Association of New Zealand and regards himself as a supporter of both organizations.

As a teacher, head of department, and secondary principal Bali was often been called on to work with the Ministry of Education and NZQA on matters relating to a wide variety of educational issues, the most important being in the development of NCEA, of which he has always been a high profile supporter.

In 2006 Bali joined the NZQA as a Deputy Chief executive responsible for the NCEA. In this role he had significant responsibility for rolling out a suite of reforms to the qualification which were widely welcomed by the sector as addressing major ongoing concerns.

His various roles in the sector over many years have allowed Bali to build strong connections not only with teachers, principals, and parents throughout New Zealand, but also senior public servants, and education ministers in Wellington.

Preface

This book will be of interest to parents, teachers, principals, government officials and even politicians. It is based on the premise that although our secondary schools are already good by international standards, they have the capacity to be great. I suspect it will upset lots of people. I can assure you that the analysis is as honest as I can make it and the proposals for further debate in Part 4 as sensible as I can think of.

As someone who has led four secondary schools, been an executive member of the Post Primary Teachers' Association, National President of the Secondary Principals' Association of New Zealand (SPANZ) and Deputy Chief Executive of the New Zealand Qualifications Authority in Wellington, I hope that the multiple perspectives I bring will provide readers with food for thought and inspiration for taking action, particularly in the secondary school sector.

The book is divided into four parts.

Part 1 explores what we mean by quality in schooling, and shows that though making judgements about schooling systems—internationally and within New Zealand—is problematic, one thing is clear: New Zealand, while performing relatively well, has a significant problem of educational disparity, which if not addressed could rapidly consign the country to a has-been status within a generation.

The extent to which schools and teachers can reasonably be expected to address this problem of disparity is discussed, and some conclusions are drawn about the important part schools and teachers *can* and *cannot* play in improving student achievement outcomes.

Given the importance of schooling and teachers in addressing these issues, Part 1 ends with a discussion about how we might go about identifying quality in schooling, and to what extent we can sensibly compare schools with each other to make judgements about their quality.

Part 2 examines some relatively recent educational reforms aimed at improving the quality of our schooling (Tomorrow's Schools, the National Certificate of Educational Achievement (NCEA), the revised *New Zealand Curriculum* and National Standards) and comes to a worrying conclusion: despite millions of dollars of expenditure and major reform efforts, none of the reforms have been as successful as one might have hoped. One important reason for these continued failures is made clear: as each reform has been rolled out, the *same*—sometimes catastrophic—mistakes have been made, again, and again, and again.

Part 3 explains why politicians, the Ministry of Education, the Post Primary Teachers' Association and school leaders all need to take some responsibility for this unfortunate situation.

Part 4 provides an integrated and radical set of proposals for debate and further analysis, which might begin to address the problems highlighted in Parts 1, 2 and 3, and thus improve the quality of our schooling system.

Given that there is an intent here to build and develop an argument for reform and change, it is best if the book is read from the beginning to the end. However, the various chapters could be read on their own, or skimmed if desired, depending on the particular interests of the reader.

Bali Haque, October 2014

Part 1: Looking for quality

How well we educate our children is of interest to most people. As parents, we are keen to ensure that our children attend good schools, and as citizens we know that education is an investment in the future of the nation. This is why the search for quality in education attracts so much interest.

When the results from international tests are published, such as those for the 2012 OECD PISA[1] reading, mathematics and science tests for 15-year-olds, many of us analyse the results and our placing on the published league tables as if they were our own personal examination results.

Similarly, in New Zealand the National Certificate of Educational Achievement (NCEA) league tables draw much attention when they are published each year, and many of us avidly search out the latest Education Review Office[2] (ERO) report about a school and read this very carefully. Both NCEA results and ERO reports are used to make judgements about the quality of a school.

In Part 1 of this book I will question the extent to which the judgements we make about the quality of New Zealand schooling in general, and of individual schools, based on this evidence are valid or helpful.

---

1 Organisation for Economic Co-operation and Development Programme for International Student Assessment.

2 The Education Review Office is a government department charged with reporting publicly on the quality of education in all New Zealand schools and early childhood centres.

How much attention should we pay to international PISA test results, or NCEA results, or ERO reports? What do these data really tell us about how good our schooling system is and how well individual schools within the system are doing compared with one another?

As part of this discussion I will examine the impact of family background on student achievement and ask to what extent this determines how well a student can do at school, and how much difference schools and teachers can really make. As part of this discussion I will explain how our current decile system works and how it is badly misused to compare schools.

Finally, I will review various ways we can make judgements about the quality of a school, and conclude that currently in New Zealand this is a very difficult thing to do with any degree of accuracy or certainty.

Chapter 1: How good are we?

Introduction

New Zealand schools are the envy of many overseas. The vast majority of parents and students in New Zealand support their schools and think they are doing a good job. We have a well-regarded national curriculum and qualifications framework, and New Zealanders are often sought after overseas in competitive job markets.

By and large, internationally administered PISA tests support this positive view of our education system. The latest testing of around 5,000 randomly selected New Zealand 15-years-olds across 177 schools in July 2012 came to the conclusion that our scores in mathematics, reading and science were above the OECD average in tests that covered 65 countries and around 500,000 students. The tests were a mixture of open-ended and multiple-choice questions, and were intended to assess students' understanding of basic concepts by solving real-life problems. They were not directly related to the curricula of the countries concerned, but rather designed to evaluate the ability of the students to apply knowledge to solve problems in real-life contexts.

All the tests are administered every 3 years with a different primary focus. For example in 2000 the focus was on reading, in 2003 on mathematics and problem solving, in 2006 on science, in 2009 on reading again, and in 2012 the focus was again on mathematics.

The good news, as stated above, is that New Zealand scores well above the OECD averages. The bad news, however, is that we have dropped in the country rankings since the last tests in 2009. In reading we dropped from 7th to 13th, in science we dropped from 7th to 18th, and in mathematics we dropped from 13th to 23rd.

It is not just a matter of falling rankings, however. According to the PISA test results we are a country with "low equity". This means that the gap between students from poorer, lower socioeconomic status (SES) homes and better-off, higher SES homes is relatively large.[1] What is more, according to the OECD, it is our Māori and Pasifika students on average who score below the OECD average.

It is this *equity gap*, it could be argued, which presents any current or future New Zealand government with its most serious and persistent educational, social and economic problem. This problem—potentially, at least—is made worse by the fact that the proportion of Māori and Pasifika students in the population is growing.

Are PISA data valid?

The OECD is confident that the results of its testing in New Zealand and globally are accurate and robust, and that governments should therefore *take notice*. Using the data it collects from questionnaires filled in by principals and students, and its own research, it produces six volumes of findings and policy advice, and makes the following claim:

> PISA is not only an accurate indicator of students' abilities to participate fully in society after compulsory school, but is also a powerful tool that countries and economies can use to fine-tune their education policies. There is no single combination of policies and practices that will work for everyone, everywhere. Every country has room for improvement, even the top performers. That's why the OECD produces this triennial report on the state of education across the globe: to share evidence of the best policies and practices and to offer our timely and targeted

---

1 PISA researchers identify students as low, middle and high SES by way of a questionnaire given to students, which asks them about their parents' occupations and their access to educational resources and possessions. Four SES categories are created (from the lowest 25 percent to the highest 25 percent) and the scores of students in these categories are then recorded.

support to help countries provide the best education possible for all of their students. (OECD, 2012)

There is little doubt that governments *do* take notice, particularly if the rankings are dropping, as they have done for New Zealand. Poor results in Germany and England in 2009, for example, resulted in national soul searching and significant policy responses in both countries.

In New Zealand, after the publication of the 2012 results, the *New Zealand Herald* headline of 7 December 2012 referred to the "education debacle" revealed by the test results, and this was typical of much of the initial response of many journalists, union officials, politicians and even academics, who were quick to lay blame and ask for immediate remedial action. Suggestions included dumping the national literacy and numeracy standards, getting rid of NCEA, putting teachers on performance pay, setting up more charter schools, and establishing a national commission to reconsider the aims and purposes of education.

However, before New Zealand rushes headlong into a panic-stricken round of educational reforms based on the PISA 2012 results, it is worth noting that the OECD test has its critics. For example, Ofqual, the English exam watchdog, disputed the reliability of the 2009 data:

> The 'horse race' approach to the rankings produced by international studies—looking to see which position England is placed in and whether or not it has moved up or down the league tables—is not that meaningful, partly because the absolute differences in scores between countries are not that great and partly because the constituent group of comparators changes from study to study and from year to year. Overall, and over time ... it cannot be assumed that the findings provide a definitive answer about which learners are the highest performing. (Stewart, 2011)

Dr Hugh Morrison, of Queen's University Belfast, also provides pause for thought:

> There are very few things you can summarize with a number and yet Pisa claims to be able to capture a country's entire education system in just three of them (reading, writing and science tests scores). It can't be possible. It is madness. (Morrison, 2013)

For another thing, PISA results do not always correlate well with other international tests, such as the Trends in Mathematical and Science Study (TIMSS) tests in maths and science for younger children, which tend to focus more directly on curriculum subject knowledge than PISA tests do. The fact that two international tests can produce "wildly contradictory results" (Hughes, 2013) probably suggests we should take the results of neither as being entirely accurate.

So what is the basis for these concerns? One very big problem is that the processing of the test results to produce the rankings takes place in a 'black box'. The statistical models used are complex, and very few people actually have the technical expertise to understand them. In the final analysis, teachers, educational bureaucrats, government policy makers, politicians and the public have to agree to *trust* the OECD statisticians and the test writers, or not, as the case may be. This is not a satisfactory position to be in, given that the results of these tests are of such critical importance for governments and could easily drive their future educational reform agendas. However, it is only possible to provide a brief and generalised outline of the debate here.

PISA comparisons are not based on one common test, which all students take

Svend Kreiner of the University of Copenhagen points out that different students are tested using different combinations of questions. Furthermore, as we have seen, each PISA round has a focus on *one* major area. In 2009 it was reading and in 2012 it was mathematics. In PISA 2006 about half the participating students were not asked *any* questions on reading and half were not tested at all in mathematics, although full rankings were produced for both subjects. Science, the main focus of PISA that year, was the only subject that all participating students were tested on. According to Kreiner, only about 10 percent of the students who took part in PISA were tested on all 28 reading questions. What is more:

> Eight of the 28 reading questions used in Pisa 2006 were deleted from the final analysis in some countries. The OECD says that this was because they were considered to be 'dodgy' and 'had poor psychometric properties in a particular country'. However,

in other countries the data from these questions did contribute to their Pisa scores. (Stewart, 2013)

OECD officials are not at all concerned about this. In fact much of this critical information is in their own technical reports, which are available on their website. Some of the justification for this apparent flaw is based on a widely used statistical method, called the Rasch Model, which provides a way to calculate "plausible values" for students who did not actually answer the questions.

The key point the OECD statisticians make here is that this modelling of answers is perfectly acceptable and accurate, using the Rasch scaling method, because they are attempting to measure the performance of a system (a country, or a region) as a whole, *not* particular individuals. Since individual students' results are not reported, it is perfectly acceptable to use scaling models to predict what these students would plausibly have got. According to the OECD's Schleicher:

> Pisa has convincingly and conclusively shown that the design of the tests and the scaling model used to score those lead to robust measures of country performance that are not affected by the composition of the item pool. (Schleicher, 2013)

This explanation does not convince the critics, though, who question whether the (Rasch) model has been properly used. For example, a condition of its use is that all questions must be *equally difficult* for all candidates. Given the enormous diversity that exists across 65 participating countries, this will be a challenge for any attempting to write the test. The OECD response makes clear that considerable trialling was done for all questions, and that "dodgy" questions were weeded out.

PISA tests are culturally biased

Harvey Goldstein, professor of social statistics at the University of Bristol, has argued that the tests are culturally biased. This apparent cultural bias is what caused India to withdraw from the testing programme after a disastrous showing in 2009. Its education ministry claimed that the topics covered in PISA questions were particularly difficult for students in rural areas of the country.

Certainly the massive disparity of cultural and economic conditions across the countries involved does raise questions about whether just one test instrument can possibly provide really reliable data on the quality of the schooling as a snapshot once every 3 years, let alone over 6 or 9 years. However, the OECD view is that this is one very important reason why all countries do *not* use exactly the same questions. Those questions that, as a result of testing, are found to be culturally biased are simply removed from the country in which they are biased. The absence of these questions, the OECD claims, does not mean that plausible results cannot be calculated using the accepted scaling model.

In fact, according to the OECD, having exactly the same questions for all countries could well lead to a set of questions that fails to properly test the strengths and weaknesses of each country, and would only test the lowest common denominator across all countries and fail to identify the nuances and differences in performance between different countries.

In the case of both the above debates (that the same tests are not administered to all students and that they are culturally biased), Professor Kreiner has argued that the substitution of some questions used by one country and not by another can lead to very significant changes in the final outcomes, scores, and rankings, and that therefore these outcomes scores and rankings are worthless.

PISA tests should not be used to measure performance over time

Goldstein also points out that PISA tests a *different* group of 15-year-olds every 3 years. Since it is a different group of students, differences in achievement rates could be explained by a range of factors that could have little to do with the education system. For example, differences in achievement rates might be explained by changes in a range of social and economic factors affecting the particular group of students being tested at a particular time.

Rankings are misleading

According to the OECD itself, the rankings allocated to countries are not as finely tuned as is implied by their published league tables. Because of the scaling methods employed and the use of 'plausible' values, the OECD warns that there is a "small inaccuracy" in ranking. For example, a country with a top ranking might actually be ranked second or third. Given this, we should not be too concerned about small changes in rankings over time. However, according to the OECD, New Zealand's drops in the 2012 PISA rankings are significant and substantial, and certainly beyond a "small inaccuracy."

The equity gap, especially the ethnicity gap, is not as significant as is claimed

According to a Massey University report (Snook, O'Neill, Church, & Rawlins, 2013), the argument from the OECD that New Zealand's equity gap is larger than in most other countries is misleading. These authors argue that although a large gap does exist, it is a result of our high-achieving students doing better than those in most other countries. Therefore, the New Zealand equity gap is a result of our top-end students doing particularly well, rather than our less able students doing particularly badly. In fact, according to the authors, our bottom-end students are roughly on a par with those in other similar countries.

From another angle, Brian Easton argues that the *ethnicity* differences the PISA points to may not be as serious as suggested because the students who sit the tests are asked to *self-select* their ethnicity. According to Easton, this is not a particularly objective way to measure ethnicity differences:

> Students were asked their ethnicity. It is a self-categorization and is not an objective measure. It may even have a different meaning for boys and girls; it is possible that an individual's ethnic choice is influenced by educational achievement.

Even if this potential problem is ignored, Easton goes on to argue that the ethnicity gap is not as serious in New Zealand as is painted by some because it is significantly influenced by socioeconomic status:

> The group of those who describe themselves as either sole Maori or Maori and Pakeha score lower than the OECD average. *When their scores are adjusted for socioeconomic status* they are very near the OECD average. They may be said to be in receipt of an 'OECD average education'. (Easton, 2013a, emphasis added)

According to this argument, ethnicity is conflated with socioeconomic status (SES), and proportionately more Māori students perform poorly in PISA tests largely because of their SES status, not their ethnicity.

School decile and NCEA achievement data

NCEA achievement data are based on *The New Zealand Curriculum*, and the assessment processes used for NCEA are completely different from those used for PISA. NCEA cannot, therefore, be used to make any international comparisons. However, the data can shed some light on the New Zealand domestic equity issue, highlighted by the PISA results, which showed that New Zealand is a country with low equity, based on both socioeconomic and ethnicity factors.

One way of doing this is to examine the relationship between school decile and achievement, whereby we use school decile as a proxy for SES.[2] Broadly speaking, the higher the decile of a school, the higher the SES of many students at the school; the lower the decile, the lower the SES of many of the students at the school.

Looking at the NCEA data in relation to the decile rating of schools, we discover that:

- 51.3 percent of the students who began Year 11 in 2011 in decile 1–3 schools achieved NCEA Level 2 in 2012
- 64.0 percent of the students who began Year 11 in 2011 in decile 4–7 schools achieved NCEA Level 2 in 2012
- 77.8 percent of the students who began Year 11 in 2011 in decile 8–10 schools achieved NCEA Level 2 in 2012. (NZQA, 2014)

Data from the Ministry of Education show a clear correlation between decile and student achievement (see Figure 1).[3]

---

[2] Decile 1 schools are the 10 percent of schools with the highest proportion of students from low socioeconomic communities, whereas decile 10 schools are the 10 percent of schools with the lowest proportion of these students

[3] See http://www.educationcounts.govt.nz/indicators/main/education-and-learning-outcomes/1781

Chapter One: How good are we?

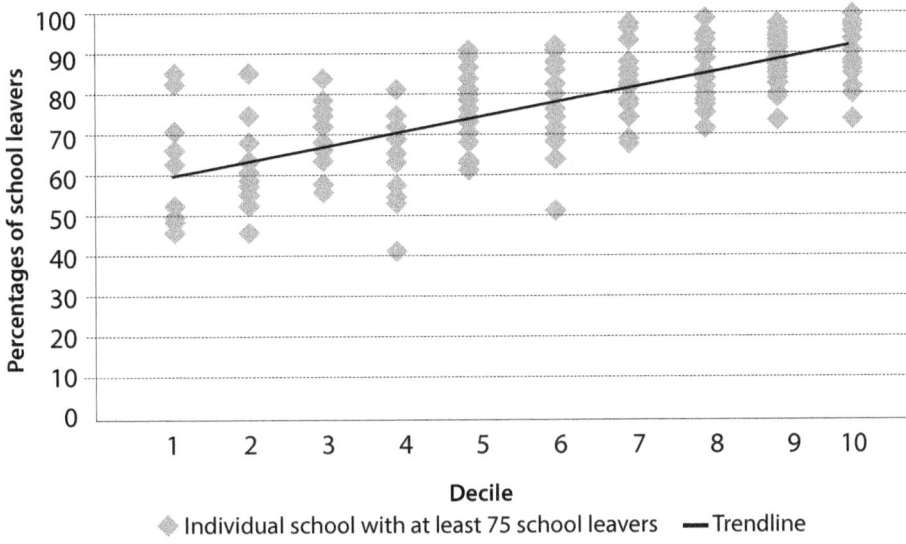

Figure 1: Percentage of school leavers with at least an NCEA Level 2 or equivalent, by school decile (2013)

According to the Ministry of Education:

> In 2013, 90 percent of students from schools in the highest deciles (deciles 9 and 10) left school with at least an NCEA Level 2 qualification. This was 31.4 percentage points higher than the percentage for school leavers in deciles 1 and 2.

The data also show there is a wide variation in achievement *within* deciles, a phenomenon we will discuss in Chapter 3.

The rates of Excellence certificate endorsement[4] at Level 2 NCEA in 2013 tell much the same story:

- 4.4 percent of students in decile 1–3 schools gained an Excellence certificate endorsement
- 10.5 percent of students in decile 4–7 schools gained an Excellence certificate endorsement
- 18.7 percent of students in decile 8–10 schools gained an Excellence certificate endorsement.

---

4 Excellence certificate endorsements are awarded to able students who gain at least 50 credits with Excellence grades.

Given all of the above, it is clear that the existence of a significant achievement gap, based on the SES factors highlighted by PISA, is clearly supported by NCEA and decile data.

Ethnicity and NCEA achievement data

Ethnicity NCEA data also confirm the PISA equity conclusions about New Zealand:

- 48.1 percent of Māori students who began Year 11 in 2011 gained NCEA Level 2 in 2012
- 53.2 percent of Pasifika students who began Year 11 in 2011 gained NCEA Level 2 in 2012
- 72.7 percent of European/Pākehā students who began Year 11 in 2011 gained NCEA Level 2 in 2012 (NZQA, 2014).

Ministry of Education data also show that "the gaps between ethnic groups are reducing slightly over time but a large achievement gap remains for Māori and Pasifika students" (see Figure 2).

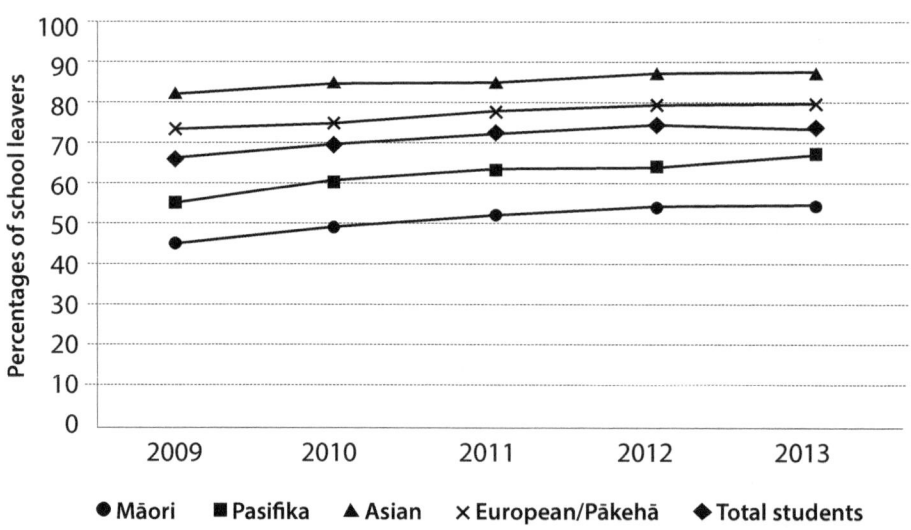

Figure 2: Percentage of school leavers with at least an NCEA Level 2 qualification or equivalent, by ethnic group (2009 to 2013). (Retrieved from www.educationcounts.govt.nz/indicators/main/education-and-learning-outcomes/1781.)

Much the same story about ethnicity is demonstrated by the proportions of certificate endorsements in 2013:

- 5.4 percent of Māori students gained a Level 2 NCEA Excellence certificate endorsement
- 3.6 percent of Pasifika students gained a Level 2 NCEA Excellence certificate endorsement
- 15.4 percent of European/Pākehā students gained a Level 2 NCEA Excellence certificate endorsement (NZQA, 2014).

Given this brief analysis of both the PISA and NCEA data, what can we reasonably conclude?

- New Zealand 15-year-old students are *not* doing as well as they have done in the past in their reading, mathematics and science, as measured by PISA, although we still score above OECD averages. Rankings, though, are quite a blunt instrument. We should be careful about trying to be too precise here.
- We have a serious achievement gap, even if we accept (the Massey University report) that the gap is partly a result of our top students doing particularly well.
- Ethnicity and SES are conflated, and the ethnicity gap may therefore be strongly influenced by socioeconomic factors. In other words, Māori and Pasifika students come overwhelmingly from low SES homes, and it is this that causes the equity gap, not ethnicity.[5]

Concluding comments

The New Zealand education system is a good-quality system. On average, we clearly do well in international tests, but we are slipping in the world rankings. More seriously, we also appear to have a significant quality problem related to equity. Both PISA and NCEA data confirm that we live in a community where educational achievement, and therefore the future success of our learners, is related strongly to their SES and ethnicity. We should note, however, that ethnicity and SES are conflated in the data. In other words, many Māori and Pasifika

---

5   NCEA data suggest that the SES–ethnicity gaps may be slowly closing. This change, though not strongly supported by the PISA data, is of course welcome, but it has stirred debates about the extent to which schools are better managing the flexibilities of NCEA to boost the NCEA results of some of their students. Of course this is what the purpose of NCEA was in the first place. This phenomenon is discussed fully in Chapter 5.

students live in homes with a low SES.

No Government can afford to walk away from this equity issue. If it is not addressed, not only do we waste valuable human resources, we also risk significant social and economic consequences, which will threaten our long-term future prospects for a better quality of life for all of our citizens.

Chapter 2: More about the deciles

Calculating deciles

As we have seen, in New Zealand we use the decile system to classify schools into 10 decile groups, based on a selection of socioeconomic characteristics of the students who attend each and every school in the country. Broadly speaking, high-decile schools have the *lowest* proportions of students with parents who are poor and poorly educated, with low-skill/low-income jobs, while low-decile schools have the *highest* proportion of students with parents who are poor and poorly educated, with low-income jobs.

Having said this, we should note that the decile of a school is not *only* about income and jobs. The specific indicators used are as follows:

1. the proportion of households with equivalent income (adjusted for the number of adults and children in the household, and the age of the children) in the lowest 20 percent nationally
2. the percentage of employed parents in occupations that are at skill levels 4 or 5 (of the 1 to 5 levels in the Australia and New Zealand Standard Classification of Occupation), which include all labourers, all machine operators and assemblers, and others who work in

occupations at these lower skill levels, irrespective of the sector or type or profession involved

3. the percentage of households with an equivalised crowding index greater than one—this index is the proportion of household members per bedroom, adjusted for the presence of children under 10, every two of whom are assigned to share a bedroom; couples, and others are each assigned their own bedroom
4. the percentage of parents with no tertiary or school qualifications
5. the percentage of parents who directly (i.e. not as a partner) received a Domestic Purposes Benefit, Unemployment Benefit or Sickness and Invalid's Benefit in the previous year, which does not include parents receiving the Family Tax Credit (Ministry of Education, 2009).

In order to calculate the decile of a school the following steps are taken (PPTA, 2013a):

- The school provides its students' addresses to the MoE and these are used to determine the "mesh blocks" these students live in. A mesh block is a group of around 50 households.
- The characteristics of the "mesh block" are examined using census data and scored against each of the five defined SES indicators.
- All schools are ranked against each other for each indicator, weighted for the number of students who live in particular mesh blocks, and then all five rankings are added up to give one overall ranking for each school in the country
- Schools are allocated a decile (1–10) according to their ranking.

Whilst this approach to calculating deciles is certainly robust, insofar as it goes, it is also misleading. In my own years as a school principal in three different New Zealand schools and as President of SPANZ, I regularly talked with experienced principals and teachers who complained that the assigned decile for their school just did not "seem right".

There are often good reasons for such misgivings.

Deciles are not averages

A decile does not indicate the *overall* socioeconomic mix of the students attending a school. It is not an average. It simply calculates the proportion of students who can be classified as coming from particular SES communities using specifically defined indicators. Put another way, the statisticians are only interested in the number of students who fit a particular profile as defined in the indicators (the number who comes from the *lowest 20% of household income*, the percentage that are at *skills level 4 and 5*, the number who live in households with an equivalised *crowding index greater than one*, the percentage who have *no school or tertiary qualification* and the proportion who are on *specified benefits*). The SES characteristics of any other students who do not fit these particular definitions are completely ignored.

This is important because it means that two schools with the same decile which have the same proportion of students who fit the specified indicators could actually have very different mixes of students *when the entire school roll is accounted for*. To put it another way: school A and school B may have exactly the same proportion of students which classifies them (say) as decile 2 schools, but school B may well have a far higher proportion of high SES students than school A, because the decile calculation takes no account of students who do not fit the defined indicators.

It is worth noting here that the calculation of the decile rating is based on very specific cut-off points. For example, in the first category, the proportion of households with equivalent income in the lowest 20 percent nationally would make no allowance for people who might be at 21 percent. A mesh block of people who did not meet the 20 percent threshold and perhaps were slightly better off at the 21 percent would score zero for this category. The same specific cut-off points would apply to overcrowding, for example, and also for definitions of occupations.

There are further complexities here: even if two schools have exactly the same SES mix of students, the nature of the students could still be very different. According to research carried out in two decile 8 schools (Alcorn & Thrupp, 2011), the nature of the middle-class families attending a school can make a huge difference to the nature of that school. Two high schools are described by the authors: Gandalf High School which serves middle class families who were often small business owners relatively well off, and 'more entrepreneurial than academic', and Tolkien High School which has a largely well-educated professional intake and prides itself on being an academic school. There are also significant differences in ethnicity between the two schools. Whereas Gandalf has a slightly greater proportion of Māori students, Tolkien has more students from Asia, Middle East, Latin America and Africa.

Such different mixes of students, with consequential difference in motivation and goals, mean that comparing schools in the same decile, even if they have exactly the same socioeconomic mix, creates significant difficulties. The research concluded that:

> Schools can serve different fractions of social class in a way that although they have intakes within the same socio-economic bracket, they are teaching ... different kinds of class-located families with different aspirations and levels and types of achievement. (Alcorn & Thrupp, 2011, pp 67–68.

Finally it is important to note that in our competitive school environment the possibilities of "school bias" can also result in misleading conclusions being drawn. For example a location with several schools within travelling distance of one another could easily draw from very similar mesh blocks, resulting in all the schools receiving similar decile ratings. However it is entirely possible that one school (maybe a single sex school or an integrated school) actually draws higher SES students than another (maybe the coeducational school). The decile ratings based on mesh blocks in such a case would not take account this possible "drift" to preferred schools by students from higher SES backgrounds even though they reside in mesh block which may contribute more to lower decile ratings.

Decile and school funding

Decile ratings were first introduced into New Zealand in 1995 as part of an attempt by the Government of the day to provide additional resources to those schools that had to cater for students who needed support and were at risk. The decile system was a mechanism for *funding* schools, and in particular, for providing 'poor' schools with more money.

For example, the 2013 targeted funding for educational achievement—decile-related funding—for Papakura High School, a decile 2 school, was $487 per student. The equivalent decile funding for

Rosehill College, a decile 6 school in the same town, was $90 per student. Pakuranga College, on the other hand, a decile 8 school, received only $45 per student, while MacLean's College, a decile 10 school in Howick, received no decile funding at all (Teddy, 2014).

In other words, higher-decile schools receive less, or no, decile funding on the grounds that schools with a very low proportion of students from low-income homes do not need targeted assistance and can tap into their own well-off communities for extra funds if they so desire. For example, in 2014 the annual 'donation' parents of Maclean's students were expected to make was $495.[1] Pakuranga College asked for $340, and Rosehill College $160. Papakura High School asked for a donation of $100.

Of course donations are not necessarily paid by all parents. The anecdotal evidence is that as well as the amounts charged being generally smaller, the actual collection rates are much lower for low-decile schools. It is also worth pointing out that higher-decile schools also tend to attract far more fee-paying international students than lower-decile schools, which can add substantially to their total income.

The point to be made here is simple enough: decile funding, to some extent anyway, is designed to provide lower-decile schools with *additional* funding, which can be used to address the *particular* problems these schools have to deal with—students from low-income, low-skills and/or overcrowded households. Higher-decile schools appear to be quite good at accessing resources from their communities and have less need for the funding.

School decile and school population

It is important to be aware that the decile system classifies *schools*, not *students*.

It is *not* true to say that 10 percent of New Zealand students attend decile 1 schools, or that 10 percent of students attend decile 10 schools. It would be a big mistake to assume this, since schools vary in size considerably. As the data below show (these data relate to all schools, not just secondary schools), there are actually far more students in high-decile schools than in low-decile schools. For example, there are more than

---

1 The donation at Auckland Grammar in 2014 was $1,050.

twice as many students in decile 10 schools than there are in decile 1 schools. The main reason for this is that decile 10 schools are considerably bigger, in terms of student population, than decile 1 schools.

Decile	Number of students
1	53,139
2	59,572
3	54,617
4	65,876
5	72,493
6	79,428
7	69,217
8	87,949
9	91,734
10	117,146
Not assigned	8,789
Total	759,960

Table 1: School decile and student population, all schools, 2013

Source: Adapted from figures retrieved from www.educationcounts.govt.nz/statistics/maori_education/schooling/6028. Note: Unassigned schools are generally private schools that do not have decile ranking.

School decile and school ethnicity

Table 2 shows the ethnicity of students who attend higher- and lower-decile schools.

Decile	European/Pākehā	Māori	Pasifika	Asian	Other	MELA	Fees	Total
1	2,623	26,557	22,227	1,378	93	250	11	53,139
2	12,828	28,812	12,791	4,022	186	817	116	59,572
3	16,553	21,046	9,555	6,026	283	993	161	54,617
4	28,915	20,308	7,735	6,819	269	1,365	465	65,876
5	42,026	18,698	4,698	5,022	292	1,196	561	72,493
6	50,336	15,736	4,226	6,451	484	1,451	744	79,428
7	44,801	11,034	3,744	6,348	426	1,362	1,502	69,217
8	61,707	11,244	3,714	7,908	593	1,565	1,218	87,949
9	61,627	9,621	3,313	12,674	723	1,910	1,866	91,734
10	84,278	7,695	2,606	16,828	929	2,534	2,276	117,146
n/d	5,346	2,260	391	269	450	57	16	8,789
Totals	411,040	173,011	75,000	73,745	4,728	13,500	8,936	759,960

Table 2: School roll, by decile and ethnicity, all schools, 1 July 2012

Source: Adapted from figures retrieved from www.educationcounts.govt.nz/statistics/maori_education/schooling/6028

Note: MELA = Middle Eastern, Latin American and African; Fees = international fee-paying students; n/d = no decile (private schools are not assigned a decile).

There are some fascinating statistics hidden in this table. For example, in 2012:

- 84,278 European/Pākehā students attended decile 10 schools, but only 2,623 attended decile 1 schools
- 48,784 Māori and Pasifika students attended decile 1 schools, but only 10,301 attended decile 10 schools
- 22,227 Pasifika students attended decile 1 schools, but only 2,606 attended decile 10 schools
- 26,557 Māori students attended decile 1 schools, but only 7,695 attended decile 10 schools

- 16,828 Asian students attended decile 10 schools, but only 1,378 attended decile 1 schools.

It is pretty clear that decile 1 schools are overwhelmingly populated by Māori (49.9 percent) and Pasifika (41.8 percent) children. European/Pākehā children feature only minimally (4.9 percent).[2] Conversely, decile 10 schools are overwhelmingly populated by European/Pākehā (71.9 percent) and Asian (14.3 percent) students, with Māori (6.5 percent) and Pacific (2.2 percent) students featuring only minimally.

All these data are interesting, but essentially they reveal what many of us are aware of already: there are lots of Māori and Pasifika students who come from low-income homes who end up in low-decile schools, while European/Pākehā and Asian students from higher-income homes end up in high-decile schools.

It is important to think about what these data actually mean, in a very practical sense. We know that decile and student achievement are related, and we also know that SES and ethnicity are conflated: in other words, many Māori and Pasifika students have low SES. This means we live in a highly stratified country which operates what can only be described as a form of educational apartheid, particularly if we compare decile 1 schools with decile 10 schools. Certainly an argument could be made that too many Māori and Pasifika students live in poor, ghettoised communities and attend increasingly stressed and ghettoised schools, while rich European/Pākehā and Asian students live in separate, well-off communities and attend privileged schools.

---

2 The situation looks slightly better if we expand our analysis to compare students who attend low-decile schools, defined as decile 1–5, and those who attend higher-decile schools, defined as decile 6–10: of the 173,011 Māori students counted, 115,421 went to decile 1–5 schools. This means that over two-thirds of our Māori students attend lower-decile schools. On the other hand, only 102,945 European/Pākehā students attended decile 1–5 schools, which is about a quarter of the total number of European/Pākehā students. The equivalent figure for our 75,000 Pasifika students is 57,006, which means that 76 percent of our Pasifika students attend decile 1–5 schools. Of the 411,046 European students counted, 308,095 went to decile 6–10 schools (plus the unassigned deciles, which generally means private schools). This means that three quarters of European/Pākehā students attend decile 6–10 schools. However, only one-third of Māori students attend decile 6–10 schools. It should be noted here that there are more students in higher-decile schools than in lower-decile schools. It should also be made clear that the percentage distributions quoted in a given decile should be examined in the context of the proportion of students of various ethnicities in the population as a whole.

Concluding comments

The decile system is rather blunt. Even calculating a school's decile is based on some fairly arbitrary methodologies. It is important that we understand that the system has very significant limitations, the most important of which is that even similar-decile schools can be very different. The decile of a school does not provide us with an *average*, or a description of the whole school community.

Having said this, it is clear that low-decile schools are populated with more Māori and Pasifika students than high-decile schools, and that there are far more students in high-decile schools than in low-decile schools. We live in divided communities, and our schools reflect these divisions.

Chapter 3: Do schooling and teaching matter?

In Chapter 1 we established that PISA and NCEA data confirm that student achievement is strongly correlated with socioeconomic background, and that we have a significant equity issue in New Zealand. The facts are clear: Māori and Pasifika students are, on average, likely to do badly at school.

Cultural capital

The French socialist Pierre Bourdieu, working in the early 1960s, argued that cultural habits and dispositions inherited from the family are critically important to school success. Aspiration and values, and the knowledge students arrive at school with, all add up to a disposition to value learning and to maximise the benefit from schooling, and as such add to the sum of *cultural capital* possessed by an individual (Sullivan, 2002).

This argument is not about traditional economic capital; it is about social habits and dispositions. For example, some families will set aspirational goals for their children, ensure that reading and writing skills are developed early in life, and attend parent–teacher interviews. They will also be alert to learning problems, be insistent on remedial action if there is a problem, and be competitive and willing to help with homework. These are the parents, *and therefore* students, with lots of cultural capital, because it is these sorts of dispositions, values and attitudes that do indeed contribute to success at school.

However, students with parents who are traditionally 'working class', such as construction workers, even plumbers and electricians, may be well off in the economic sense but may still lack cultural capital. Before readers protest, I accept that this is treacherous territory. It is entirely possible—and increasingly likely—that those with plenty of what has been defined as cultural capital are deliberately opting for these occupations because they now provide higher incomes than more traditional, middle-class occupations. Having said this, in general there *is* a link between cultural capital and economic factors, in that people on low incomes in unskilled and semi-skilled jobs will *tend* to have low cultural capital as well. To this extent, it could be argued that cultural capital and SES are strongly, though not completely, related.

Cultural capital, then, though an elusive concept, is really about a whole mix of attitudes about learning and being educated, which we might think of as being related to what we have already referred to as SES, but with the emphasis on social attitudes and social class.

We are back in treacherous territory here: it is obviously not true that those who come from disadvantaged homes do not want to learn. However, those with low cultural capital tend to come from poor and deprived homes, and they will, according to the evidence, tend to do worse in the education system because of certain attitudes and dispositions they have learnt, often from their families.

Bourdieu actually takes the argument a step further. His view is that cultural capital not only gets passed on through families and generations, but also through the very institutions of the state, including schools. According to Bourdieu, cultural capital pervades every aspect of our society and institutions.

In the case of schooling, his view is that the policy makers working in the education sector and the teachers that work in the schools are, by definition, successful people who have benefited from large dollops of cultural capital themselves. As such, those in control of our schools inevitably try to replicate their own values and ways of seeing the world. For teachers, this is inevitably reflected in their teaching styles, the content they choose, the teaching activities they select, and their judgements of, and relationships with, their students. In fact the entire institution of the school—the values it promotes, the expectations placed on students and parents, the curriculum, and the assessment methodologies—all reflect and meet the needs of only those who enter with lots of cultural capital (Tzanakis, 2011).

For those with less cultural capital, the institution of the school feels alien, unhelpful and disconnected from their actual lives and lived experiences. Taken to its logical conclusion, this argument predicts that the entire schooling system inevitably reflects the habits, dispositions and aspirations of those who control it, and therefore (and this is important), those likely to succeed in it.

Given the fact that school and consequential tertiary study success will tend to lead to higher-paid and more influential jobs (such as policy makers and teachers), the concept of cultural capital, according to Bourdieu, provides an explanation as to why the rich and powerful *stay* rich and powerful, and society effectively replicates itself—and the power relationships that hold it together—generation after generation. Put bluntly: those with cultural capital are 'doomed' to succeed in the system, and those without it, to fail.

Cultural capital and New Zealand Māori

It is worth pausing here to make clear that this interpretation of cultural capital may have some connection with the current plight of New Zealand Māori in New Zealand mainstream schools. In New Zealand, many Māori have argued strongly that schooling does not reflect the values and culture of Māori.[1] Māori, it is argued, are a colonised people who have had Western culture, and its associated economic and social values, imposed on them. Their land, so central to their own culture, has been stolen, their people gradually urbanised and their language almost lost. The way that Māori view the world, the way they learn, the way they view learning and assessment, and the way they see their important relationships with adults and others is just *different* from that of middle-class Pākehā New Zealanders.

It is this difference that provides the best explanation for why many

---

1 The use of the term 'culture' here should not be confused with Bourdieu's 'cultural capital' (though of course there will be some similarities).

Māori are not succeeding in mainstream schools, and why mainstream New Zealand schools are viewed by some as untenable and doomed to fail their children, despite the best efforts of well-intentioned Pākehā teachers.

Although this is a contentious view, it has, at least partially, been the main driver for the development of kōhanga reo, a total-immersion, Māori-language programme for young children, which, it is claimed, has so successfully raised Māori achievement. Kōhanga reo programmes have been successful, it is argued, because they have provided an appropriate cultural environment for their students.

It should be noted that some researchers, such as Professor Elizabeth Rata from Auckland University, would dispute this, arguing that it is socioeconomic forces that are at work, and that the cultural explanations are unproven (Rata, 2011). However, even in mainstream schools, much of the current focus on improving the achievement of our Māori students has been on Māori within the context of their cultural and social environments.

This argument should not be confused with Bourdieu's theory of cultural capital. Bourdieu argued that those with less cultural capital are disadvantaged, and that to succeed in the current environment they need to get more of it: without cultural capital it is difficult to learn, because a particular set of values and dispositions is required in order to succeed. The argument about Māori, as expressed above, is that that there are *different* sets of cultural capital, all of which might be considered valuable and effective depending on one's perspective. Therefore, it is the job of the school and the institutions of the state to reflect these different cultural sets rather than focus solely on the one dominant (Western) paradigm.

The impact of cultural capital and socioeconomic status on achievement

This chapter asks the question 'Do schooling and teaching matter?' If we accept Bourdieu's argument, the answer would be: "it depends". Students who are well endowed with cultural capital will be well placed to take advantage of a school system and teaching that is designed to meet their needs. However, those *not* well endowed will continue to fail because of the way the system works against them.

Is this a reasonable argument? Are we prepared to accept that schooling and all the work teachers do every day in the classroom is really of value only to those students already doomed to succeed, and that the prime determinant of educational success is largely predetermined by cultural capital and related SES factors?

We already know from Chapter 1 that the educational achievement gap in New Zealand is strongly related to socioeconomic factors, which in turn are closely related to notions of cultural capital. To this extent, anyway, there is a case to support the notion that schooling in New Zealand is not addressing the needs of those not well endowed with cultural capital and with low SES, and that therefore Bourdieu was right.

However, international evidence relating to SES (but not cultural capital specifically) provides us with a different view: some countries are better at addressing the problems associated with socioeconomic background factors than others. In other words, in some countries, schooling and teaching may have a bigger impact on lifting student achievement of those in low socioeconomic groups than in other countries. Some countries have policies in place that mitigate the impact of socioeconomic background more than others.[2] This means the SES and cultural capital 'doomed to fail' scenario may not be completely immutable, and that Bourdieu is not entirely correct.

According to the OECD PISA data, in 2009 New Zealand had the widest achievement gap (over 50 points) in reading of all OECD countries when performance of high SES students was compared with the performance of students with low SES. The figures have improved slightly since 2009, but the gap remains large. The 2012 PISA data still show that although disparity attributable to SES factors is evident in all countries, in New Zealand it appears to be wider than in many other OECD countries.

According to the New Zealand Treasury:

> the socio economic background of NZ students exerts a much larger influence on their achieving than in most other OECD countries. In other words New Zealand's education system

---

2 It should be emphasised here that these data refer to SES factors directly, and not cultural capital, although it has been argued that the two are related.

does not appear to be very good at enabling students to succeed regardless of their background. (New Zealand Treasury, 2012, p. 2)

We have already noted (see p. 9) that this equity issue is controversial, with some researchers arguing that the gap is not as large as has been portrayed by the OECD or the Treasury. The debate will no doubt continue. For our purposes it is perhaps enough to say that we do have an equity gap, the size of which is still the subject of some academic debate.

In-school and between-school differences in achievement

There is some further evidence in this regard. Both the OECD and the New Zealand Ministry of Education point out that disparities of achievement *within* schools in many countries are wider than disparities *between* schools. To spell it out: the average difference in achievement *between* low- and high-decile schools in New Zealand is smaller than the average spread of achievement *within* schools in New Zealand.

This may be important: if the variation in achievement is bigger within schools than it is between schools, it could mean that variations in achievement are related more to the variation in the quality of the teaching going on within schools than the decile of the schools. According to this logic, the SES/cultural capital predetermination argument does not entirely hold up: evidence of both high and low achievement exists within all schools, regardless of their decile. This may mean that at least some teachers in *any* school can produce students who can do well, regardless of their background.

According to the New Zealand Treasury:

Both PISA and school leaver data show that low attainment is not just confined to a few schools, or to schools serving the most disadvantaged communities, but is widely distributed across schools (although Maori, Pasifika and low socioeconomic background students are most at risk of low attainment). This suggests that all schools could do better at lifting the achievement of their lowest performing students. (New Zealand Treasury, 2012)

The fact that New Zealand has a very large in-school variation compared to many other countries could well be used to support the view that cultural capital/SES issues can be overcome. The fact that other countries (for example, Finland) have relatively small *within* school differences in achievement may indicate that these countries have found the right approaches and policies to overcome problems related to cultural capital and SES, while New Zealand clearly has not.

If we accept the arguments here, the best way to address disparity of achievement in New Zealand is to ensure that teachers and schools find better and more effective approaches and policies to support failing students.

There are, of course, opposing arguments. The variation in between-school achievement is measured on the basis of *average* achievement of the individual schools. Comparing the average performance of, say, two schools may well show a smaller difference between the two schools than the variation within each school, but this is only because we are comparing an average value across more than one school with a range of values within a particular school. The fact that *within*-school variations are larger than *between*-school variations therefore is hardly a surprise. It is, statistically speaking, a very likely scenario.

This argument does not explain why New Zealand appears to have a *wider* achievement gap than many countries. The issue is not that within-school variations are larger than between-school variations—this could be expected. What is important is the relative size of these variations.

The relatively large variation of within-school scores in New Zealand may simply reflect the fact that New Zealand has become a more unequal society than most. According to Brian Easton,

> New Zealand was 9th out of 34 in the OECD ranking of *inequality* in 2009, after adjustment for population and per capita GDP. It was about 20th in 1985, so it moved from being in the bottom half of the OECD to the top half. (Easton, 2013b) (Emphasis added.)

Furthermore, our schools are required to take *all comers*, unlike many other countries, which place students into different technical/

vocational and academic schools.³ According to this argument, New Zealand's relatively large *within*-school variation is mainly due to the fact that we are an unequal society operating a 'comprehensive' schooling system. Individual schools, regardless of decile, have to deal with a wider variety of students than most other countries.⁴

According to this argument, even though schooling and teaching are important, the major reasons for variation of achievement both within schools and between schools is largely related to socioeconomic and cultural capital factors. Bourdieu is correct after all!

If we accept this argument, the best way of overcoming achievement disparities in a country such as New Zealand is by applying more enlightened economic and social policies than are currently in place. For government to focus solely on schooling and teaching as the key instrument to address these disparities is unhelpful and misleading. Teachers and schools should not be required to work magic and fix wider societal and economic problems. Rather than complaining about school and teacher underperformance, government needs to stop abdicating its responsibility and directly address the social and economic issues that are the real root causes of poor achievement.

As an aside, it is worth pointing out here that the reverse argument is also true. Since teachers cannot entirely be blamed for the lack of achievement of their students with low SES, they cannot entirely take the credit for the achievement of their high SES students either. Students who start life with privileges and support, who attend high-decile schools and who succeed are likely to do so independently of the capabilities of their teachers. The fact of the matter is that some principals and teachers in higher-decile schools are guilty of overstating their contribution, which is generally far less significant than the contributions of family home and income.

This is a complex and ongoing debate, but there are some common-sense conclusions we can arrive at, and I discuss these below.

---

3 New Zealand also has a relatively small private school sector compared with many comparable countries.
4 New Zealand Māori and Pasifika students' underachievement may well be the source of these large variations.

Socioeconomics or schools and teachers?

There is a need for government to address the deeply rooted economic and social issues that create disadvantaged students who are more vulnerable to becoming uninterested in learning at school. There is no getting away from this fact. Simply blaming teachers and targeting schools for their poor performance will not address these issues fully. This is, after all, where the problem *begins*: in homes where children are deprived, lack opportunity, are hungry and have caregivers who do not possess the cultural capital to support their children. Addressing these issues is fundamental to long-term success.

However, there can be no doubt that good schools and good teachers can reduce the impact of SES and cultural capital. There is plenty of research evidence to show that teachers and schooling can compensate for the cultural and SES disadvantages their students bring with them to school. By doing this, they can at least *narrow* the achievement gap—certainly in New Zealand, where it is relatively big compared to other countries.

Marzano (2000) brings the arguments together in a substantial piece of research carried out over a decade ago in which he synthesised and analysed a large number of studies carried out by researchers during the previous 40 years. According to Marzano this research suggested that there are at least three factors that can have a powerful impact on student achievement:

1. *the school*—this could include the school's leadership, curriculum, resources and assessment processes, the time available for instruction, and the school climate, policies and procedures
2. *the teachers*—this could include the quality of the teachers, the classroom curriculum and classroom management
3. *the students*—this could include their socioeconomic background, cultural capital, prior knowledge, aptitude and interest.

Marzano looks at these impacts based on a *value added* approach. Put simply, he asks: given the fact that some students start the educational race with handicaps, and some start with advantages, what can teachers and schools add to what the students start with? This value add approach helps develop another dimension to the ongoing debate about the impact of teachers and schools.

According to Marzano, *student background* determines 80 percent of achievement outcomes, the *school* determines 6.66 percent of achievement, and the *teacher* determines 13.34 percent of student achievement outcomes. All of this would support those who argue that it is vitally important to address the SES factors—what the *student* brings with him/her to school. However, given that we *start* with this, what does the research tell us about what schools and teachers might be able to change?

Marzano looks at the *value* added impact on student achievement of a variety of combinations of school and teacher quality for some hypothetical students who enter the schools or classrooms with a range of achievement scores, from very low to very high. The relative *initial* positions of the hypothetical students on a distribution of scores are proxies for SES. For example, students who come with low initial scores are assumed to come from low SES backgrounds, and students who come with high scores are assumed to come from high SES backgrounds.

The students are placed in schools and with teachers in the following combinations for a course of study:

- average teacher in an average school
- ineffective teacher in an ineffective school
- ineffective teacher in an exceptional school
- exceptional teacher in an ineffective school
- exceptional teacher in an exceptional school
- average teacher in an exceptional school.

Marzano's findings (p. 80) are, perhaps, not surprising.

- Average teachers in average schools do little to influence the relative position of any students on the final scores distribution. Those students who enter the school or class with a relatively low score (low SES) on the overall distribution remain at that same point on the distribution at the end of the course.
- The ineffective teacher and ineffective school actually have a negative impact, and all students lose ground and slip down the distribution, regardless of their initial positions.
- Students in an exceptional school with ineffective teachers lose ground.

- Students with an exceptional teacher in an ineffective school either maintain their relative position or improve on it.
- The average teacher in an effective school produces good progress.
- The exceptional teacher in an effective school produces the greatest gains for all students.

His conclusions are worth quoting in full:

> Exceptional performance in terms of school level factors overcomes the average performance of teachers, but not the ineffective performance of teachers. However exceptional performance on the part of teachers not only compensates for average performance at the school level, but even ineffective performance at the school level. (Marzano, 2000, p. 81)

The key point is this: although student factors, such as socioeconomic background, have a huge impact on achievement, this can be compensated for by a combination of effective schools and exceptional teachers, and exceptional teachers in particular. The size of the effect can be substantial. However, those who enter the school or class with higher scores given the same combinations will retain their relative potions compared with those who come in with lower scores, though the gap can be substantially reduced.[5]

Further evidence of the powerful effects of exceptional teachers, using a value add approach, are provided by Raj Chetty and John Friedman at Harvard University and Jonah Rockoff of Columbia University, as quoted in *The Economist* in 2013. The researchers drew on a massive American database of student achievement, which included 2.5 million students and covered over 20 years of results. They developed a value add score of student achievement, which took account of SES factors. They then correlated this achievement data with the quality of the teachers teaching those students. *The Economist* reports that the authors found that the quality of the teachers is directly linked to the value adds of their students:

---

[5] I accept that this is American-based research. However, the conclusion that effective teaching and schooling do make a significant difference is hardly disputed anywhere in the world. The argument is about the extent to which governments, including the New Zealand government, try to absolve themselves of their economic and social responsibilities by focusing too much on the teacher and school impacts, thus effectively 'blaming' schools for matters that are well beyond their control.

When the average quality of teachers in fourth grade falls from one year to the next, for example, the performance of the fourth graders also drops as expected.

What is even more interesting, according to *The Economist*, is that good teachers are identified across most schools:

the quality of the teachers varies more within schools than among them: a typical school has teachers that span 85% of the spectrum for the school system as a whole. Not only do teachers matter, in other words, but the best teachers are not generally clumped within particular schools (*The Economist*, 2013).

According to these researchers, differences in student achievement *between schools* are *not* due to teacher quality, because good teachers are spread reasonably evenly across all schools. However, improving teacher quality in low-performing schools *would* have a significant impact. By moving higher-performing teachers into low-performing schools, it is likely that the impact on those low-performing schools would be substantial.[6]

Concluding comments

It is important to point out that much of the research that has been discussed in this chapter comes out of a 'black box'. The methodologies used and the conclusions drawn by the OECD, the Ministry of Education, ERO, Marzano and *The Economist* (citing the work of Chetty, Friedman and Rockoff) are, for most of us, difficult to understand.

Furthermore, a number of tacit assumptions have been made in the research. How are 'good teachers' or 'effective schools' identified in the first place, and is this a credible process? These questions will be examined in the next chapter.

Importantly, even the researchers would advise caution in drawing firm conclusions. However, the findings, tentative though they are, do help provide us with a workable theory of action that most readers would probably accept.

---

6 The research is from the US and so needs to be treated with caution when applying it to the New Zealand environment. Nevertheless, it does make intuitive sense 'on average'. Moving *one* highly effective teacher into a low-performing school may not make a lot of difference. However, changing the *average quality of teachers* in a school is clearly likely to be a successful strategy.

- SES clearly matters, and New Zealand may not be as good at mitigating the negative effects of this as many other OECD countries. However, schools and teachers matter as well. From a school or teacher or even parent point of view, the SES is a given, at least for the short to medium term. Therefore we should concentrate on encouraging *schools and teachers* to lift student performance. We may need to consider ensuring that our best teachers are placed in low-performing schools to maximise opportunities.
- However, we should be clear that though schools and teachers can help close the gaps between high and low achievers, it is unlikely that those who come from low SES homes will, on average, outperform those that come from high SES homes.
- Only governments and voters can make many of these challenges much more manageable by putting in place policies that remove social and economic handicaps and privileges, and allow all our students to start the life–education race from the same starting point.

This chapter posed a simple question: does schooling and teaching matter? We have come, taking something of a circuitous route, to a working conclusion in the affirmative, and of course no one will be surprised. If we really thought that schooling and teaching did not matter we would hardly spend millions of dollars educating our children.

It is precisely this belief in the power of schooling and teaching that has been the engine for large-scale educational reform in New Zealand over the past three decades. Changes have been initiated by Governments with the expectation that they would improve educational outcomes. The list of reforms is impressive: Tomorrow's Schools, at least two major curriculum reviews, the introduction of an entirely new assessment system,[7] the establishment of new watchdogs (ERO and NZQA), new initiatives in strategic planning and reporting of school performance, the development of new teachers' performance standards, new national literacy and numeracy standards , new ICT[8] policies, school improvement projects, new approaches to funding and the professional development of teachers, countless restructures at the Ministry of Education and NZQA—and much more.

---

7 The New Zealand Qualifications Framework and NCEA.
8 Information and communication technology.

Despite all these initiatives, the following facts should be a source of concern.

- Socioeconomic and decile effects remain very strong in New Zealand. Students who attend low-decile schools do not do well, in general.
- Many low-achieving students are Māori and Pasifika, and the gap between Māori/Pasifika performance and European/Asian performance, although closing slowly (as measured by NCEA data), is still very large.
- PISA data tell us we are doing well, though in decline, and that we have a persistently wide achievement gap compared with other OECD countries.

This leads us to something of an uncomfortable conclusion: if we accept that teaching and schooling *can and do* make a difference, we are forced to conclude that the educational reforms put in place over many years have not worked as well as we would all have hoped for. Why is this? And what can we do about it?

Before we answer these questions we need to take a brief detour. If schooling and teaching are important, how much do we know about what an effective or quality school looks like?

Chapter 4: School effectiveness

The school effectiveness movement

If we are willing to assert, as we have done in the last chapter, that schools and teachers can to some extent trump the effect of socioeconomic factors, then we need to be very clear what it is about a school that makes it a high-quality or effective one capable of doing this.[1] Readers will not be surprised to learn that there is a global industry based around identifying and answering this very question. It is, in a sense, the holy grail of education.

The effective schools movement arose in the US after the US Office of Education produced a paper written by one James Coleman. Coleman concluded, on the basis of his research, that public schools made little difference to student outcomes and that the important determinants of student success were family background and SES (Association of Effective Schools, 2013).

The appalled response from more optimistic researchers was to identify plenty of schools with students from poor and deprived backgrounds who were successful, thus immediately contradicting Coleman's basic thesis. The problem was that no one really understood

---

1 For the purposes of this chapter we will assume that the two terms, 'high quality' and 'effective', mean the same thing.

why some schools were more successful than others, even when they had identical mixes of poor and deprived students. What was it that these successful schools were doing that was so effective?

It was to answer this question that the effective school movement began and developed. The outcome of this work was often a list of descriptors or, using the original terminology, 'correlates', which were intended to describe the common characteristics of effective schools. In the 1980s, in response to Coleman's original thesis, these descriptors or correlates were:

- a clear school mission
- high expectations for success
- effective instructional leadership
- frequent monitoring of student progress
- the opportunity to learn, and student time on task
- a safe and orderly environment
- strong home–school relations.
  (Association of Effective Schools, 2013)

There are plenty of other descriptors, or correlates, of effective schools available in the literature, some very similar to the list above and some quite different, depending on the nature of the research done. There is no doubt that they provide school leaders, teachers, parents, the media and government officials with plenty of scope to initiate and drive school and national educational reforms.

Effective school research methodologies

We should, however, be careful about accepting this sort of research at face value. To understand why, it is necessary to explain *how* the research is carried out in the first place. Researchers generally need to:

1. establish a set of quality criteria or proxies, which schools need to demonstrate to prove their effectiveness/high quality in the first place
2. identify and examine schools that can demonstrate they meet these criteria
3. identify the common key 'working' characteristics of these schools

4. produce a list/set of correlates that summarises the characteristics identified.

The initial selection of the criterion or proxy to be used (step 1 above) obviously needs to be based on some sort of data. These data most often—but not always—focus on some form of common standardised testing. High test scores are presumed to demonstrate that the school is effective and that students are learning. Test scores, in other words, are used as a proxy for quality. This approach may provide some useful information, particularly since test scores tend to remove elements of subjectivity in any judgements made by the researchers. However, using test scores alone as a measure of quality can be a very limited and misleading approach to take.

Other proxy data could just as easily be used to demonstrate effectiveness/quality. For example, high retention rates, or level of community support, or even high rates of entry to tertiary study might well be regarded as indicators of an effective/quality school. We should be clear: in order to find an effective school we need to decide on the criterion or proxy we are using as the measure of effectiveness/quality, and only then search for the correlates. Without the first, it is not possible to determine the second.

So, in the example above, schools with high test scores have been considered effective, and *then* the common characteristics or correlates (such as instructional leadership and clearly articulated mission/vision) of these schools have been documented. Put another way, researchers must start by looking for schools with high test scores, not schools that demonstrate the correlates.

The problem is that once researchers use a criterion such as high test scores (which is by far the most common) as a proxy for identifying effective/quality schools, the final list of correlates produced will logically and inevitably reflect this criterion/proxy. In other words, if the sole criterion used to establish whether a school is effective or not is high test scores, the final set of correlates will obviously identify the characteristics of the schools that deliver these high test scores.

There is nothing really wrong with this, and it is an entirely logical approach as far as it goes, but before we rush into school reform mode we need to be clear about a few things.

- The tests (if tests are the agreed criterion/proxy) that are fundamental to the entire process need to be carefully designed to compare school performance across the full range of SES homes, locations, gender and school types. Furthermore, they need to do this over a period of time to ensure the data are consistent.

- Large-scale testing for quality can have perverse effects. For example, schools may decide to focus their energy on 'teaching to the test'. Teaching to the test may be fine if the test is broad and uses a range of assessment tools. However, if the test is narrow, or unduly focused on rote learning, it may have a negative impact on the quality of learning taking place and on the motivation of the students. Furthermore, such testing can drive out useful and worthwhile curriculum areas that are not tested—often in the arts and liberal studies.

- Simply establishing a relationship between high test scores and a set of correlates does not necessarily mean there is a causal link between the two:

> It is not necessarily valid to argue that, just because, for instance, instructional leadership is correlated with high test scores, that one directly causes the other. It might be that principals who focus on instructional leadership also hire effective teachers. It might also be that the causal relationship works the other way around; for example, schools in which students are gaining high test results (for whatever reason) might also tend to require less of a principal's time to be spent on administration relating to students' welfare, leaving more time to engage in instructional leadership.[2]

There are other significant problems with research on effective schools. For example, as mentioned, what if researchers select a different criterion/proxy for quality? For instance, researchers might decide that the sole criterion/proxy for quality is the rate of entrance to tertiary study, not test scores. This might be an entirely reasonable indicator of quality for many schools because it might indirectly take account of not only test scores but also a range of other personal attributes and learning developed through the entire schooling system.

---

2 Dr Michael Johnston, Victoria University of Wellington, personal communication, November 2013.

If this were to be the sole criterion/proxy, it is possible that researchers will identify a different set of schools from those selected by the researchers who are concentrating solely on test results as the effectiveness/quality criterion. These selected schools, when examined, could easily exhibit a different set of correlates from those identified for the high test score schools. Researchers might therefore publish a different list of correlates to describe effective/quality schools. For example, for schools selected for effectiveness solely on the basis of a high rate of tertiary study criterion, one correlate might be a broad curriculum, offering multiple pathways to polytechnics and other tertiary training establishments. On the other hand, for schools selected for effectiveness solely on the basis of high test scores, the correlate might well be a narrower, more specialist curriculum.

What if researchers select high retention rates as the sole criterion/proxy for effectiveness/quality? Once again, they may identify another, different, set of schools, create a different set of correlates, and set principals, officials and consultants on a different path of school reform.

It should be noted that researchers could search for schools with multiple criteria/proxies. For example, they could search for schools that have high test scores *and* high rates of tertiary study *and* high retention rates, and then identify the common characteristics/correlates of these schools. It may well be that strong school leadership or vision/mission could appear on this list.

This multiple criteria approach is worthy of attention, but suffice to say that one difficulty with multiple criteria is that correlates are likely to become less useful and more complicated to write because some of the policy implications of the various criteria might be contradictory. For example *low* retention rates (often regarded as a negative) may well be a sign of *high* quality if a school is intent on developing strong links with tertiary institutions and placing students in work. Including both high retention rates *and* rates of entrance to tertiary study as key (multiple) criteria may therefore lead to erroneous conclusions about the schools in question.

OECD PISA effectiveness judgements

It is useful to consider the OECD PISA data in the light of this discussion. The PISA report claims to describe what successful educational systems do. In other words, it describes the correlates. According to the OECD, successful schooling is demonstrated by those countries that score well in their tests. However, we must be clear that the effectiveness proxy the OECD uses as the key success effectiveness indicator is a written test administered once every 3 years. The characteristics of those countries that do well on these tests are examined, and their common characteristics distilled for the rest of the world to try to emulate.

We should be cautious: in any effectiveness research and reform process we need to be clear what criterion or proxy is being used as an indicator of effectiveness or quality. If it is standardised test, is the test instrument technically reliable?[3] Will an emphasis on that one test have a longer-term perverse impact, such as future teaching to the test and a narrowing of the curriculum? If other proxies are being used, what are they and how reliable are they? And finally, whatever the criterion/proxy used, is it reasonable to expect there is a causal link, and not just a random relationship between the criterion and the correlate?

The ERO perspective on quality

The New Zealand ERO criteria for quality appear at first to present a broader and more detailed approach to identifying quality. In its 2011 synthesis of its own reports over a 5-year period,[4] ERO concluded that quality schools are places where:

1. there is a focus on the learner
2. leadership is promoted in an inclusive culture
3. school decisions enhance effective teaching
4. the school engages with its community
5. policies and practices are implemented in a cycle of continuous improvement.
   (Education Review Office, 2011, p. 2)

---

3 We have already noted that the methodologies used by the OECD for the PISA testing have been criticised for being technically *unreliable* (see p. 4).

4 These were compiled using the results of 36 national evaluations and reports of good practice between 2007 and 2010.

ERO has identified schools that meet these criteria and has compiled a hefty report which tells us what characteristics these schools have. For example, in the case of the first criterion, in quality schools where there is a 'focus on the learner', we will find the following:

- the focus is school wide, on all students not just a few
- learners are engaged in their learning
- assessment information is carefully analysed and acted on
- assessment practice is effective
- decision making is evidence based
- curriculum implementation is well advanced
- programme and resource selection is effective
- learners are encouraged to take responsibility for their own learning
- progress and achievement are monitored
- results are communicated.

(Education Review Office, 2011, pp. 7–25)

Under *each* of these headings the reader is provided with good practice examples and advice. The report then goes on, in equal detail, to repeat the analysis for each of the other four indicators.

This is all useful material for a school. However, it is important that we understand that the initial five indicators for quality were broadly established *prior* to the research being carried out. In other words, ERO reviewers went looking for schools that, in *their view*, demonstrated the five indicators and *then* documented examples of good practice from the selected schools.

ERO accepts this in its report and frankly states that "these findings were the only possible outcomes given ERO's focus and the questions asked" (p. 6). However, it goes on to suggest that the "evaluative" questions it asked in its research were broad enough to pick up other relevant indicators as appropriate. Presumably this means that its researchers remained open to the possibility of changing or adding to their initial list of quality indicators based on the data they collected in the research process.

The point is this: some potential alternative quality indicators did not appear on the ERO initial list, which other researchers might well have added. For example, some might argue that schools need strong and principled leadership, *not* inclusive leadership, given the propensity of some schools and teachers to resist change, but this was never examined because it was not on the list of criteria to find "good practice schools".

ERO might well argue that its initial selection of indicators was based on its own reviews of New Zealand schools over several years and the best international research: ERO is simply applying its findings. However, this still leaves various questions unanswered, such as on what basis was this international research done, and were ERO's own previous reviews (which were used as the basis of the report) properly carried out and credible?

We are not given any information about the nature of the international research used in the report, but it is likely that a significant part of it was based on standardised test results. This is understandable given the problems of analysing, standardising and collating more subjective or complex data. However, if test scores are the prime proxy for these ERO conclusions about quality and effectiveness, we need at least to acknowledge the bias this places on the research finding. Standardised testing, as has already been suggested above, may or may not be the best way of establishing a universal quality indicator, or a proxy for quality.

If ERO is using its own previous reviews to identify effective schools, are the criteria used appropriate and credible, or is ERO simply summarising its own previous—possibly unreliable—findings? If, as seems the case, ERO selected its five indicators of quality on the basis of its own school reviews of New Zealand schools, along with international research, and if, as seems entirely possible, the international research was primarily focused on test results, ERO has provided us with what is effectively just another set of *correlates*. This represents much the same process as the other effective schools research we have looked at.

None of what has been said thus far should be taken to suggest that research on what makes a quality school is not worthwhile. It is, because it provides very helpful information about what might be termed 'good practice'. Whatever the criteria established, the research provides us with information about schools that do it well. However, the point that should be clear by now is that identifying just what makes a high-quality school is not as easy as it sounds, and this is perhaps as it should be.

Schools are incredibly complex organisations involving a large number of variables, and are required to meet a wide and sometimes conflicting range of expectations from their communities. Agreeing what makes for quality depends on some initial subjective value judgements about what is important.

If we add to this the fact that *socioeconomic* characteristics of those attending the school have a far bigger impact on student outcomes than the school does, it becomes clear that research about quality schools (and the abundant advice about what makes for quality) needs to be used with care.

Using proven teaching strategies: a different perspective on quality

Given that the concept of quality is slippery and that we need to be very clear about the criteria we are using, can we say anything useful about quality schools if we focus directly on the quality of *teaching* going on in the schools? If we can identify what good teaching involves, will this help us say something more about the quality of schools, and, perhaps more importantly, will it help us improve schooling?

Not surprisingly there are plenty of researchers who have come up with evidence-based prescriptions for quality teaching. The focus of this research is on examining the relationship between what teachers do in their classrooms and the learning taking place, rather than setting out to document the characteristics of effective/quality schools. The aim, using a variety of data—both test-based and more subjective and observational—is to help teachers understand what works in classrooms. In other words, this approach puts the magnifying glass on the classroom and tries to establish what good teachers do, rather than on the school as whole, or the schooling system.

New Zealand is a leader in this sort of research, with some of the best work coming from the Ministry of Education. A fairly complex set of answers emerges clearly from the Ministry's Best Evidence Synthesis (BES) research programme. The characteristics of quality teaching are summarised below.

1. Quality teaching is focused on student achievement (including social outcomes) and facilitates high standards of student outcomes for heterogeneous groups of students.

2. Pedagogical practices enable classes and other learning groupings to work as caring, inclusive and cohesive learning communities.
3. Effective links are created between school and other cultural contexts in which students are socialised, to facilitate learning.
4. Quality teaching is responsive to student learning processes.
5. Opportunity to learn is effective and sufficient.
6. Multiple task contexts support learning cycles.
7. Curriculum goals, resources including ICT usage, task design, teaching and school practices are effectively aligned.
8. Pedagogy scaffolds and provides appropriate feedback on students' task engagement.
9. Pedagogy promotes learning orientations, student self-regulation, metacognitive strategies and thoughtful student discourse.
10. Teachers and students engage constructively in goal-oriented assessment.
    (Alton-Lee, 2003, pp.67–68)

Marzano (Marzano, R., 2003, pp. 67–68) has identified nine key teaching strategies:

1. identifying similarities and differences
2. summarising and note taking
3. reinforcing effort and providing recognition
4. homework and practice
5. non-linguistic representations
6. co-operative learning
7. setting objectives and providing feedback
8. generating and testing hypotheses
9. cues, questions, and advance organisers.

There is no doubt that reference to the mountain of research about quality teaching and what works in classrooms, which we have barely touched on here, is vitally important. However, some teachers and researchers may have a nagging concern about what appears to be a rather *mechanistic* approach to what is an incredibly complex process.

The problem with research like this is that it implies that teaching is a purely scientific enterprise, and that a 'tool box' of teaching strategies can be constructed; all that is required is to train teachers to understand, and use, the tools in the box. The implication is that all teachers need do is apply these 'proven' strategies. If we can write these strategies down, and prove they work, all that is left is for teachers to implement them. Teachers can be treated as the *delivery* mechanism, rather than as the highly skilled practitioners they are.

Most teachers know that this toolbox/delivery approach is a nonsense. They know, from their experience, that teaching is essentially more of an art than a science, and is better characterised as a form of street (improvised) theatre. What works or does not work in a classroom (as in street theatre) is inextricably linked with the nuances of human interaction and the interplay between all the parties involved. The task of the teacher, the 'director', is to provide the spark to transform all these interactions into meaningful, deep, learning experiences for all those involved—even though every performance is likely to be different.

The great challenge for teachers, of course, is that the toolbox, if it exists at all, is very hard to use and is incredibly complex. As with street theatre, although there may be a rough plan, what actually happens will depend on the action of the moment.

Shifting the focus to the quality of the teacher

It may be that we need to shift the focus again. We have already shifted from outcomes (such as test results) to inputs (quality of teaching). Another possible shift could be from quality of the teaching to the quality of the *teacher*. Quality teaching, I want to argue, is far more about a *state of mind* than a set of strategies in a toolbox. In other words, what is crucial is the teacher himself/herself and his/her personal dispositions, attitudes and assumptions.

This helps to explain why so many experienced teachers show signs of extreme cynicism when presented with the latest fad tool from researchers about what works in classrooms. They know perfectly well that the latest 'silver bullet', though it may well be interesting and worthy of attention, is certainly not the panacea that researchers and government officials sometimes suggest it is. They know perfectly well that it is the quality and state of mind of the teacher that matter most. If that state of mind remains unchanged, no reform effort will succeed, regardless of what the research says and no matter how many new fancy strategies are produced by newly inspired principals and university professors.

Of course readers will be asking: What exactly is this state of mind teachers are meant to have? Surely if we could describe and define it, it could then become the silver bullet we are all seeking. It, too, could go into a newly designed and special tool box and be sent out with a covering note to all principals. If the argument proposed here is to be taken seriously, it is important to try to explain what the state of mind approach looks and feels like, even as we make it clear that it is far too complex to be the elusive silver bullet solution to the challenges of teaching.

Teaching as inquiry

The teacher as inquiry model appears in *The New Zealand Curriculum* (Ministry of Education, 2007). The core of the model is that really effective teachers need to have a state of mind[5] that constantly asks questions about the effectiveness of what they are doing in the classroom, that seeks honest answers to these questions, and then is willing to change practice accordingly. In order to be able to do this, teachers need to be honest, willing to accept they might get things wrong, and, most importantly, be able to constantly monitor their performance and success, based on the impact of their teaching on their students.

The inquiry model depicts three phases of inquiry

Using the inquiry model, teachers would start with a *focusing inquiry* and ask themselves what they know about the students in front of them and where the evidence is to support any conclusions they come to. Only by understanding students' starting point regarding any learning can teachers determine what is important to focus on.

Given the data and evidence from the focusing inquiry, teachers would then move into the *teaching inquiry* by identifying and trying teaching strategies that are likely to work, based on their own understandings and the research evidence available. As the teaching and

---

5 The phrase "state of mind" is not used in the official explanations of the model.

learning progresses, teachers will constantly be checking to see whether the strategies are working and are achieving the intended outcomes. If they are not, teachers will be reviewing and re-evaluating their teaching inquiry and going through the cycle again (Ministry of Education, 2007a).

There is nothing in this cycle that suggests that one teaching strategy is identified as being better than another. Putting students into groups is not necessarily better than lecturing them; self-reporting grades is not necessarily better than teacher marking and ICT is not necessarily better than using a textbook. In my years observing teachers as a principal I can certainly recall many teachers who lectured, used textbooks heavily, and focussed on rote learning, who were regarded by their students and their colleagues as very good, even great teachers.[6] Having said this, it is obviously important that "inquiring" teachers be aware of the research available and use it wisely. The aim will be to constantly and honestly evaluate and respond, rather than simply deliver.

There is perhaps one caveat here: although the inquiry model does require teachers to be open, honest and fallible (this is what is meant by the phrase 'state of mind'), it does perhaps lack a broad philosophical/moral framework. For example, what would happen if a teacher has developed stereotypes about certain students in his/her class? The teacher may assume that particular students or groups of students are simply not capable of achieving anything significant because of their family background or culture. Applying the teaching as inquiry model for such a 'deficit thinking' teacher is unlikely to produce quality teaching and learning, because the teacher's expectations could easily cloud and impede their inquiry process.

It is clear that the teaching as inquiry model will only be successful if teachers do possess a higher moral purpose about the possibilities for what they can do. They will need to believe that all students *can* achieve, and will strive at all times to make this happen. The inquiry model in the hands of a teacher with no sense of purpose or *passion*, who believes that schools make little difference, is unlikely to be any use at all.

John Hattie, in his book *Visible Learning* (Hattie, 2012), appears to

---

[6] Not all of these methods would necessarily feature very prominently in a toolbox produced by the worthy researchers we have referred to earlier in this chapter!

endorse and build on the teacher as inquiry model, but also adds some passion and moral purpose. Hattie tells teachers they need to develop the following "mind frames":

a. *Teachers need to believe that their fundamental task is to evaluate the effect of their teaching on students' learning and achievement.* According to Hattie, this mind frame is about the need for teachers to be constantly evaluating the impact of their teaching by seeking feedback from the students, checking assessment data, and then making changes to the teaching approaches being used, as necessary. Does the teacher know what is working, and how well it is working? Where is the evidence to confirm, or perhaps refute, these judgements? What does the teacher do about it? This is probably a pretty good summary of the teaching as inquiry model we have already discussed above.

b. *Teachers believe that success and failure in student learning is about what they as teachers did or did not do; teachers are change agents.* Hattie's argument is that teachers need to believe they can and do make a difference. There is no place for deficit thinking or blaming students for matters that are most probably out of their control.

c. *Teachers want to talk more about learning than teaching.* Hattie implores his readers to move from debates about teaching strategies to a focus on learning: How do people learn? How do we know students have learnt something? According to Hattie:

> Teachers need to be adaptive learning experts, to know multiple ways of teaching and learning, to be able to coach and model different ways of learning, and to be the 'best error detectors in the business'. (p. 163)

d. *Teachers see assessment as feedback about their impact.* Teachers not only give feedback to students, but receive feedback about their impact from student assessment. Teachers need to seek and use this feedback as an integral part of their job.

e. *Teachers engage in dialogue, not monologue.* Hattie wants teachers to be prepared to enter dialogues with their students,

> to listen to their questions, their ideas, their struggles, their strategies of learning, their successes, their interactions with peers, their outputs and their views about teaching ... This is

about finding the right balance between teacher talk and more rich interaction with learners. (p. 163)

f. *Teachers enjoy the challenge and never retreat to 'doing their best'.* Teachers need to focus on ensuring that the challenges that students face engage their interest. If students can see what is expected and what the success criteria are, they are more likely to meet the challenges and, by implication, do *better* than their best.

g. *Teachers believe that their role is to develop positive relationships in classrooms.* This is not just about developing a warm and friendly classroom atmosphere. It is more about ensuring a classroom climate that encourages students to ask questions, take risks, and express their concerns about not understanding something that has been taught.

h. *Teachers inform all about the language of learning.* Teachers need to ensure that parents understand the language of education and the classroom so that they can be equally involved in the education of their children:

> Parents who understand the importance of deliberate practice, concentration, the difference between surface and deep knowing, and the nature of the learning intentions and success criteria are much more likely to work with their children and their teachers more effectively. (p. 165)

Hattie's mind frames, as briefly described above, and the teaching as inquiry model, as outlined earlier, bring us to an interesting conclusion in our discussion about quality. Quality teaching is about possessing a state of mind, and that state of mind is something we can describe. Combining this state of mind approach with what research tells us about quality teaching could well deliver results. We will return to this issue in Part 4.

Concluding comments

Given the importance of good schools and good teachers, this chapter has shown that defining good quality is not as easy as it might first appear. There are a number of important points we can summarise here.

- Any approach that lists the characteristics/correlates of effective schools will produce information based on the initial criterion chosen as a proxy for quality/effectiveness. For example, test results might be such a proxy, but retention rates may be another equally valid one. It is important to note that whatever the criterion/proxy chosen, if the measurement is based on large-scale standardised tests, there are almost always perverse and unintended impacts on learning. We need to be careful, therefore, when we are debating the quality of a school to ensure we know what we are measuring. It is possible to have multiple proxies, which can result in the broadening of characteristics/correlates. This approach is certainly worth investigating further, but it, too, may have problems, relating to consistency.

- Another way of looking at quality is to look at the input side rather than the output side. Rather than focus on test scores, it might be useful to look at the *quality of teaching* going on in schools. This approach avoids the need to choose proxies, and probably reduces the need to run large-scale tests. It is important to select successful teaching strategies based on evidence from a range of sources, not just test scores.

- There are plenty of data and research, both qualitative and quantitative, about the teaching strategies that work well and thus contribute to quality teaching. These data are informative and useful. However, such tool box approaches to quality can become quite prescriptive. Teaching is not about tool boxes and fool-proof strategies that can be wheeled out and applied, in the process turning teachers into a 'delivery mechanism'. Teaching is not a science: it is more an art, akin to improvised street theatre.

- Therefore, the question of what contributes to quality teaching is better focused on the *quality of the teacher*. Quality teachers need to have an inquiry approach to teaching and a particular set of mind frames.

It is important that the current research base about quality teaching and effective schools is not abandoned. This research base is large and valuable. What is being suggested here is that it is only part of the picture. Without quality *teachers* who possess the personal, moral and philosophical framework necessary to ensure that all students are given an opportunity to maximise their potential, it is difficult to imagine success.

Current approaches to educational reform to improve quality/effectiveness, and many reform efforts since the 1980s, as we will see in the next chapter, derive from the tool box approach: the focus has been more on the quality of teaching, or the quality of the school, or the quality of the assessment or administration, rather than the quality of the teacher. Arguably, as a result, much of this reform has failed to address the key issue of educational disparities and underachievement in New Zealand secondary schools. There is a need now to focus more of our reform efforts on the mind frame approach to the quality *of teachers*, because this approach is more likely to have lasting and deep impacts.

There is another fundamental question that arises out of this argument: If we accept that it is a mind frame we are looking for, what do educationalists, school leaders, politicians and government officials need to do to produce, support and nurture it? This critical question will be addressed in Part 4 of this book. But before we do this, we need to examine how we in New Zealand attempt to *measure* quality in schooling.

Chapter 5: Measuring quality in schools

Introduction
Readers will recall that in Chapter 1 we addressed the issue of the quality of the New Zealand education system as a whole. It was concluded that, on the basis of data from PISA and NCEA, our educational system is a good-quality one. However, PISA data also point to a long-term decline, and we urgently need to address the issue of disparity based on SES and ethnicity.

In the previous chapter we considered how we might identify quality schools, quality teaching and quality teachers. In this chapter our focus will be on whether we should, or can, make robust judgements about the quality of a school that will allow us to reasonably compare it with another.

NCEA data
Looking at NCEA data is probably the most common way the community make judgements about particular secondary schools and their teachers. Schools that have improved their NCEA pass/endorsement results are lauded by ERO, the Ministry of Education and the commu-

nity, while schools with poor pass/endorsement rates are often pilloried. The problem is that NCEA data cannot easily be used as a measure of teacher or school quality, and certainly cannot be used to compare schools—or even to measure performance over time. Let's look at why this is so.

School-to-school comparison

The best way to explain the pitfalls involved in using NCEA data for school-to-school comparison is to compare two different types of school: School A and School B.

A comparison of two hypothetical schools

School A

School A is a small, low-decile school in a rural area. Traditionally the school has offered a reasonably standard programme, which requires students to complete full-year courses in English, maths and science at Level 1. Students have to choose two or three additional subjects from a range that includes history, geography economics, accounting, food technology, computing and physical education. Teachers assess the students using achievement standards and encourage them to take at least two or three externally assessed standards per subject, if they are available.

Because the school is situated in a quiet, rural area, there are limited opportunities for work experience or for developing any links with other educational (tertiary) providers.

Parents are traditional in their approach to schooling and are keen to ensure their children have the opportunity to be exposed to a 'basics' type of curriculum.

It is clear from an analysis of the results from previous years that students do not do well in the external examinations. Often they don't show up at all, and when they do, they find the pressures of a written examination under time pressure hard to cope with. However, the principal and board believe that external assessment by way of a written examination is a vitally important skill that needs to be developed.

Although they are interested in broadening their curriculum, they don't feel they have the resources or staffing to, for example, develop work-related programmes or tertiary links. Given its isolation, there are few alternative schooling options available to students.

At Levels 2 and 3 the curriculum and approach are much the same.

The principal is concerned about his school's poor NCEA results compared with other similar-decile schools. However, he feels he is 'holding the line' on educational standards.

> **School B**
>
> School B is a larger, urban-based school, also low decile, which has taken a different approach. A wide range of programmes have been developed with the help of the local tertiary institution and industry training organisations (ITOs). The size of the school and the fact that it is located in an urban area help a lot. There are a large number of students participating in the school's Building and Construction Academy, where students can gain industry-based unit standard credits for a range of practical and work-related activities.
>
> The school also offers a basic literacy and numeracy programme, through which extra credits can be gained. There is also a sports academy on site, and several national certificates are offered through ITOs using unit standards. These include programmes in tourism and hospitality, as well as computing and business technology.
>
> The school, having analysed its NCEA data, has come to the conclusion that external assessment does not work for all of its students. The board and principal argue that school-based internal assessment is much nearer the reality of workplace requirements. As a result, external assessment is only required if students are intending to go on to university. A significant number do this because they are aware of university requirements. Many students are also keen on gaining course endorsement, and external assessment is offered to these students also.

A media reporter or parent comparing the NCEA results of these schools will find that School B has better NCEA results than School A. Readers may have their own opinions about the decisions made by the principals and boards in each school, but under the New Zealand system of governance, school boards and principals do have the right to make these decisions. School A is clearly more traditional and perhaps suspicious of schools like school B, which seem to be offering a smorgasbord of programmes, which (they might argue) fail to address the basics. School B might well be offended by the smorgasbord criticism and argue that it is providing integrated and useful vocationally based programmes for many of its students, which will help them get qualifications and jobs. School B is focused on acknowledging the achievements of its students rather than simply consigning them to failure. School A might argue that the best way to properly educate students is to make them focus on the basics, set high expectations and not "dumb down" the curriculum.

Whatever view one takes, it is clear that the difference in NCEA results probably has little to do with the quality of the teaching going on in the two schools and not a lot to do with the quality of the school either. The difference is largely explained by the differing programmes offered by the two schools.

- External assessment is much more heavily used in School A. Since pass rates for externally assessed standards can be half that of internally assessed standards, Schools A's results overall are likely to be worse than those of School B.
- Similarly, School B uses ITO competency-based unit standards. Pass rates for these standards are generally much higher than the pass rates for internally assessed achievement standards, and considerably higher than for externally assessed achievement standards. Once again, School A will be doing worse than School B based on their programming decisions.

Of course it may be reasonable to view this difference in programmes as an indicator of quality by arguing that School B offers its students a better opportunity to succeed in NCEA than School A, and in this sense is a better school. However, this needs to be stated very clearly when such a judgement is made, otherwise unwarranted assumptions about the quality of teaching and teachers will be made.

Within-decile comparisons

The media often like to compare the performance of schools with the same decile. However, even if two schools offer identical programmes, thus addressing the issues raised above, comparison of schools within the same decile is fraught with problems, as has already been suggested in Chapter 2.

Readers will recall that decile ratings are based on the proportion of students who fit a particular set of (low socioeconomic/poverty) criteria. The measurement therefore does not take account of the *entire* mix of students at the school. Some schools, particularly in Auckland, draw students from a wide variety of households, so it is entirely possible for a school to be mid or even low decile and still have a substantial number of students who actually are in the higher socioeconomic brackets. This means that two schools with exactly the same decile rating could have very different mixes of students. The result could easily be very different NCEA results, which are more related to the socioeconomic status of the students in the school than to any useful measurement of the quality of the school or its teachers.

Longitudinal measures of NCEA performance

If we cannot be confident about school-to-school comparison, even within the same decile, what about comparison *over time*, both for individual schools and for aggregated data for the nation as a whole? The analysis of longitudinal data for a particular school is subject to the same concerns as explained above for school-to-school comparisons. Simply changing programmes can lead to better pass rates. It may be that schools should indeed take credit for the initiatives, but to claim that the improved pass rates are a result of better *teaching* is quite another matter.

Some schools have substantially increased their pass rates over relatively short periods of time by managing the opportunities NCEA offers more effectively. For example:

- a holiday course during which students pick up extra credits by participating in a range of activities, including demonstrating team skills and writing a CV—while these may well be genuine credits, they are used to get borderline students over the bar, students who might well have failed if left to their mainstream class work
- withdrawals of entries—teachers and students may decide that a student is unlikely to gain credits, particularly in an external assessment, so the student is withdrawn and asked to concentrate on other internally assessed credits, thus potentially improving final percentage pass marks and grades
- shifting the focus of assessment from external assessment to internal assessment, as has already been suggested, which will raise pass rates, often dramatically; offering more vocational ITO unit standards will have the same effect.

To what extent does the better pass rate that may well eventuate from these initiatives reflect better-quality teaching, and to what extent does it reflect better management of NCEA? There is absolutely nothing wrong with using the flexibilities provided by NCEA, but observers, parents and the media need to be clear about what is actually going on, and not jump to conclusions about a 'miracle' school with an outstanding principal who has finally 'got the answer'.

The improved national NCEA pass rates published by the Ministry of Education, particularly in recent years, may not therefore be proof of better-quality schooling and teaching in New Zealand. Instead, they may simply be a result of schools being better able to use the flexibility provided by NCEA.

The debate about NCEA will no doubt continue, but it should be said that the flexibility it has provided has allowed many students some success whereas in the previous system, School Certificate and University Bursaries 'failed' thousands of learners simply because they did not gain a magic mark (around 50 percent), regardless of what they actually did know and had learnt.

It should be noted here that being flexible with regard to qualifications is not a particularly new idea. Schools in the previous School Certificate/University Bursaries system were often guilty of blatantly unethical behaviour. Students in many so-called élite schools were simply not allowed to enter the examination and were sent off to 'alternative courses'. At the same time local or regional 'qualifications', of very limited value were offered by a variety of other schools (for example the Taranaki Maths Certificate). Whilst these certificates might have had some credibility locally and regionally, they had very little credibility nationally and absolutely no credibility internationally. Alternatively, these same students were politely asked to get a job. Once these poorer-performing students were removed from the picture, the resulting pass rates appeared to be outstanding and were dishonestly marketed as such.

The way that School Certificate and University Bursaries were scaled added to the problem. With University Bursary results, raw marks in some subjects were regularly in the 30–40 percent area. However, prevailing policy required a higher pass mark, and as a result students often had their marks scaled up considerably, allowing for a pass mark of around 50 percent.

The point is this: comparing schools with each other using NCEA data (and previously School Certificate and University Bursaries data) is fraught with difficulties. Any attempt to do this is likely to result in conclusions that could misleading. Trying to make judgement calls about whether particular schools have got better, or the entire education system has improved, based on these data is very dangerous indeed.

At best the public, the media and parents are left to interpret complex data based on individual school programmes, which are almost impossible to compare. At worst, we are required to sift through what can only be described as 'untruths' propagated by some overzealous principals and journalists.

ERO and differentiated reviews

The Education Review Office (ERO) is an independent government department charged with monitoring the quality of schools. ERO reports comment on the quality of individual schools, and also aggregate and analyse data from their observations to provide advice about the quality of the education system as a whole.

One of the key judgements ERO reviewers make when they visit a school is whether the quality of the school merits special status. High-quality schools, according to ERO, exhibit the following characteristics:

- learners experience a coherent and rich curriculum that provides them with relevant choices and pathways and supports their successful transition through schooling and on to further education and training
- learners are actively engaged in their learning, and are progressing and achieving well; and the progress of priority groups of learners is being accelerated
- Māori learners are actively engaged in their learning, progressing and achieving well and succeeding as Māori
- there is a well-sustained culture of high expectations for students and staff
- a school-wide culture of rigorous critical reflection and self-review contributes effectively to sustaining the school's positive performance and continuous improvement
- leadership is highly effective and strategic, and is consistently improving student learning and achievement
- teaching consistently demonstrates high-quality practices, makes very good use of student achievement information, and is highly effective in promoting outcomes for learners
- the school has taken all reasonable steps to provide a safe and inclusive environment

- governance is highly effective in self-review, direction setting, decision-making and ensuring school accountabilities are met
- the school is highly effective in engaging the community in partnerships for learning and in the life of the school.
(Education Review Office, 2013)

Schools that meet these criteria are regarded as high-quality, special status schools and are rewarded with a further ERO review after 4 to 5 years. Average schools are revisited every 3 years. Schools that are regarded as poor-quality schools are punished with a further review after only 1 or 2 years. In these schools there is a problem with one or more of the following:

- student engagement, progress and achievement
- Māori student engagement, progress and achievement
- provision of effective teaching
- leadership and management
- governance
- the provision of a safe and inclusive school culture
- engagement of parents, whānau and communities.
(Education Review Office, 2013)

Readers should note that the 4–5-year return visit and the 1–2-year return visit are extremes. Most schools are of average quality and qualify for the normal 3-year return visit.

It would seem that this differentiated approach to reviews provides parents and the community with a useful way of comparing schools: schools with a 1- to 2-year return date presumably are poor quality, and schools with a 4- to 5-year return date are much-better-quality schools, with the normal 3-year return date schools performing to an acceptable standard.

An analysis of the extremes is instructive and sheds some light on how judgements about quality are made. It also raises some serious doubts about the usefulness of this approach in making comparisons between schools. The tables below have been constructed using ERO data. They show the number and decile of schools visited by ERO over a 3-year period for 2010/11, 2011/2012 and 2012/13. Given that the dangers of using decile as a robust descriptor of a school's student pro-

Chapter 5: Measuring quality in schools

file have already been discussed, this analysis uses just two categories (deciles 1–5 and deciles 6–10). Some reference is also made to decile 1–3 schools as a group.[1]

1- or 2-year return visit required		
Decile	Decile of individual schools	Total
1–5	4,3,1,1,3,1,2,3,3,3,4,1,2,3,2,5,2,1,2,2,4,3,1,1,1,4,1,4	28
6–10	7,7,10,6,9,6,6,6,7,10	10
4- or 5-year return visit required		
Decile	Decile of individual school	Total
1–5	4,1,5,4,5,1,1,2,	8
6–10	10,8,7,10,7,7,9,9,9,10,9	11

Table 3: Number of return visits, 1 or 2 years versus 4 or 5 years, by decile, 2010/11. (Sargent, 2012)

1- or 2-year return visit required		
Decile	Decile of individual schools	Total
1–5	3,4,2,4,3,2,3,1,3,2,2,2.4,2,5,5,5,4,1,2 2,3,4,1,1,4,4,2,3,2,2	31
6–10	10,6,8,6,6,7	6
4- or 5-year return visit required		
Decile	Decile of individual school	Total
1–5	5,5,4,5,5,	5
6–10	9,10,10,10,9,7,9	7

Table 4: Number of return visits, 1 or 2 years versus 4- or 5-years, by decile, 2011/12. (Sargent, 2012)

---

1 These data were provided to the author in response to email information requests made to ERO in 2012 and 2013.

1- or 2-year return visit required		
Decile	Decile of individual school	Total
1–5	2,3,3,2,3,5,2,1,4,3,4,3,1,3,2,2,1,1,1,4,2,4,3,2,2,	25
6–10	9,10,8,6	4
4- or 5-year return visit required		
Decile	Decile of individual school	Total
1–5	5,5,1,3,3	5
6–10	9,6,9,10,8,7,9,6,9,8,	10

Table 5: Number of return visits, 1 or 2 years versus 4 or 5 years, by decile, 2012/13. (Sargent, 2012)

Decile	1- or 2-year return	4- or 5-year return
Decile 1–5	84	18
Decile 6–10	20	28
Total	104	46

Table 6: Three-year summary, 2010–2012. (Sargent, 2012)

An analysis of the data throws up some fascinating conclusions. Schools that ERO visits after 1 or 2 years (presumably the poor-quality schools) are overwhelmingly low-decile schools. Over the 3-year period covered here, of the 104 schools that had to be revisited in a 1- or 2-year period, 84 were lower-decile (decile 1–5) schools. That is, just over 80 percent. Of these 84 schools, 55 were decile 1–3 schools.

Schools that ERO visits after 4 or 5 years (presumably the better-quality schools) are more evenly spread, though there is a significant bias towards higher-decile schools: of the 46 schools to be rewarded with a 4- or 5-year revisit, over the 3 years 28 were higher-decile (6–10) schools and the other 18 were lower-decile (1–5) schools, though only seven of these schools were in the lowest 1–3 decile range).[2]

---

[2] Raw comparisons of NCEA achievement data are not a cause of the decile/return-visit correlation shown in the table. Although most low-decile schools will have poorer results than higher-decile schools, a 1- or 2-year return visit could reasonably be imposed only on schools that have NCEA results lower than could be expected for similar decile schools and not simply on the basis of NCEA results compared with all schools.

The most worrying aspect of these data is that, assuming that ERO reviewers know what they are doing, one could conclude that parents are *correct* when they assume decile and quality are related, especially when it comes to lower-decile schools. This is despite assurances from educators, the Ministry of Education and ERO staff that decile does not indicate anything about quality and is only a funding mechanism.

The key question is this: how can the *quality* of a school, as defined by ERO, be so closely related to the socioeconomic status of the *students* that attend it, as measured by the decile ratings of the school? Surely all of these socioeconomic factors exist independently or develop independently of any deliberative action taken by the school or its teachers. Given this, how can ERO justify or explain the clear correlations between its quality judgments and the lower end of the decile ratings of schools? Just as important, how can ERO explain the relative *absence* of higher-decile schools in its 1- or 2-year return visits?

One possible explanation might be that low-decile schools, *because* they have more students from poorer and disadvantaged backgrounds, do not attract enough high-quality staff and do not access enough resources, while high-decile schools do. As a consequence, low-decile schools perform poorly for ERO reviews. If we accept this argument it might be possible to argue that decile and quality are related to each other *causally*. That is, one factor (socioeconomic deprivation) causes the other (low-quality schooling). If we accept this, then the methods used in the ERO review process become a little murky. What exactly is being reviewed and why is it being reviewed if the problem is actually outside the control of the school?

The argument gets more complicated: there are plenty of low-decile schools that perform well enough to be placed in a normal 3-year cycle, along with schools from higher deciles, and there are also plenty of low-decile schools that achieve the 4/5-year revisit. Take the following examples:

- In 2010/11, of the 78 decile 1–5 schools reviewed by ERO, 28 had a 1- or 2-year return period, but 42 had a 3-year return and eight had a 4–5-year return. This means around one-third (35 percent) of decile 1–5 schools were in trouble, but the rest were doing well or exceptionally well.

- In 2011/12, of the 89 decile 1–5 schools visited, 31 had a 1- or 2-year return period, but 53 had a 3-year return and five had a 4–5-year return. Once again, around one-third (34 percent) of decile 1–5 schools were in trouble, but the rest were doing well or exceptionally well.

Therefore, *any causal* link between low decile and quality is not proven or clear: some low-decile schools can and do perform well, according to ERO.

Are low-decile schools underperforming?

In 2012/13 ERO stopped publishing the decile of a school in its reports, arguing that decile ratings are a blunt instrument and were being used as an *excuse* for poor performance by low-decile schools. Some cynics might regard this change as a rather neat way of ERO avoiding the very issues that have been outlined above: ERO seems to penalise lower-decile schools in its review process and, by implication, to favour higher-decile schools. But this seems hardly fair: decile ratings, while ERO might not publish them, are freely available anyway.

Graham Stoop, the chief review officer at the time, in an article for the *New Zealand Herald*, confronted the issue head on:

> I understand the power of socio-economic advantage and the oftentimes sad implications of socio-economic disadvantage. But I also believe in the power of education; the power of teaching; and the power of leadership to lift a person's sights, raise a person's or a school's performance to a higher standard, and to build a school beyond its perhaps expected limitations. Good schools can do this. Good schools, wherever they are, can provide high quality education and produce highly successful students—no matter what their socio-economic background. (Stoop, 2012)

To suggest that all schools, regardless of their decile rating, should be expected to perform equally well is clearly nonsense, and Stoop must be well aware of this. What Stoop is presumably saying here is that good schools with low-decile ratings can, to some extent, overcome the disadvantages their students start with, and that teachers, principals and the community as a whole need to work hard to make this happen. In Chapter 3 this basic argument was accepted.

However, one is led to an uncomfortable conclusion: given the return visit data presented above, and Stoop's view that it is possible to "build a school perhaps beyond its limitations", ERO is really saying that many low-decile schools are simply not performing and need to do better. For many hard working and dedicated teachers and principals of low-decile schools who I know such a conclusion is outrageous. From their point of view the problem is not with the school but with the expectations built into the ERO review process, which does not take enough account of the unique issues that many schools (even within the same decile) face on a daily basis. This is shown by the relative preponderance of low-decile schools that fall into the 1- or 2-year revisit category. Accepting this argument would strongly imply that the ERO methodology penalises low-decile schools for shortcomings that are simply beyond their control. This includes their ability to attract and retain sufficient numbers of quality teachers.

These are not easy issues to address, and they raise a fundamental question about whether ERO has sensible, fair and helpful ways of measuring the performance or quality of low-decile schools, given the disadvantages that many of these schools face.

Problems with the ERO review process

If we put aside the differentiated review as at least a question mark, can we rely on the mainstream 3-year return visit review process? Will this help us compare schools sensibly? The ERO review methodology focuses on six dimensions:

- Governance
- Leading and managing.
- Teaching
- Student learning and achievement
- School culture
- Engaging families.

A reading of the copious information provided by ERO about this methodology emphasises that the six dimensions are clearly inter-related, with student learning and achievement being a key indicator:

> The Six Dimensions of a Successful School ... shows how student achievement connects to effective governance, professional leadership, high quality teaching, school culture and engagement with whanau and communities. All the six dimensions directly or indirectly contribute to creating conditions that promote student learning and achievement.
> (Education Review Office, 2014, p. 29).

ERO provides a set of evaluative questions for schools for each dimension, and schools are encouraged to review themselves against these questions. The approach taken by ERO is to try to work co-operatively with schools as far as possible.[3] This model reflects ERO's own take of quality. To this extent, the six dimensions are really just a set of what we have already referred to as correlates. There is nothing new here that should surprise readers.[4] But we have another problem related to this model: can it be used to compare schools? If student learning (engagement, progress and achievement) are key and central components of being a quality school, what data are collected from schools as evidence of this?

In the case of secondary schools, the main national achievement and progress data collected are NCEA results.[5] Given this, since we know now that comparing NCEA results over time and across schools is at best problematic, we are left with an important question: are the judgements ERO makes about school quality based on these achievement data in any way credible?

ERO may well argue that NCEA results are only one aspect of their review process, and this is certainly true. A reading of an ERO review provides a range of information and judgements relating to governance, teaching, leadership, involvement of families, and so on. However, question marks about the usefulness of achievement data do leave a

---

[3] ERO has moved to what it terms a "complementary approach" to its work, which requires schools to demonstrate their capabilities in self-review.

[4] As with other sets of correlates, it is still possible to challenge the basis of the research ERO has conducted to determine why these particular dimensions are important, but we have already traversed this issue in Chapter 4.

[5] There is very little national standardised achievement information collected from all Year 9 and 10 students in secondary schools, so comparison between schools at these levels is not easy. PAT (Progressive Achievements Tests) and asTTLe (Assessment Tools For Teaching and Learning) data are used in the junior school but are limited in their coverage of subjects and are not used by all schools, so school-to-school comparisons are likely to be difficult.

significant problem if, as is presumably the case, judgements about the other dimensions are based on the extent to which they contribute to student achievement.

It is true that ERO reviewers ask schools to justify and explain the achievement data they present to their reviewers: one of the key evaluative questions ERO poses is whether the achievement data presented by schools are in fact "robust". This is wholly appropriate. ERO reviewers are no doubt perfectly aware of some of the complexities of NCEA. The problem is that decisions about what is appropriate and robust and what is not appropriate or robust in relation to NCEA are complex, and sometimes probably well beyond the brief of an ERO reviewer.

For example, in our hypothetical example of School A and School B discussed earlier in this chapter, the judgement about whether School A is underperforming is not a simple one. If a school is boosting its NCEA results by running holiday programmes to allow students to pick up credits in areas unrelated to their curriculum, will the school be seen to be outperforming a school that views this as inappropriate? Some schools have elected not to allow students second assessment opportunities, while other schools have actively encouraged this. How can the performance of two such schools be compared?

The problems do not stop here. Although ERO no longer publishes a school's decile in its reports, it certainly does take account of its decile when it makes judgements about its performance. For example, in the 2012 review of Burnside High School the reviewers commented that "student achievement in NCEA was higher than in similar schools". By "similar", ERO means of a similar decile (Education Review Office, 2012). We know now that two schools with the same decile could easily have students who have very different student profiles and motivation, thus making comparisons highly questionable.

The point here is simple enough: ERO must use NCEA as measure of student achievement in secondary schools, but the ruler is not designed to do the job that ERO is using it for.

Concluding comments

Comparing schools with one another with regard to their 'performance', particularly secondary schools, is fraught with difficulty. NCEA has brought huge benefits to thousands of our students because it is a flexible qualification designed to meet the needs of our diverse population However, it is not designed to provide precise and credible information upon which to base judgements about the performance of one school in comparison to another.

Using NCEA improving pass rates over time to claim that a school, or the system as a whole, is improving is also problematic. Parents trying to find out more about particular schools are often told to look at the ERO reviews of the schools they are interested in rather than rely on the NCEA league tables published in the newspapers. Although this is good advice, it has been shown in this chapter that some of the evidence from the ERO differentiated review process suggests that the ERO review methodology tends to penalise at least some lower-decile schools.

Furthermore, the mainstream ERO review methodology, which places student engagement, achievement and progress at its centre, is problematic for secondary schools because the achievement NCEA data the reviewers must rely on are not designed to be used for comparison purposes. The conclusion is inescapable: trying to measure the quality of schools in order to *compare them*, using our current achievement data, is not sensible or appropriate, and can lead to some unwarranted conclusions.

Is there another way? How *should* we compare and measure quality effectively? Should we even try? Before we develop these ideas it is important to understand how attempts to improve our education system have foundered over the years and to ask what lessons, if any, can be learned.

PART 2:
Educational reform in New Zealand: What goes wrong?

New Zealand, like many other countries, has a history of significant attempts to reform its education system. The big issue remains the persistent disparity of achievement within the country. It appears that attempts to address this issue have not been successful. Why is this? And, more importantly, what can be learned for future reform efforts?

In Part 2 I will examine four major recent attempts at educational reform in New Zealand:

- Tomorrow's Schools
- NCEA
- *The New Zealand Curriculum*
- the National Standards.

My purpose will be to analyse the reform *process* in the hope that lessons can be learnt for future reform efforts. Therefore, for each reform:

- some background will be provided, to place the reform in a context
- a judgement will be made as to whether the reform achieved its objectives
- an analysis and critique of the reform process will be presented.

As each reform is examined the messages will become clear and will be repeated. Educational reform has been relatively unsuccessful in New Zealand since the 1990s because of consistent:

- poor-quality policy development and research
- poor implementation, and an absence of proper evaluation of the reforms
- absence of leadership from government agencies and school principals
- failure to focus on the essentials—the teacher and what the teacher does in his or her classroom.

Chapter 6: Tomorrow's Schools

Introduction

Tomorrow's Schools was a bold administrative reform introduced by the Lange Labour Government in 1989. The consensus at the time was that the education system was not delivering, particularly to Māori students. It was argued that part of the reason for this was that it was over-regulated and heavily bureaucratic.

The impact of Tomorrow's Schools has already been commented on by many academics and observers, so it is not necessary to present a detailed history in this chapter. The purpose here is to critically examine the *reform process*. In order to do this, though, a brief background is necessary so that we can understand why the reform has not been as successful as might have been hoped.

Background

The key assumption of the proponents of the reform was that devolution of decision making and accountability would improve the education system, particularly for Māori students, by freeing up enterprise and innovation. According to David Lange, it represented a

> good mixture of responsiveness, flexibility and accountability ... the government is certain that the reform it proposes will result

> in immediate delivery of resources to schools, more parental and community involvement, and greater teacher responsibility. It will lead to greater learning opportunities for the children of the country ... particularly the needs of Māori education. (quoted by Wylie, 2009, p. 7)

Lange also made it clear at the time that the reform was an administrative one and that it would be complemented by both curriculum and assessment reform in the future, as indeed it was, in the form of the new New Zealand curriculum and qualifications frameworks, which were rolled out in the 1990s. Some of the initial key aspects of the reform were captured in *Administering for Excellence*, otherwise known as the Picot Report, which was published in 1988. This report needs to be read in the context of major public sector reform throughout New Zealand at the time. The Post Primary Teachers' Association (PPTA) summarises it as follows:

> Schools were to enter a new world of mission statements, priorities, and accountability, all of which would make them more efficient and effective. They would be kept up to the mark by 'consumers' who would choose to send their children elsewhere if dissatisfied, and by the review and audit agency that would monitor performance. (PPTA, 2009)

This major re-tooling of the education system included the following changes (Wylie, 2009; NZCER, 2013).

- Education boards were abolished and boards of trustees took over their functions, with the right to hire and fire and determine school policies.[1]
- Schools were to establish their own *charters* to define their purpose and aims. The school charter would be supported by a range of school policies, which set out the school's position on all educational, administrative and operational matters. Charters were specifically required to address equity issues.
- The Department of Education was to be replaced with a much smaller Ministry of Education, whose role was to be largely *policy*

---

1 Secondary schools already had boards of governors with significant powers, so the bigger change here was for primary schools.

based, so that schools could get on with their jobs without undue central government interference or involvement.
- A new Review and Audit Agency (later known as ERO) was to be established to monitor school performance.
- A Teacher Registration Board was established to register and regulate teachers.
- The New Zealand Qualifications Authority (NZQA) was established to quality assure schools' assessment policies and practices and to (later) administer NCEA.
- Schools were to be given considerable freedom with which to spend their operational budgets without Ministry of Education interference, by way of an operational bulk grant.

A number of other proposals got started but did not last, including:
- the establishment of community education forums, which were to feed into a national education policy council—the concept here was to provide community input into national policy development, but the council was never established and the community forums barely started before they were abolished
- the setting up of a parent advocacy council, which was abolished in 1991
- the establishment of a form of zoning, which allowed students the right to enrol at their nearest school, but also allowed schools to take anyone else—this was done away with in 1991 and schools were allowed to determine their own zoning rules (which effectively removed any zoning rules) although zoning regulations were tightened again in 1998 and again in 2001.

The original Picot Report also included proposals to:
- bulk fund teachers' salaries as well as the operational grant—various attempts were made to do this, but it was done away with in 2001
- remove teacher registration, thereby freeing up entry to the profession—this was done briefly in 1991 but registration was soon reintroduced
- employ teachers and principals on fixed-term contracts—principals were placed on fixed contracts briefly, but the policy has since been shelved

- introduce performance pay—this had not been put in place at the time of writing.

National Education Guidelines (NEGs) and National Administration Guidelines (NAGs) were introduced in 1993 (Ministry of Education, 2013a). Although not part of the original Tomorrow's Schools package of measures, these guidelines documented the legal requirements placed on all schools regarding the delivery of the curriculum and school administration. They continue to exist today and form an important part of the legal framework within which schools are required to work.

The key issue increasingly recognised by the Ministry of Education from the mid-1990s was that the highly devolved system set up under Tomorrow's Schools could not easily operate effectively as a *national* education system. The Ministry and the Minister lacked significant central or regional power. As a result, bureaucrats in Wellington often ruefully complained that all they could do was "influence". Schools were independent Crown entities. Therefore, addressing poor performance of an individual school relied very heavily on the capabilities, propensities and resources of these individual schools. The reform had essentially swept away almost all the central and regional support networks that schools previously had access to, particularly poorly performing or high-needs schools.

Apart from the major policy function, the one significant regulatory tool left for the central authorities in the initial Tomorrow's Schools package was that of accountability, in the guise of ERO and NZQA reporting. It is probably true that a poor ERO or NZQA report did galvanise some action by a failing school, if only to ward off the media.

However, the actual means of improvement was to be provided largely by the school itself, regardless of its capabilities and resources. Poorly performing/high-needs schools were therefore to be held accountable for their performance, even if they did not have the capabilities and resources to meet expected achievement levels or other targets. The Ministry of Education could take little responsibility to help them build the capabilities and resources required to achieve these targets. The reality was that it had little ability to intervene meaningfully from the centre, *other* than to hold schools accountable through its sister agencies, ERO and NZQA.

The logic became rather circular: simply holding a school board and principal of a poorly performing/high-needs school accountable produced no meaningful solutions or answers because the school was poorly performing and had high needs, and as a result did not have access to the required capabilities and resources.

The system has evolved over the years and it is clear that the original very constrained role assigned to the Ministry of Education has been allowed to expand. According to Wylie, through the 1990s into the 2000s it became apparent that the hands-off approach from the Ministry, and the associated lack of support for schools, was not working, particularly for those schools that were actually in need of support. As a result, the Ministry gradually took on an expanded role in curriculum development, literacy and numeracy, ICT, Māori education and evidence-based teaching/assessment practice (Wylie, 2009, p.14).

In 2010 the Ministry began its most significant and overt intervention by introducing what was called the Student Achievement Function. In a letter to all principals, Karen Sewell, the then Secretary of Education, stated that the Government intended to take a "much stronger frontline focus on lifting student achievement". She went on to say that "while there is much to be proud of in our education system too many students aren't achieving even the minimum qualifications they need". Finally, she explained that the aim of this "refocused approach is to ensure all schools have the capability to improve outcomes for all students" (Sewell, 2010).

It is clear from Karen Sewell's letter, and subsequent actions from the Ministry, that the original hands-off approach has evolved, and the current Ministry is very much more active in the sector, working with and supporting schools far more than was the case even 10 years ago. However, it should be made clear that despite this watering down of the Tomorrow's Schools philosophy, New Zealand remains one of the most devolved education systems in the world, with individual schools given far wider powers and responsibilities than most overseas jurisdictions could conceive of.

School boards remain as Crown entities: they are required to meet the National Administration Guidelines (NAGs), National Educational Goals and National Educational Guidelines (NEGs) which set out their major responsibilities. However, they are, to a great extent, free to decide *how* they will do this.

New Zealand still does not have a strong regional or district education structure, as is the case in almost every other similar nation in the world.[2] Boards appoint principals as chief executives and are then required to performance manage that chief executive. The Ministry has no part to play in this process, or in the process of hiring and firing teachers.[3] It is the job of ERO to monitor the performance of boards and schools. ERO evaluates the performance of the board against the requirements of the NEGs and NAGs, and it is up to the board to address the issues raised, not the Ministry.

Rather than an education *system*, New Zealand has more of a market place, where schools operate relatively independently within broad guidelines set by government.

Has the Tomorrow's Schools reform achieved its objectives?

It is true that the reform did reduce much Wellington-inspired micro-management and compliance-driven behaviour. School principals of the time will no doubt recall the school manuals, which contained all that was necessary to get anything done, down to the most mundane school maintenance tasks. The freedoms gained were well received and there would be few who would want to return to the pre-reform days of central control, administration and micro-management. Many schools have developed a pride in what they do, and many boards consider that they have forged new and innovative ways of operating.

Furthermore, as indicated above, the system has evolved so that there is more support for schools and a greater role for the Ministry than first intended by the original reformers. The Ministry has encouraged schools to use evidence-based research to redesign their teaching programmes. A large number of important teaching initiatives have been designed and supported through the years by the Ministry—some more successful than others. The Student Achievement Function, men-

---

2 The Ministry of Education does have the authority to dismiss a board and place a commissioner in its place where there is a major failure. However, it is generally the objective to replace the commissioner with a new board as quickly as possible.

3 The Teachers' Council, another government agency, retains the role of registering and disciplining teachers.

tioned above, has been an important and worthwhile development, at least in intent.

Also, ERO has moved from being an audit agency to one that has tried to develop a role for itself that is capacity building as well as accountability based. And yet, as Wylie states:

> There is no evidence that giving schools control of their budgets and employment decisions *per se* led to system-wide gains in student performance or learning, or new approaches to learning, or greater equality.
>
> Student performance in the international tests generally showed little change; and the New Zealand results for mathematics and science were termed 'mediocre and disappointing' (Minister of Education, 1998). No major progress had been made in reducing the number of low achievers or closing the gap between students related to differences in their home.

Since 2002, of course, some might argue that there have been improvements in achievement as measured by NCEA results. However, the point is that these improvements, if they are meaningful, are not attributable to the Tomorrow's Schools reform. According to Wylie:

> Secondary qualifications levels and the retention of students in secondary schools either dipped or showed little improvement *until the introduction of a standards based qualification in 2002.* (Wylie, 2007, p. 2) (Emphasis added.)

To this extent, the contention is that Tomorrow's Schools has failed to deliver any improvement in student outcomes. In fact, although some might argue that it has provided schools with certain freedoms to act, which have made for a more responsive and less bureaucratic system, it may well have done considerable harm.

Despite the evolution (or watering down) of the model, its bedrock philosophy remains based on individual schools acting to further their own interests. This has turned out to be a real problem for many of our schools, particularly low-decile schools. In my experience, both as a principal in provincial New Zealand and in Auckland, and as a as senior NZQA leader overseeing NCEA, lower-decile schools inevitably find it difficult to compete in this market environment.

Here is how it still works in the market place of 'Schooling New Zealand Incorporated':

- Low-decile schools have far more educational and social challenges than higher-decile schools. No amount of complaining from principals of high-decile schools about how demanding their middle-class families are can change this fact. Low-decile schools are harder to teach in than high-decile schools because they have more students who are having to cope with significant educational, economic and social problems.

- Many teachers who choose to work in low-decile schools are often passionate, dedicated and committed. However, in the reality of the market place, principals of many low-decile schools tell me that they often attract fewer high-quality teachers than high-decile schools. Many know perfectly well that they sometimes have to settle for their second or even third choice, even from the limited range of applicants they receive for some of their jobs. A number of these principals also admit that some of their teachers are caught in a trap of low expectations and poor performance as a result of battling hugely difficult educational issues for years with only limited help.

- Many low-decile schools find it harder than high decile schools to attract board members with the required skills. This is hardly surprising. Sometimes there are few contenders. Some of these parents have to do two jobs and they are exhausted. Sometimes they are willing and have the time but have limited understanding of their governance roles. Although they are offered some training, it is limited. These board members often do not have access to the kinds of networks and resources that their high-decile counterparts are likely to have.

- High-decile schools often draw more motivated students from low-decile schools. There is nothing quite so frustrating for a principal and teachers of low decile schools as to watch students drive or bus past their front gates because they or their parents believe that they will obtain better academic support from the higher decile neighbouring school. Unfortunately, however, the fact is that high-decile schools, on average, have better NCEA results than low-decile schools. This is the reason that they continue to attract more academic students, ensuring that low-decile schools continue to perform poorly.

- Many parents think that placing their children in a high-decile school will improve their life chances (and they may well be correct, as we have seen), and pleas from teachers and principals to send children to the local school do not wash. The government supports the local school argument with enrolment scheme legislation, but these enrolment rules can be avoided. Sometimes high-decile schools offer sponsorships or other incentives to poach more able students for their sports teams or music programmes.

- Low-decile schools, as we have seen, are more likely to be penalised by ERO, and yet they have limited financial or personnel resources to address the issues they face. High-decile schools have more discretionary money than low-decile schools and are better able to address problems.

- Low-decile schools are overwhelmingly populated by Māori and Pasifika students, have more social and discipline issues than high-decile schools and therefore are not attractive options for some families. As a result, low-decile schools often get into a vicious spiral: falling rolls result in less money from the Ministry of Education and inadequate resourcing, and this in turn causes the roll to drop further. Middle-class flight from low-decile schools is now normal. The reverse is true for high-decile schools, with burgeoning rolls attracting more resources and more students.

I am not suggesting that low-decile schools cannot add huge value to their students. There are some very successful low-decile schools, and this is confirmed by ERO's differentiated reviews, as we have already noted. The point nevertheless stands: the current competitive Tomorrow's Schools model advantages higher-decile schools and disadvantages lower-decile schools. As a result, lower-decile schools are often marginalised and ghettoised. This is good for high-decile schools and bad for many students left in low-decile schools, who suffer stigmatisation and continued failure. It is truly awful for the cohesiveness and social and economic wellbeing of New Zealand as a whole.

This situation, perpetuated by the reform, is arguably a major reason for the continuing disparity of achievement in New Zealand noted by the OECD and highlighted by our NCEA results. How, one might ask, do we expect to address this problem when we place our most needy and disadvantaged students into a system that further disadvantages them?

The reform process

We move now to the most important part of this chapter by asking what it was about this reform process that resulted in massive problems for thousands of our children and many of our schools so soon after its implementation?

Poor-quality policy development

A key assumption of the initial reformers was that freeing up schools from unnecessary bureaucracy and making them each accountable to their community[4] would drive school quality and achievement up. Nowhere in the Picot Report or the following Tomorrow's Schools report was any evidence or research cited that could be used to support this assumption. Although one of the key purposes of the reform was to improve learning for children, *particularly the disadvantaged*, the reformers assumed (wrongly) that changes in the administration and organisation of our schooling system would *somehow* lead to educational benefits.

To put it more bluntly, this massive change in the way the education system was organised was based on nothing more than a political ideology, which was being applied across much of the state sector at the time. The package of proposals— complete with bulk funding, freeing up enrolment zones and community input—was certainly internally consistent: this was a business model of education, whereby schools would compete, and the good ones would attract customers, the bad ones would gradually wither away, the 'customers' would get what they want, and quality would improve.

Unfortunately, not enough policy work was done to predict and then analyse the actual likely downstream consequences of the implementation of the package. How would schools access support if they required it? What would the consequences be in communities of schools competing with each other? If there were to be 'winner and

---

4 Through their boards, ERO and NZQA.

loser' schools, how would students left in loser schools be supported? What would be the impact of the reform on the role of principals? How would principals manage their workload? Would boards of trustees be able to sustain and develop the skills they needed? What would be the effect of creating over 2,500 independent entities on collaboration between schools? On what basis was the promise of better outcomes for Māori students made?

Of course all these questions are asked with the benefit of hindsight, and yet one would have imagined that someone, somewhere, in the Minister's office or the Department of Education would have been tasked with thinking some of these issues through before the reform was unleashed on the country.

What is staggering is that this was not done. This lack of foresight and good policy development helps explains why so many of the building blocks of the original reform concept came and went, or did not eventuate at all. For example, as stated above, community education forums, something that Lange regarded as a key aspect of the reform, were never properly established. The Parent Advocacy Council had come and gone by 1991. The joint council to co-ordinate the many new government agencies, born out of the demise of the Department of Education, was never established. Enrolment schemes were initially put in place to ensure students could attend their local school, and then effectively removed in 1991—and then reinstated in 1998. Bulk funding came and went. The new Ministry was to be hands off, but gradually grew to become more hands on.

Although some of these apparently arbitrary changes occurred as a result of a change in Government, the problem was that the entire policy framework that should have underpinned the reform *did not exist*, and as a result the coherence of the vision for Tomorrow's Schools, which was evident in the Picot Report, was never fully implemented. Instead, the nation was presented with a range of *ad hoc* decisions, which were a response to *political* imperatives rather than policy or educational ones.

Given the very limited policy work that was done for an incredibly radical experiment in a highly charged political setting, this reform was essentially a leap of faith. Tellingly, although it has created interest overseas, no other jurisdiction in the world has cared to emulate it in over three decades.

Poor implementation and absence of evaluation of reforms

No account was taken of the changes that were required in schools to actually put the reforms into place. Although the Ministry did set up an implementation unit, the implementation process was rushed and chaotic. Concerns expressed by principals, the PPTA and teachers at the time were generally ignored as teachers and principals embarked on a massive exercise in writing mission statements, policies, property plans and management documents. Some of these may have been necessary, but the process involved in producing them was terribly flawed.

As the change process unfolded it was obvious to everyone that the implementation was putting immense pressure on principals, teachers and boards, as one might have expected given the magnitude of the changes. According to Wylie (2012):

> There was just 14 months between the Tomorrow's Schools policy document and the changeover date of 1 October 1989. (p. 89)

> Insufficient time or support also marred the development of ... charters. They were to be given to the Ministry of Education at the end of 1989—by boards that did not start work until June. Five or six months was nothing like the time needed, ... (p. 91)

As they focused on the administrative requirements of coming to grips with property and financial management, and as they fought their way through the development of charters and policies, it was very clear that the focus on classroom teaching and instructional leadership waned. Although the Ministry tried to help with a variety of training programmes and communication strategies, those in schools felt that the process was poorly planned and far too fast. Inevitably, the quality of what was done at this time by many schools was variable, to say the least.

The proponents of the reform did not establish any mechanism for evaluating its impact on the performance of schools in terms of improving student achievement. This is staggering! No one knew if there was a *causal* link between an administrative reform of this type and student achievement, and no commitment was made to find out. In fact, no data were produced that served as a baseline or a means to make a judgement. Given this, is it not surprising that in 2014, more than two decades on, there has never been an official comprehensive government review of the effects of Tomorrow's Schools on the education system as a whole?[5]

Absence of leadership from government agencies and school principals

Once the Department of Education disappeared and boards of trustees took up their new roles, there was little opportunity for government agencies to provide leadership.[6] The whole point was that local communities and boards were expected to step up, and many boards and communities did. The difficulty was that each community and each school around the country was working independently to achieve its goals, its charters, its own policies, its own interpretations of what was required. Nationally, by the very nature of the reform, coherent educational leadership was conspicuous by its absence.

Within schools the change in role for most principals, particularly in the smaller schools, was largely unrecognised. Some training was offered, but far too little and too late. The critical qualities required to lead an effective school in the newly devolved environment were highly sophisticated and nuanced. Principals in this environment needed to retain instructional leadership but also become a human resources, property and finance manager. Principals found themselves overwhelmed, overworked and unprepared for what was to come. Given that the entire system was built around principals providing strong leadership and becoming more responsive to their communities, this lack of support and training was a very important reason why no real progress was made in the critical area of student achievement.

Many principals did not understand—and some did not accept—that their leadership role had fundamentally changed. They were no

---

[5] We should note that a series of surveys, based on questionnaires, were administered by the New Zealand Council for Educational Research and funded by a purchase agreement with the Ministry of Education through the 1980s and 1990s. These surveys, using a sample of primary and intermediate schools (not secondary schools), questioned teachers, principals, board members and parents about how they felt the reform had affected their schools. Although the data collected were interesting, they did not in any way constitute a proper evaluation of the reform of the education system. The Lough Report, produced 6 months after the establishment of the Ministry of Education, was a Treasury view of the unfolding new system, and suggested that the original pure "business model" of the reform was being thwarted by officials during the implementation process.

[6] One might argue that the overarching policy leadership role had already been exercised in establishing the structure for Tomorrow's Schools. However, from this point on the intention was for the Ministry of Education and the government to be hands off.

longer simply the lead teacher of an institution that was highly regulated and in which their powers were constrained and their performance closely scrutinised. They were now chief executives, who had enormous powers and who had been given a very demanding leadership role.

Lack of focus on the essentials of teaching and teachers

Regardless of the lack of any evidence or research base, nothing was done to transfer the assumed benefits of the *administrative* and market-driven reforms into better teaching and learning. No mechanisms or support for schools were established in this regard other than making boards and principals 'accountable'.

In fact many administrative structures that previously existed to support the improvement of learning and teaching in schools, such as the school inspectorate and subject experts, were removed. The assumption was that giving schools responsibility and accountability in an environment where the consumer could choose which school to attend—or even set up their own school—would release a spirit of innovation and responsiveness to the community in schools, which would in turn lead to better educational outcomes for all students. Innovation and enterprise may well have been released, but there was scant support for schools to convert this into actual better classroom practice and teaching.

What is perhaps even worse, the new structures actually incentivised schools to act in a manner that may have taken focus away from teaching and teachers, since it encouraged competition between schools and teachers and discouraged greater collaboration. Teachers were more and more on their own, with little support from either their peers in other schools, the Ministry of Education or other government agencies.

To cap it all, during the implementation process teachers and principals were called away from their functions of teaching and learning to spend hours, weeks and months writing policies and accountability documents, which, ultimately were largely a waste of time.

Concluding comments

Tomorrow's Schools was introduced to New Zealand as part of a wider public sector reform. Its purpose was to free schools to innovate and be responsive to their local communities. The aim was to improve education for our students—it was not just an administrative reform. It was *hoped* that such a reform would, by freeing up the system, improve learning outcomes, particularly for Māori and Pasifika students.

Since the 1990s the Ministry of Education has gradually been trying to re-establish more hands-on involvement, and has over the years worked to provide leadership to the sector and schools in a range of critical areas related to curriculum, ICT, assessment, planning, and evidence-based professional development for teachers. More recently, the Student Achievement Function has marked another determined effort to intervene in and support schools.

Despite this, the basic competitive structure remains in place. The reform process was flawed because of poor policy development, an almost complete absence of research prior to implementation, poor implementation, and a complete absence of evaluation. This was compounded by an absence of appropriate leadership, both at the centre and in schools, and a failure to focus on what should be the essential part of educational reform: teaching and teachers.

Given this, it is not at all surprising that the reform has not improved learning in schools, and that it continues to cause harm to many of our students, particularly the most disadvantaged and needy, who, it was claimed, it was actually designed to support.

Chapter 7: NCEA

Background

NCEA came about because of growing dissatisfaction with the existing School Certificate, Sixth Form Certificate and University Bursaries system. New Zealand could not afford to continue with a qualifications system that was *designed* to fail approximately half the population. This approach might have been entirely acceptable in the economic and social conditions of the 1960s and 1970s, but it was no longer tolerable, sensible or economic in the 1990s.

It is important at the outset to be clear that NCEA was not really 'introduced' at all. It evolved, rather tortuously, out of a myriad of political compromises engineered by the Ministry of Education and NZQA in an attempt to satisfy two broadly opposing views in the sector and the nation. Before we can examine the reform, it is necessary for the reader to understand at least some of the issues that were being debated at the time.

On the one hand, there were those (we might call them traditionalists) who had the following beliefs:

- Competitive, time-bound examinations, set externally by a central examination authority, are better than school-based internal assessment because examinations are fairer than school-based assessment. With examinations, all candidates sit the same assessment, at the same time, and it is assessed using the same marking schedule. School-based internal assessment, on the other hand, does not require all candidates to sit the same assessment, since schools write their own assessment. As a result, the assessments can be of variable quality. The quality of marking can also vary depending on the marker and the school the assessment is taking place in.

- Assessment should be norm based and provide a rank order. With norm-based assessment, the aim is to pass a predetermined proportion of the candidates. This overcomes the problems associated with variation in the difficulty of assessments from one year to another, and also allows better discrimination of candidates because they are ranked, usually by giving them a percentage-based mark or grade. The most common way of achieving this predetermined pass rate is referred to as scaling. Scaling can result in marks being moved up or down depending on the pass rate required or the level of difficulty of the examination.[1]

- Standards-based assessment, which sets an expected standard of performance and allows all candidates who achieve it to pass, and does not set a predetermined pass rate or rank students, is not at all rigorous. The problem is that setting and writing clear standards of performance is not possible in academic subjects. Assessing a student's understandings involves considerable professional judgement from the assessor, *particularly* in academic subjects. While it is possible to write clear standards of performance for practical activities such as changing a tyre or driving a forklift truck, it is not possible to write a standard to assess a student's understanding of more intellectual activities, such as the intricacies of the origins of World War I or creative writing. Another problem with standards-based assessment is that it often requires a subject to be broken down into smaller parts, so that the assessment and grading can be directed at discrete units of learning. This breaking down of a subject into component parts discourages students from identifying the *interconnectedness* of the subject as a whole. In norm-based assessment, using one examination and one percentage mark, the component parts are subsumed

---

[1] Scaling does not change the rank order of candidates

into one holistic mark or grade, and there is no need to break the subject into smaller units.

- Academic subjects are quite distinct from vocational subjects, and vocational subjects are likely to be less cognitively demanding than academic subjects. There is a canon of academic subjects, such as English, mathematics, physics, biology, chemistry, history and geography, and it is these subjects that form the basis of what could be termed true and tested knowledge. These disciplines encapsulate something that is fundamental and unchanging. Generally speaking, students who are successful in academic subjects should go on to university and those who are more successful in vocational subjects should go on to polytechnics or paid employment.

On the other hand, reformers believed the following:

- School-based, or internal, assessment is fairer than competitive, time-bound external examinations. Teachers and schools can ensure that assessment is properly related to what has been taught in the curriculum. The assessment can be carried out in an environment that is more likely to give the candidate the maximum opportunity to succeed rather than create a stressful, time-pressured situation that is unlikely to be suitable for clear thinking. Furthermore, most assessments or tasks in the real word are not based on sitting students down to write about what they know. It is far better for students to be able to *show* what they have learned; for example, by *giving a speech*, not writing about how to give a speech; or by completing a research project on an environmental or scientific issue, rather than writing about how this might be done. More importantly, internal/school-based assessment is more likely to focus on higher-level competencies, such as analysing and synthesising, rather than rote learning, which is a feature of external assessment examinations. Issues around consistency of grading and variation in the level of difficulty of internal/school-based assessment can be addressed by high-quality training of teachers and quality learning and teaching resources. New Zealand teachers, by and large, are highly professional and can be trusted to maintain appropriate standards of assessment and marking.

- Norm-based assessment, whereby a predetermined proportion of students pass and students are ranked, usually based on a percentage mark, is inappropriate since a pass or a fail under this system provides no information about what students know or do not know. Assessment should not be about ranking students: it should be about recognising what students know and can do. This is why assessing to standards, or standards-based assessment (SBA), is better than norm-based assessment. If students can show they have reached a given standard of performance, they should be rewarded for this.
- The distinction between academic subjects and vocational subjects is not real and is irrelevant. For example, a subject such as automotive engineering or media studies could draw concepts from many academic subjects such as maths, physics and English, allowing students to understand the interconnectedness of knowledge. Furthermore, providing students with more practical ways to *apply* academic concepts is likely to engage them more purposefully in their learning than is the case in many traditional academic classrooms.

What has been described above represents an ongoing and developing national debate, but when NZQA introduced the National Qualifications Framework (NQF) in November 1991, the prevailing political philosophy was firmly in the reformers' camp.

All qualifications were to be recognised on the NQF, regardless of whether they were deemed academic or vocational. School Certificate, Sixth Form Certificate and University Bursary qualifications were to be placed on the framework at Levels 1, 2 and 3 respectively. The scholarship exam, traditionally designed for very able students, was to be placed at Level 4. The intention was to provide a national, comprehensive, quality-assured database of qualifications categorised by level of difficulty—initially to eight levels, and later (in 2001) to 10 levels.

The then Minister of Education, Lockwood Smith, stated:

> Barriers [will] no longer exist between schools and post school education and training, all courses will lead to national qualifications regardless of the place of study. (Quoted in Lee & Lee, 2001.)

Crucially, many qualifications that were to be placed on the NQF were to be assessed using *unit standards*, originally called 'units of learning', which were essentially standards based, and which provided a competency scale with just two grades: Achieved or Not Achieved. Unit standards were to be *internally* assessed (in the school or the workplace): there were to be no *external* formal written examinations.

A given qualification would be assessed using a number of specified unit standards.

A credit system allowed learners to collect credits across the entire framework, which were to be of comparable value. So, for example, (after NCEA was introduced) if four credits were to be awarded in physics at Level 3 in a school environment, they were deemed to be equal and comparable with, say, four credits awarded for demonstrating ability to provide customer service in a work situation.[2]

The NQF was to include what were deemed nationally registered qualifications only, and excluded what were termed "local qualifications". Local qualifications were all those qualifications that did not use unit standards as their method of assessment. For example, the universities opted out of the NQF, arguing that the unit standard approach would not be appropriate for university study. University degrees, therefore, were not considered to be "national qualifications".[3]

The expectation was that School Certificate, Sixth Form Certificate and University Bursary subjects would all be converted into unit standards by 1997 and placed on the NQF. The Ministry of Education began trials in a number of school curriculum subjects to begin this process.

For most teachers, and the public, the extent of the change was astonishing and revolutionary, though some aspects of it had already

---

[2] For example, the work-based, NZQA-registered, Level 3 unit standard 5886 v5 ("Demonstrate customer service and communication skills in the electronic security industry"), which requires learners to demonstrate communication skills, compose written communication, present a professional appearance and demonstrate care of the working environment, is worth four credits. Another Level 3, NZQA-registered standard 91521 Physics 3.1 ("Carry out a practical investigation to test physics theory relating two variables in a nonlinear relationship") also carries four credits.

[3] Between 2001 and 2006 the New Zealand Register of Quality Assured Qualifications (the Register) was established. The Register was to list and categorise all quality-assured (by NZQA) qualifications regardless of whether they used unit standards or not, and thus included university degrees and a huge number of other qualifications provided by a range of institutions including polytechnics. The key purpose of the Register was to provide the public with a robust way of comparing qualifications and levels, regardless of whether they used unit standards or were regarded as national qualifications.

been signalled, for example, by the 1985/86 Committee of Inquiry into Curriculum Assessment and Qualifications, established by the then Minister of Education, Russell Marshall (Department of Education, 1986).[4]

Supporters argued that this reform focused on the core business of education by *unifying* vocational and academic pathways, something that had not been attempted anywhere else in the world. The shift to standards-based assessment, and the flexibility it allowed learners in the demonstration of their learning, along with the move away from external assessment (generally formal written examinations), would ensure that all learning was rewarded and fewer learners were 'failed'. Furthermore, making this vast menu of standards available for all learners would make it possible for those who were failed by the previous system to access a much wider range of knowledge and qualifications than had previously been valued or regarded as useful.

Given the scale of the proposed change, it was not at all surprising that growing concerns around the issues outlined above were expressed by many teachers and principals, in the secondary schools sector in particular. Significant numbers of teachers and the PPTA were worried about the "atomisation" of learning as unit standards broke subjects into small learning units. Concerns were also expressed about the lack of student motivation resulting from only having two grades (Achieved and Not Achieved). Many teachers felt the inclusion of all learning, both academic and vocational, in one form of assessment (unit standards) was unworkable. Some wanted to see external assessment (examinations) as a key and compulsory part of any school qualification. Others went further and challenged the whole notion of standards-based assessment.

---

[4] The report called for internal assessment at both Form 5 and Form 6 (Years 11 and 12) and criterion-based assessment, which was essentially a form of what became known as standard-based assessment. It was at this time that that the University Entrance examination was removed and replaced with a fully internally assessed Sixth Form Certificate. The Department of Education consequently actually carried out some school-based trials in Achievement-Based Assessment (ABA) between 1986 and 1988.
Employers and the PPTA were also at the time calling for a wider range of subjects to be offered in schools, as well as more internal school-based assessment. Internal assessment was not an entirely new concept either, given that fully internally assessed options in School Certificate art, maths, science, English and workshop technology already existed in the 1970s.

It was in response to these growing concerns about the NQF that NCEA appeared in a paper entitled *Achievement 2001*,[5] published in November 1998 by the then Minister of Education, Wyatt Creech. NCEA essentially combined existing ideas on the new framework with some new ones.

New standards, called achievement standards, were to be written for all school curriculum subjects. Achievement standards were to be standards based. There would generally be only between four and seven standards written for each subject (this partly addressed the atomisation argument, for which unit standards were criticised). Each standard would be assigned a credit value related to the amount of work a student would need to do to complete it. Each subject at each level would have standards totalling 24 credits. At least half of these credits would be externally assessed, by examination.

Reporting one grade or percentage mark for an entire subject was to be dispensed with. Instead, each standard would be graded and reported separately on a four-point scale: Not Achieved, Achieved, Achieved with Merit, and Achieved with Excellence. This new four-point scale was a major change from unit standards, which had only a (two-point) Not Achieved/Achieved scale. The new four-point scale, it was hoped, would provide more motivation for students to excel rather than just settle for a pass grade.

Students at school were to be assigned their own personal Record of Learning (RoL), and all grades from all their learning, throughout their life, would be recorded on this RoL, standard by standard. In this way, employers or tertiary providers could view a detailed profile of a person's learning. For example, in English a learner might have achieved an Excellence grade in creative writing but only an Achieved grade in formal writing.[6]

Rolling out the new achievement standards

Writing the new achievement standards was a massive job, and the Ministry of Education elected to use teachers to do this. Time was short. Standards had to be written, resources prepared, policies devel-

---

5 An early version of NCEA was actually launched in 1996.
6 This level of detail was missing under the old School Certificate/University Bursaries system, which merely reported one mark/grade for the entire subject.

oped, computer systems set up, quality assurance process enhanced, and training completed for teachers, all in time for a phased introduction of the new certificate in 2001 at Level 1.[7]

This was not just a matter of writing down some content for teachers to deliver. New Zealand was moving to *a standards-based* system of assessment, which required outcomes of learning to be clearly documented. On top of this already challenging task, the writing parties were required to assign a credit value to each standard and to specify outcomes for the extra grades of Merit and Excellence.

The standards *were* written, and this must count as a big success in itself. However, given the very tight time frame allowed for this process it is hardly surprising that they were not all of the same quality or even consistently written across different areas.

Supporting assessment resources

The story was similar with regard to *the teacher assessment resources*, which were to be developed to support the newly written standards. The Ministry of Education accepted that teachers would need quality assessment resources to support them through the roll-out process. This was done by contracting teachers to do the required work on a part-time basis. Not surprisingly, given the enormous amount of work required to write assessment resources and the very short time lines, many of these resources were not of the highest quality.

Internal assessment and moderation

Internal (school-based) assessment was to be increased in most subjects at Levels 1 and 3.[8] This decision was an important and controversial one. Critics argued that internal assessment would be prone to 'gaming' by schools, that there would be no consistency in marking across different schools, and that it would increase the workload of teachers because they would have to do more marking.

---

7 In the event, Minister Mallard postponed the start until 2002.
8 With the introduction of NCEA, the amount of internal assessment was actually *reduced* at Level 2, since Sixth Form Certificate, prior to NCEA, was entirely internally assessed. With the introduction of NCEA at least half of the assessment was supposed to be externally based at all three levels, including Level 2, where Sixth Form Certificate was delivered. The problem was that the way internal assessment was carried for Sixth Form Certificate was tightly controlled, and grade allocations were based on the performance of the students from the *previous year's* School Certificate examinations, thus destroying any notion that Sixth Form Certificate was in any way standards based.

As the new qualification was rolled out it was important that NZQA ensure that the quality of internal assessment was credible and rigorous across the nation. This matter was addressed in a number of ways. First, schools had to be *accredited*[9] to be able to offer NCEA. Gaining accreditation was a massive exercise for most schools, and required an entire systems check to ensure they had good policies and procedures in place to deliver the qualification. This meant that most schools had to write a whole suite of policies, relating to assessment matters in particular, but personnel, financial and property issues had to be addressed as well. If a school gained accreditation, it had effectively been awarded a 'quality licence' to deliver the qualification.

The second important way NZQA tried to assure the public that the quality of internal assessment in schools would be robust was through what was called the 'moderation' process. The term 'moderation' has a number of different meanings, even among educators. For our purposes here, moderation provides a mechanism to ensure the grade awarded by teacher A in school X for a *particular piece of student work* will be the same grade as awarded by teacher B in school Y. Moderation, in other words, is about ensuring *consistency* of assessment judgements between teachers, wherever they are.[10]

The view taken by NZQA on this matter was a perfectly reasonable one. The best way to ensure internal assessment is consistent and of a high quality is to ensure teachers understand the standard required. Getting consistency across schools was best achieved through professional development and feedback to teachers. Teachers would therefore be asked to select work they had graded and submit it for checking by moderators. Teachers would be encouraged to submit graded work which they were *least* confident about, so that they could be provided with feedback to help them make the best assessment decisions possible

---

9 The term 'accreditation' in this context has now been replaced by 'consent to assess'.

10 External assessment (mainly by examination) needs less moderation than internal assessment, because with external examinations all students sit the same assessment task and it is marked by a small number of external markers. On the other hand, with internal assessment the assessment tasks can vary across schools and are marked by teachers in their own schools.

in the future.[11]

These part-time moderators (mainly teachers) would make judgements about how accurately the teacher had graded the work and return it to the school, often with a 'score'.[12] Because the process was meant to be completely objective and free of bias, moderators' names were not published in any official documents or circulars for fear they may be pressured or otherwise influenced in their moderation decisions by teachers in their own schools or regions.

The third way to provide assurance to the public about the quality of internal assessment was the NZQA Managing National Assessment (MNA) school visit and report. The purpose of this audit was to check school quality assessment systems, generally every 3 years, so that the school could maintain its accreditation.

MNA visits were essentially document and policy checks. Senior staff were interviewed and questioned about how they carried out their assessment and moderation. Commendations and recommendations were made, and where serious problems were discovered it was possible for NZQA to effectively withdraw permission for the school to assess until it had addressed the identified problems.[13]

Other than the moderation and MNA reporting, as described above, no real attempt was made to provide an assurance to the public that teachers were assessing accurately and that students were not being awarded grades that were either too high or too low. This was clearly a high-trust model of moderation. The public and the community as a whole were to trust that the professionalism and expertise that schools and teachers brought to the process would ensure fairness and consistency of assessment decisions across the country. As a result, no national measures were put in place to measure the robustness of grading in individual schools or across the country. Even the judgements made by

---

11 Although teachers received feedback about their assessment decisions, students' grades were not altered, even if moderators disagreed with the teachers' decisions. The logic here was that teachers would 'do it better' the next time. Changing students' grades *after* moderation would have caused major logistical problems as well as being unfair to all those students whose work had not been submitted by teachers for moderation.

12 For example, teachers might be informed that "6 out of the 10 pieces you have submitted were at the right standard while 4 were not".

13 MNA visits did not involve classroom visits and certainly did not involve looking at samples of student work. Essentially, MNA visits focused on ensuring the school had appropriate and robust assessment policies and systems in place. The extent to which these policies and systems were properly *used* was not a strong focus.

moderators about the work submitted by teachers were not particularly useful as a measure. The samples of work collected were hardly typical, given that *teachers themselves* selected the work they wished to submit.[14]

External assessment

A huge amount of work had to be done by NZQA to ensure that external assessments by way of examinations were ready for all subjects at the end of the year. Examination standards were to be treated in the same way as internally assessed standards. They would be assigned credit values and would be graded using the NAME categories (Not Achieved, Achieved, Merit and Excellence). Many subjects had three standards to be examined in a 3-hour period, but a number had more than three and some had fewer than three. All examinations were 3-hour, regardless of the number of standards to be assessed.[15]

In general, the final NAME grade awarded was to be based on an intricate process of counting the subsidiary NAME grades awarded for each sub-question or section of the standard. For example, to receive a final grade of (say) Merit may have required a student to gain at least three Merit grades for particular parts of the standard, as this would have been assumed to reflect the overall quality of the answer given. Although this approach mostly worked, it was cumbersome and sometimes penalised good answers for minor mistakes.

Since this was a standards-based system, as with internally assessed standards students would be awarded the grade they were deemed to have achieved regardless of how many or how few students had achieved the required standards nationally. There was to be no predetermined pass mark. If students achieved the required standard, they were to be rewarded with the appropriate grade.

NCEA as a multi-field qualification

An early decision was made to make NCEA a *multi-field qualification*,

---

14 Critics were quick to point out that if teachers themselves were selecting the student work they wished to be checked, they were likely to protect themselves against criticism by only selecting work they were very confident about regarding their grading decision, in which case the school would look better than it actually was. Alternatively, teachers might choose to send in work they were not confident about, as they had been asked to do, in which case the school would look worse than it actually was.

15 A student being assessed against one standard was given the same amount of time as a student who was being assessed against three standards. This is still the case at the time of writing.

one of only two qualification of this type on the framework. This meant that any combination of standards—academic or vocational—using achievement and/or unit standards could be used to gain credits that could contribute to the 80 required to be awarded the qualification.[16]

This created a flexible qualification that could be adapted to meet the needs of all learners and gave most a better chance of success. So called 'non-academic' students could gain NCEA using a vocational pathway, while so-called 'academic' students could gain the same qualification using an academic pathway. Other students could combine academic and vocational pathways.

Students would leave with a Record of Learning, which would provide a comprehensive listing of the standards a particular student had used to gain the qualification. This ensured that employers and tertiary institutions were made aware of the standards used to gain the qualification by that student.

Policy and implementation issues

NCEA was introduced level by level, with Level 1 in 2002, Level 2 in 2003 and Level 3 in 2004. It would be fair to say that the implementation process was problematic, with NZQA and the Ministry of Education both facing growing criticism of their handling of the policy development and implementation process. The problems were wide-ranging:

- The achievement standards in a number of important subjects were poorly written, so that the outcomes were not clear enough for teachers to assess or write assessments. Furthermore, the complexity of the marking process for externally assessed standards, already referred to above, meant that some students were penalised for a minor mistake. This nit-picking version of standards-based assessment did considerable damage to the early credibility of the qualification.

- The assessment resources to support the internally assessed standards produced by the Ministry of Education were often of variable quality. NZQA moderators who had to check these tasks often told teachers that the tasks produced by the Ministry were not up to

---

16 However, there were some specified literacy and numeracy requirements at Level 1 that had to be met before the qualification could be awarded at Level 1. These now apply at Levels 2 and 3 as well.

the required standard of quality. Teachers, understandably, were not impressed that the two government agencies charged with implementing NCEA couldn't agree on fundamental issues of quality.

- The unit standards written as part of the original unit standard trials were allowed to remain on the framework and be available to schools. This meant that in many subjects, both unit standards and achievement standards existed *for the same or similar content*. The problem was that there was little 'parity of esteem' between unit standards and achievement standards in the eyes of many in the secondary sector. Many parents, students and teachers felt that unit standards, particularly at Level 1, were less challenging than the achievement standards, though they often generated similar numbers of credits.

- This was not surprising given that the industry-based Level 1 unit standards, in particular, had been deliberately designed to be 'entry level' and basic. Achievement standards, in contrast, were designed to reflect *The New Zealand Curriculum*, which did prescribe higher levels of difficulty than many of the unit standards at Level 1, often for a similar number of credits. The result of all this was a *perception*, at least, that an easy pathway for achieving NCEA existed, which required no external assessment and simpler unit standards-based assessment. The impact of this parity issue was significant, raising questions about the fairness and credibility of the qualification itself.

- The whole concept of NCEA as a multi-field qualification provided fodder for much debate and angst. Was it right that vocational and academic standards could contribute to the same qualification, and if they did, how would this affect the academic credibility of the qualification? For many, this mixing was completely unacceptable. Furthermore, the whole idea of breaking subjects down into standards and somehow describing expected outcomes continued to be hotly debated.[17]

- When NCEA was first introduced, the expectation was that at least half the assessment for curriculum-based subjects would be external,

---

17 For supporters of the reform, however, this was not an issue; the old School Certificate and Sixth Form Certificate were essentially also multi-field qualifications in that students could select from a range of school subjects to fulfil the requirements of the qualification. As to the idea of breaking up subjects into standards, this, it was argued, was hardly new: teachers have always broken down their subjects into topics or units for teaching purposes.

mainly by examination. In practice, this requirement did not last since NCEA was a *multi-field certificate*. This meant that any standards—external or internal, Achievement or Unit—could be used to gain the qualification. Since pass rates for internally assessed standards were much higher than for externally assessed standards, some students (on mainly internally assessed Unit Standards courses), it was argued, were being awarded 'easier' qualifications than those working with externally assessed standards.

- The credibility of school-based, or internal, assessment, which was such an essential element of the new qualification, soon became a big issue, with some high-profile cases of what appeared to be very high pass rates. Teachers and schools were accused of cheating and gaming the system by marking too easily and/or inappropriately helping students with the answers.

- The fact that there were no real guidelines from NZQA about *reassessment* opportunities continued to be controversial. Under a standards-based assessment system it is perfectly acceptable for students to be given further opportunities to pass their assessment if they do not pass it on their first attempt. Some schools took advantage of the re-assessment option and allowed multiple opportunities, while others elected not to offer reassessment at all.[18]

- The fact that failure (Not Achieved) in internally assessed standards was not reported on the student Results Notice or their Record of Learning (RoL) became something of a philosophical touchstone for the qualification as a whole. On the one hand, supporters of the policy argued there was no point in reporting what was *not* achieved on a Results Notice or an RoL. On the other hand, the critics argued that a Not Achieved result did inform a user of the qualification about an important part of the student's whole performance—what was attempted and not achieved.[19]

- The combination of some poor standards, poor resources, increased

---

18 Giving students another chance to pass an assessment they had already failed was considered by some 'traditionalists' to be unfair. Reassessment also constitutes a significant additional workload for teachers.

19 For the critics, the rather inaccurate throwaway line was that under NCEA no one failed: this was patently not true, given the 50–60 percent failure rates in some standards and in the failure rates for NCEA as a whole.

internal assessment, reassessment opportunities and an entire new qualification system was a huge issue for teacher workload. Many teachers (and their union) at the time complained bitterly that they had been dealt a very poor hand by the government and the agencies. Teachers had little choice but to make the system work as best as they could, while the government and the agencies looked on and offered what was felt to be minimal support.

- NZQA's moderation system was heavily criticised since it was based on teachers submitting work for moderation which they themselves had selected, thereby, it was claimed, allowing them to 'cheat' on all the *other work* they did not send in. The fact that there was no national system of checking teacher marking or reporting how robust it was created another big question mark about the credibility of the qualification. The issue relating to the credibility of internal assessment was given a very high profile as a result of the continued publication of NCEA results in league tables.

- The four-point grading system (NAME) was a concern for some, who argued that it did not provide as much motivation for more able students as did a percentage-based system.

- On the external assessment front there were major problems, as NZQA found itself dealing with huge variations in grades awarded for a large number of standards from year to year.[20] For example, over the period 2002 to 2004 the proportion of Merit and Excellence grades in one standard went from 51.3 percent to 35 percent to 16.1 percent. In another, the proportion of Merit and Excellence grades went from 6.1 percent to 9.9 percent to 21.9 percent (Martin, 2005). Such massive variations demonstrated that there was no consistency in the quality of the exams and/or in the marking of them from one year to another. This was, of course, catastrophic in terms of the credibility of the new qualification.

- Finally, the new system required that students be given a separate grade for each standard for which they were assessed. Since some students were being assessed against up to four standards in a 3-hour examination, this meant that examinations for each separate stan-

---

20 The problem was widely spread across many subjects and many standards, at all three NCEA levels.

dard had to be quite short—often less than 1 hour. Writing short examinations of *equal difficulty* from one year to another has always been a difficult task. In the old School C/Bursary system these difficulties were hidden because all the marks for the various questions in a 3-hour exam paper were added up and the students given one overall mark for the whole paper. This aggregation had the effect of cancelling out the impact of too easy or too hard questions on the final result.[21] The new system essentially required that students be given a separate grade for each standard. There was no opportunity to aggregate the grades to produce one overall grade for the entire 3-hour paper. As a result, each individual result had to be reported separately, without any check on the level of difficulty of the assessment. This is what caused the variations in pass rates, and Merit and Excellence grades, for individual standards from one year to another.

NCEA improvements put in place to address sector and public concerns

It was this variation, and major problems with the 2004 scholarships exams,[22] that finally led to a major public outcry. The then Minister of Education, David Benson-Pope, asked the State Services Commission to review both the adequacy of the Scholarship exam and the delivery of NCEA, particularly with regard to the apparent variability of results in NCEA. By 2006 a number of the recommendations from the review had been implemented, particularly as they related to the governance and management of NZQA.

Equally importantly, in 2006 the new Minister, Steve Maharey, announced a significant overhaul of the qualification designed to address some of the more important causes of sector and public concern. The State Services Commission review and the Maharey overhaul and consequential work done by NZQA resulted in a large number of very important changes.[23]

---

21 Scaling the final results was also widely used to mitigate the impact of exams that were too hard or too easy. Scaling moved the middle mark of those sitting the exams up or down without changing the rank order.

22 The Scholarship problem was also one of variation related to a widely differing number of awards per subject.

23 The changes are not documented here in chronological order.

- There was to be a rewrite of all the achievement standards. There were at least three reason for this.
    i. The new national curriculum was to be implemented, and it was important that NCEA achievement standards reflect this new curriculum.
    ii. Existing standards, many of which (as has been explained above) were of relatively poor quality, had to be "cleaned up".
    iii. The duplication of unit and achievement standards in curriculum subjects had to be addressed. All unit standards that covered curriculum subjects were to be removed or replaced with achievement standards. The intention was to ensure that only achievement standards and *not* unit standards were used to assess the new *New Zealand Curriculum*.
- The rewrite was to be completed in 2012 (for Level 3 standards) and was to be accompanied by the publication of quality resources and exemplars.
- Internal assessment was to be given a big shake up, with the appointment of over 30 full-time moderators and the introduction of *random* sampling of teachers' graded work. Moderators were asked to provide advice to teachers as well as check their work and report back agreement rates across schools and the nation. Agreement rates were designed to show the percentage of teacher assessment judgements moderators agreed with. National agreement rates were to be published annually by NZQA.
- Schools were to be required to report their internally assessed Not Achieved results. These were to be published on students' Results Notices but not their Record of Learning (ROL).[24]
- New rules were introduced around the extent of reassessment schools could allow.
- NCEA certificates were to be endorsed with Merit or Excellence, thus providing a greater level of motivation for more able or motivated students. In order to gain endorsement, students needed to gain 50 or more credits at Merit or Excellence. Similarly, course endorsement was introduced so that students could gain Merit and

---

24 The Record of Learning (RoL) was also renamed the Record of Achievement (ROA).

Excellence awards for their subjects.

- Profiles of Expected Performance (PEPs) were introduced to monitor the variability in external assessment grades. These PEPs provided markers with information as to the expected pass rates for individual standards and alerted NZQA to situations where the exam paper or the marking was for some reason problematic, so that remedial action in the marking process could be taken.
- More training was to be provided to exam setters and markers. In addition, changes were made to the way external examinations were graded to provide markers with a more holistic and yet robust way of assessing student working so as not to penalise them too heavily for minor mistakes. A 0–8 marking scale was introduced, which provided further stability and more reliability in the grading process. Furthermore, a maximum of three standards for a 3-hour exam was established as a requirement to ensure that all students had adequate time to complete the paper.

None of these changes were without controversy, and none were implemented entirely smoothly. I can certainly vouch for this personally since it was at this time that I took up a new role as Deputy Chief Executive of NZQA with specific responsibility for NCEA. For example, teachers complained that although the new standards were mostly superior to the previous ones, the speed and quality of resource and exemplar development was still too slow and of variable quality. The new rules around reporting Not Achieved grades and reassessment have not always been adhered to by some schools, and Profiles of Expected Performance (PEPs) have been criticised as just another form of scaling.

Despite these difficulties, by 2013 the NCEA scene was more settled. Many of the improvements to NCEA had successfully addressed key issues. In 2011 an independent review by the OECD had concluded that:

> NCEA examinations have acquired a high level of credibility among students, teachers, and parents thanks to a rigorous monitoring of all the steps involved in the examination, and because of the high validity and reliability of results. (OECD (2011), p. 49)

The New Zealand Auditor General's office, which focused on internal assessment, after its review in 2012 reported that:

> Students, their parents and caregivers, employers, and tertiary education institutions can be confident that NZQA has effective systems to support the consistency and quality of internal assessment for NCEA, and
>
> NZQA is continually enhancing its processes and practices, which is helping schools to better carry out internal assessment. (p. 3)
>
> NZQA has effective systems to support the consistency, quality, and effectiveness of how schools carry out internal assessment. NZQA monitors the quality of internal assessment in schools in many ways. These methods generate useful information. NZQA uses the information well to measure the consistency and appropriateness of internal assessment and to identify and address issues within schools. (Controller and Auditor General, 2012, p. 25)

NZCER surveys of teachers and principals also showed growing support for the qualification (Hipkins, 2012).

Has the NCEA reform achieved its objectives?

A broad view of the qualification in 2014 and the reports from the OECD and the office of the Auditor General would suggest that NCEA has become reasonably successful after a deeply troubled birth. Any reversion to a more traditional external examination-based national qualification system, far from providing a more robust or valid national qualification, would probably result in more intractable problems than would be solved.[25] However, there are still rumbling issues.

- Although schools are presenting their students with a wide variety of programmes, the qualification still faces credibility issues in relation to its fundamental design intention: to provide a *multi-field qualification*, which recognises both academic and vocational pathways. There will be those who will never accept that this is desirable or possible. However, although this unitary approach is unusual inter-

---

25 External examinations are, after all, not very good at accurately identifying what students can do and know, and this fact has been recognised by most educationalists for decades.

nationally, it is gradually gaining real acceptance in mainstream New Zealand.

- Objections to the notion of standards-based assessment as opposed to norm-referenced (out of 100 percent) remain. Much more work in this area needs to be done, particularly to ensure that student motivation is maintained and, if necessary, enhanced. Course endorsement and certificate endorsement of NCEA have gone a long way to address these concerns for many, though not all, former critics.

- The improvement in achievement rates shown since the establishment of NCEA, though laudable, need to be credible, and there is a constant need to ensure that credible, school-based assessment is taking place at all times. There are still concerns about the gaming of school-based assessment, which could result in students gaining qualifications they have not properly earned. Schools are much more professional about this issue than they were even 5 years ago, and it is likely the system will continue to mature based on the professionalism of teachers and principals throughout New Zealand.

- The continued existence of *three* levels of NCEA places an unnecessary burden on teachers and students. Since almost all students stay at school to attempt NCEA Level 2, there seems little purpose in retaining a Level 1 qualification. There is, therefore, a strong case to remove the Level 1 qualification altogether, thus reducing the assessment load on both teachers and students.

NCEA: The reform process

We move now to the most important part of this chapter on NCEA. Even though we have suggested that NCEA is now well established as the national qualification, it is clear that it did not have a happy start, and that by 2006/07 it was seriously in danger of collapse. There is little doubt that the chaotic beginnings of NCEA were a direct result of a *poor reform process*, which bore many of the hallmarks of the botched Tomorrow's Schools reform we have already discussed.

Poor-quality policy development

There was very limited policy development or research work done prior to or during the implementation of NCEA. The introduction of the unitary NQF, and then NCEA, was to be a world first, and although this in itself is no bad thing (New Zealand has often been the front runner in major reform efforts), it was unacceptable that some basic *independent* government/NZQA-sponsored research related to its most significant elements was not commissioned and published prior to, or early in, its development.[26]

The fact is, the long-term implications of the proposed changes, both positive and negative, were not thoroughly examined, either in the case of the original NQF or the ensuing NCEA. Although the entire reform effort may have been seen as a wonderful opportunity to make New Zealand qualifications more inclusive, it was vitally important that those who were already 'winners' in the current system were not alienated. Officials at the Ministry of Education and NZQA were well aware of this as the reform was developed and implemented. As a result, efforts were made to include both traditionalists and opponents of the reforms in the discussions and meetings that took place. The introduction of NCEA and the initial intent to make some external assessment compulsory were the resulting compromises hammered out of this process.

My own very close observations during this period—as a principal, a strong supporter of NCEA and a member of NZQA and MoE NCEA advisory groups—is that almost all these discussions and meetings, of which there were plenty, were primarily of a *political nature*, with the protagonists attempting to reach agreement in a very compressed period of time. These were not educational or evidence-based discussions—they were *political* discussions. As a result, decisions were made

---

26 The Scottish Qualification Framework was investigated by New Zealand, but the Scottish approach at the time was far less ambitious than that adopted by New Zealand and certainly did not envisage one universal unit standard approach to assessment for all learning. Nor did it envisage a school qualification as encompassing as NCEA. Various reports about assessment and qualification in New Zealand were released in the 1980s calling for more internal assessment and more recognition of standards-based assessment. However, the concept of a unitary, all-encompassing framework of the type proposed was certainly not part of the ongoing national debate or research. In 1986 the then Department of Education did carry out some trials in standards-based assessment, but these did not last beyond 1988. A number of advocacy-based reports were also released, including the Irwin report from the Business Roundtable (1994) and the PPTA's Qualifications Framework Inquiry (*Te Tiro Hou*), 1997) probably a key forerunner for NCEA.
The 1985 Committee of Inquiry into Curriculum Assessment and Qualifications made some far-reaching recommendations, particularly in relation to internal assessment, but certainly did not envisage NCEA or a unitary framework. Nor was its work ever regarded as a substantial piece of evidence-based research.

without a proper analysis of the likely *longer-term* effects or impacts.

There is no doubt that important questions were asked by many people during the policy development process, but very little proper analysis followed. For example:

- How valid or reliable are external examinations compared with internal assessment?
- How reliable and valid would a 1-hour exam be compared with a traditional 3-hour exam?[27]
- What would be the effect of reporting results *by standard* as opposed to *aggregating* results across a 3-hour paper?
- What forms of moderation would work best?
- What impact would a four-grade or two-grade system have on student motivation?
- How might a multi-field qualification that combines both academic and vocational standards be viewed by the New Zealand public, employers, teachers and students?
- What resources would be required to support schools, and how long would these resources take to be developed and trialled?

The list could be extended, but the point is clear: had the Ministry of Education and NZQA commissioned research or accessed existing research and then completed a thorough policy analysis and development process prior to implementing the reform, many of the ensuing problems and crises from 2002 to 2007 might have been avoided.

Although some characterised these issues as "teething problems", they were not. They required continuing and major changes to the qualification as it was rolled out, to the potential detriment of a generation of our students. School-based internal assessment, for example, was a fundamental element of the new qualification but was also a major point of contention. If the qualification were to be a success, the credibility and robustness of school-based assessment was critically important. Given this, it seems almost beyond belief that so little policy

---

[27] Examinations were to be written for individual standards, most of which were designed to take around 1 hour to complete, sometimes less, and sometimes more. In some subjects three or more standards were examined separately in a 3-hour examination period. Each standard was to be marked and reported on separately.

work was done in this area.[28] As we have seen, a high-trust model was put in place with almost no regard for the objections, possible dangers and credibility issues arising out of this approach, which were being voiced across the sector. No mitigation was put in place to address these issues. The Ministry of Education and NZQA genuinely believed that somehow the public would eventually 'come round'.

There is little doubt that a proper analysis of the implications of more school-based assessment would have highlighted the dangers of a high-trust model, reviewed other options, put mitigations in place and probably changed the initial decision to use a high-trust model so early in the reform process. Such a policy development process might also have highlighted the need for some form of national monitoring of the quality of teacher grading.[29]

Although the decision to write new achievement standards for NCEA and leave similar unit standards on the framework may have arisen out of the failure of unit standards trials, this decision was another example of poor policy development, because it left so many unresolved dilemmas for the future. Most importantly, little thought was given to the downstream negative impacts of having *two* standards covering *similar* content—one with external assessment, the other *only* with internal assessment; one with two grades, the other with four grades.

It is very likely that few people understood the implications of a multi-field qualification. One is left asking whether any policy work was done to think through the consequences of allowing schools to combine standards from all sources to gain a national qualification when it was obvious that unit standards developed by ITOs were in many cases not comparable (in terms of credits) to school-based curriculum standards.

The new approach to assessment that came with standards-based

---

28 A report from an external academic or adviser was often considered adequate. For example, the Ministry of Education did commission Paul Black (Black, 2001) from King's College, London, to write a report on the proposed changes to the New Zealand assessment system. The report was supportive of the changes being proposed, while pointing out that it was a world first and predicting problems with internal assessment. Although useful, the report was written by one academic who was well known for his particular views on assessment reform. What was written would certainly not be regarded as representing a thorough policy development process for a change that would affect the entire New Zealand assessment and qualifications system.

29 A proper national monitoring process was established in 2008.

assessment, though sound in many ways, also escaped a proper policy development process. Internal assessment gave teachers much more freedom to gather evidence by observing the student at work in the classroom. If a student could demonstrate knowledge or skills that met the requirements of the standard, the student could be given credit for the standard without a formal assessment. Furthermore, if students failed to achieve what was required, it was perfectly acceptable to offer the students further opportunities to do what was required.

When teachers received an NZQA circular *Recognising Achievement*,[30] which encouraged them to give credit for qualifications through observation, collection of evidence, and further opportunities for assessment rather than a traditional test or assignment, many were concerned and even horrified. This sort of approach to assessment was light years away from what was mainstream practice for most teachers at the time. How could people be assured the teacher was being fair or even making correct judgments? How would evidence be documented? How could multiple assessment opportunities actually work? Would each assessment need to be different? Was everyone to be offered multiple opportunities? Was reassessment possible at all grades, or just at the Not Achieved/Achieved boundary? What were the workload implications for teachers?

NZQA officials made brave attempts to answer at least some—though by no means all—of these questions, but did so in response to a barrage of criticism and as a consequence without a thorough analysis of the policy implications of the advice given. Perhaps the most catastrophic failure of policy development was NZQA's inability to predict and prevent the extent of the variation in grades given for externally assessed standards during the first 3 years of examinations.[31]

The point here is obvious: how was it possible for such a catastrophe to occur to the national examinations with a new national qualification? Were experts in assessment consulted? Were trials carried out? Did anyone at all do some policy work on the implications of assessing and reporting individual standards? By all accounts the answer to all of these questions is no. Instead, it took a major scandal, a State Services Commission report and further massive denting of the credibility of

---

30 NCEA update 21 July 2004; the circular from NZQA is no longer available online.
31 See p. 102.

NCEA before action was taken to address the problem. A proper policy development process would not only have identified these issues but also put in place some form of mitigation.

It is perhaps worth pausing here to consider the role of the various Ministers of Education in the development of NCEA. I have worked with four ministers[32]—as President/Executive member of SPANZ when NCEA was being implemented, as a member of Ministry of Education and NZQA Advisory Groups, as a school principal and as Deputy Chief Executive of NZQA. My conclusion is that not a single one of them fully understood the long term implications of what was unfolding. The fact that they did not is hardly surprising given how deeply flawed the policy development process had been.

Poor implementation

The implementation of NCEA has much the same feel as most educational reforms discussed in this book: not enough time and support were provided for schools and teachers. Although Minister Mallard put back the introduction of NCEA by 1 year to 2002, this delay was clearly not enough, particularly since the following 3 years would see the rolling introduction of each of the three levels.[33]

To some extent the lack of policy and research work discussed above was a product of incredibly tight time lines. Decisions had to be made because schools required guidance and there was simply no time for the niceties of research and policy development. But the tight timelines also meant there was no time to produce the support resources required by teachers to actually implement the reforms.

Scores of achievement standards, which were the building blocks of the entire qualification, had to be written using a radically new approach to assessment which required the writers (who were almost all working teachers) to provide descriptors for three levels of achievement: Achieved, Merit and Excellence. This was a massive undertaking and had not been done anywhere else in the world.

The Ministry of Education and NZQA also failed to provide the resources to do this properly. Instead, teachers were asked to do the

---

32 Trevor Mallard (1999–2005), Steve Maharey (2005–2007), Chris Carter (2007–2008) and Anne Tolley (2008–2011).
33 Level 1 was put in place in 2002, Level 2 in 2003 and Level 3 in 2004.

work. What is staggering about this is that most were asked to do this while continuing to do their full-time jobs, rather than being formally seconded out of their usual jobs for a sustained period of time to complete what was actually a critically important job. As a result, the writing took place at weekends, during the school week and school holidays. Many teachers volunteered because they saw the process as a professional development opportunity, as indeed it was. However, the amount of time allowed for the task and the small number of teachers available to do it meant that relatively few people had enormous jobs to do in very compressed timeframes.[34]

There was not even time to establish a thorough cross-subject monitoring process to ensure that all subjects used similar approaches to the assessment process and applied the same understanding to the grading criteria or credit allocations.

The problems didn't just stop with the writing of the standards. Teachers required *assessment resources* to support the standards. The actual standards by themselves did not provide teachers with the guidance they required in the classroom. Teachers needed access to *tasks* that could be used to assess the new standards.

Providing teachers with examples of tasks was important for two reasons: the task would give them a very good idea of the level of difficulty of the work that was required for the new standard, and it would provide them with an example of an assessment task they could use or adapt in their classrooms. This support was critically important: without it, teachers would have to write *their own* assessment tasks to assess a national qualification for all their senior classes at a given level, for all topics, for 3 straight years. Quite rightly, teachers were concerned about the workload demands this made on them and, perhaps more importantly, the risks involved with the quality of what might finally be used by desperate teachers working under impossible timelines.

Teachers also required *exemplars* so that they could see examples of work at, above, and below the required standard. Teachers argued that these exemplar resources were critically important to the success of the new qualification. Without them the ability of teachers to assess to the

---

34 We should note that, unforgivably, exactly the same problems befell the agencies in the rewrite of standards started in 2008. Clearly, although lessons may have been learned from the previous cycle of writing, they were not applied.

correct standard was at serious risk.

The failure to produce quality assessment resources and exemplars for teachers was nothing short of a disaster. Teachers all over the country found themselves assessing poorly constructed standards with poorly prepared resources and, in many cases, non-existent exemplars. This is not to say that the Ministry and NZQA did not attempt to do their best. They probably did, given the time and the resources available, which were clearly grossly inadequate. The blame for this must lie squarely with the Ministers in charge at the time, and the respective leadership of both the Ministry of Education and NZQA, who clearly had not grasped the immensity of what was required.

Lack of evaluation

There are political implications in carrying out a proper evaluation of a flagship policy such as NCEA: failure cannot be an option given the potential political consequences. However, it is clear that the Ministry and NZQA were negligent in their duties because they did not establish any formal evaluation or review processes as NCEA was introduced and then implemented fully. How effectively was internal assessment being used in schools? How credible were the results? How valid and reliable were the external examinations. Was the qualification achieving what was expected? Was the multi-field nature of the qualification working as intended?[35]

The New Zealand Council for Educational Research (NZCER) was left to carry out its regular surveys of opinion about NCEA, as did the PPTA among its members. But none of this could be classed as a proper and rigorous evaluation of the reform.

Absence of leadership from school principals and government agencies

Principals failed to act in unison to facilitate a better and more coherent policy development and implementation process. The problem was that the two principals organisations, the Principals' Council of the PPTA (PC) and the Secondary Principals' Association of New Zealand (SPANZ), were busy fighting a largely ideological battle about the very existence of NCEA and were therefore unable to focus on ensuring

---

35 NZQA employed no statistician or assessment evaluation experts until 2005.

a smooth policy development and implementation process. To some extent it was the disunity among principals that allowed the Ministry and NZQA to underperform so badly.

Why a small group of just over 400 secondary school principals needs two organisations to represent them is a question we will return to. For now the point is that the leaders of New Zealand's secondary schools were impotent, unable to influence or prevent the catastrophic implementation of NCEA, which in turn had a very negative impact on their teachers and students. The debate quickly turned into a decile debate, with prominent high-decile principals (largely from SPANZ) complaining of NCEA "dumbing down", and prominent low-decile principals (largely from PC) maintaining support, albeit through gritted teeth.

The drift to Cambridge and International Baccalaureate[36] qualifications, driven by high-decile schools, turned into a marketing exercise, as unscrupulous principals played games with their communities, promising them academic international qualifications as opposed to "dumbed down" New Zealand qualifications. This disgraceful practice ensured that the implementation of NCEA became even more challenging and problematic.

The big problem with leadership being shared between the Ministry and NZQA was that they were unable to work effectively together. NZQA was the agency that was legally required to *administer* NCEA, while the Ministry was supposed to be the lead agency and policy arm. In other words, NZQA was meant to implement what had been decided by the Ministry. In practice this did not work because, as has already been shown, the policy work was woefully inadequate at the time of implementation. As a result, NZQA officials found themselves making very significant policy decisions during the implementation process, often with minimal Ministry involvement and without the benefit of any policy and research development or analysis.

Given that NZQA was effectively fronting the implementation and what there was of the policy development process, the quality of leadership provided by NZQA was critically important for success. Unfortunately it was difficult to find many signs of leadership from

---

[36] Cambridge International examinations and the International Baccalaureate offered a non-New Zealand-based alternative to NCEA.

NZQA at the time. The State Services Commission report on NZQA's implementation of NCEA stated that:

> The Executive Management Committee (which comprises the senior management team) gave scant attention to what was one of the major challenges confronting NZQA, the implementation of NCEA. The burden of implementation has fallen mainly on middle management. (Martin, 2005, p. 4)

Almost all the key decisions about NCEA were made by this group of middle managers in NZQA, who belonged to what was known as the Secondary Education Group (SEG). Unfortunately, these decisions were not properly discussed or checked by the chief executive, the NZQA senior management leadership team or the board. The worst aspect of this was that the SEG itself, left to make the major decisions on NCEA, was woefully ill equipped to do what was required of it:

> In the Secondary Education Group (SEG) more assessment expertise is required (this should include access to external advice). Its business support operations urgently need to be strengthened and made less reliant on contractors. In addition SEG should consider ways of improving its core competencies in public management. (Martin, 2005, p.4)

It is important to note that many of the decisions made by these middle managers during this period were based on what they genuinely felt was necessary to meet the very real needs of students who were currently failing in the system. Although this was laudable, the possible impact of these decisions on the entire schooling system, including those whom the current system served reasonably well—who were, by definition, in positions of influence and power—was not properly considered.

The Ministry of Education was unable to take control of the process, despite mounting concerns from 'élite' school principals, teachers and the media. All this was not lost on officials from either agency and created open resentments on both sides. Tensions became so inflamed that most teachers and principals believed neither agency was functional as a result.

An appalling example of this relates to the assessment resources the

Ministry had put online for teachers to use. It has already been noted that the quality of many of these resources was poor because of the lack of time and support provided to develop them. However, when teachers used these resources in good faith and then submitted them and student work to NZQA moderators, they were not impressed when these moderators failed the teachers for using assessment resources that were not up to the required standard. When teachers complained that these resources had been produced by the Ministry, NZQA remained unmoved.

From a school and teacher perspective this sort of disagreement between the Ministry and NZQA was unforgivable. They quite rightly had the expectation that the agencies would be professional enough to work together to ensure their customers—the teachers and students of New Zealand—could get on with the tough job they had been given of making the new qualification work.

In short, from the perspective of principals, teachers and students the implementation of NCEA was nothing short of a shambles, with poor communications, contradictory policy drivers, poor-quality support material, and poor organisation generally. The responsibility for this, partly at least, lies with the quality of leadership provided by both the Ministry and NZQA.

Lack of focus on teaching and teachers

Tomorrow's Schools was an administrative change, which reformers argued would result in better learning and teaching. By releasing schools from the burdens of petty bureaucracy and giving them the means to follow their mission, *somehow* teaching and learning would improve. We know that this did not happen because no mechanisms were created to translate the possible benefits of a market schooling system to the classroom. Accountabilities were put in place without the required support.

In the case of NCEA, proponents argued that reforming the *assessment* of the curriculum, which is what NCEA was supposed to do, would result in better teaching and learning, and therefore better pass rates and more inclusive education, particularly for those who were 'losers' in the previous system. Although NZQA and the Ministry did provide substantial professional development support for good assessment practice during the introduction of NCEA, the focus always remained on the assessment side of the equation. The assumption being made, however unconsciously, was that this would drive better teaching and that therefore better learning would take place.

However, many teachers complained that NCEA put high-stakes assessment for qualifications in the front seat of the education process and displaced the learning and the teaching, including 'formative assessment' for learning, which is the key to student progress. Teachers saw this as wholly inappropriate and damaging.

The fundamental change that teachers were grappling with was that assessment was being used simultaneously for *two* purposes: to provide informal feedback to teachers and students (for example, through multiple re-assessment opportunities, often referred to as formative assessment) *and* to gather credits for a national qualification.

For many teachers, assessment for credits and qualifications was overwhelming the more informal but vitally important formative feedback processes, which should have been a normal and integral part of teaching and learning. The result was that many teachers found themselves teaching to the specific assessment requirements of the assessment standards. It was not long before they began to complain that the NCEA reform had less and less to do with teaching or learning. Their view was that *assessmen*t was driving the teaching, and that teaching had become upstaged by the needs of an inflexible and piecemeal assessment system that required students simply to collect credits.

The big problem here was that the new NCEA standards-based system required a fundamentally different approach to teaching and assessment from the previous norm-referenced system. Teachers clearly needed much more sustained and long-term professional development than they were provided with to make the necessary changes in their approach to teaching under this new regime. They were not provided with this.[37] As a result, old-style teaching and attitudes to assessment continued to be applied, often unsuccessfully, to address the require-

---

37 NZQA and the Ministry of Education did run a series of generic and subject-based seminars and produced circulars on NCEA prior to and during the introduction of NCEA. There had been some trials in what was termed 'Achievement Based Assessment' prior to the introduction of NCEA. NZQA and the Ministry did do as much as was feasible in the time available. However, the professional development and support for the introduction of this massive reform was too little, too late and for too short a time period.

ments of a new style of assessment system.

The lack of good assessment resources and exemplars already noted made the situation even worse. The mantra from NZQA and the Ministry of Education was that teachers should prepare their own resources and thereby avoid "dependency" on the central agencies. Teachers were enraged by this attitude given the paucity of professional development support provided to them. Many were reduced to trying to *guess* at what was required and then writing assessment resources based on their guesses.

In the case of Tomorrow's Schools, teachers were expected to become more responsive to the needs of their students, but they did not, because they were overwhelmed by the administrative demands of the reform and very little was done to actually support them. In the case of NCEA, teachers were also expected to become better teachers, but they were overwhelmed by the demands of a new assessment system for which they were ill prepared. It is clear that in both cases, nowhere near enough was done to support teachers directly.

Concluding comments

The introduction and implementation of NCEA was, in many ways, doomed from the beginning. This chapter has explained the reasons behind this failure. The NCEA reform process, in echoes of Tomorrow's Schools, was flawed because of poor policy development, very limited research prior to implementation, poor implementation, an absence of evaluation, poor leadership from government agencies and school principals, and impossibly short time lines. All this was made far worse because of the limited support provided to teachers to actually change their teaching and assessment practices.

Chapter 8: The New Zealand Curriculum 2007

Background

In the foreword to *The New Zealand Curriculum* (*NZC*) (Ministry of Education, 2007b), the Secretary of Education at the time, Karen Sewell, states:

> *The New Zealand Curriculum* is a clear statement of what we deem important in education. It takes as its starting point a vision of our young people as lifelong learners who are confident and creative, connected, and actively involved. It includes a clear set of principles on which to base curriculum decision making. It sets out values that are to be encouraged, modelled, and explored. It defines five key competencies that are critical to sustained learning and effective participation in society and that underline the emphasis on lifelong learning. (Ministry of Education, 2007, p. 4)

The document provides schools with a broad enabling framework to work within, which allows them plenty of flexibility to adapt what is taught and how it is taught to their own local environment. It also, importantly, includes guidance to teachers about good teaching and assessment practice.

The curriculum itself was developed as a result of a wide-ranging and comprehensive stocktake and consultation process, which included the establishment of a high-level reference group of experts, international critiques, multiple meetings with teachers and subject experts, and large-scale questionnaire surveys seeking feedback from the community.

The new curriculum was built on the foundations of the 1993 curriculum it was replacing, and as a result there were obvious similarities between the two.

Both attempted to articulate a set of principles and values, and to identify some key skills/competencies that were considered essential for learners. They both also identified a number of "essential learning areas" and provided achievement objectives across eight levels for each.[1]

However, the 2007 version reduced the emphasis on the *content* of the essential learning areas and increased the emphasis on providing advice to teachers about good teaching and learning. The intention of the 2007 curriculum was, therefore, to move beyond subject content, towards a greater emphasis on good teaching practice. It was for this reason that the achievement objectives documented in the 2007 curriculum are broad and outcomes based, rather than full of specific content like the 1993 curriculum.[2]

The new curriculum was to be fully implemented in schools by 2010 and was launched by the Ministry of Education in 2007, after the publication of a draft in 2006. However, it was widely recognised that the curriculum's implementation would remain a work in progress for many years, given the scale of the changes that were required. According to the *NZC* document:

> Each board of trustees, through the principal and staff, is required to develop and implement a curriculum for students in Years 1–13:
>
> - that is underpinned by and consistent with the principles

---

[1] Curriculum Level 1, for Year 5/6 students, is the least difficult and Level 8, normally for Year 13 students, is the most difficult.

[2] The 1993 version produced substantial resource materials on each of the identified essential learning areas, while the 2007 version was much shorter and included sections on school-based curriculum design pedagogy and assessment.

- in which the values are encouraged and modelled and are explored by students
- that supports students to develop the key competencies.

Each board of trustees, through the principal and staff, is required to provide all students in Years 1–10 with effectively taught programmes of learning in:

- English
- the arts
- health and physical education
- mathematics and statistics
- science
- social sciences
- and technology.

Teaching programmes for students in Years 11–13 should be based, in the first instance, on the appropriate national curriculum statements. (Ministry of Education, 2007c, p. 44)

Many schools, particularly primary schools, began by talking about what became known as the 'front end' of the new curriculum, which many believed to be the more important part. This documented the vision, principles, competencies and values that underpinned it. These broadly based and deeply philosophical discussions about the nature of learning, teaching and schooling were, of course, vitally important for schools to consider before the actual practical delivery of programmes through what were known as the "learning areas".

The New Zealand Curriculum and the National Certificate of Educational Achievement

For many secondary schools, the implementation of the new curriculum was complicated by the requirements of NCEA, which had been fully implemented in schools in 2004. It is important to be clear here: all secondary schools were *required* to develop and implement their own teaching programmes based on the underpinning principles, values and competencies (the front end) of *NZC*, right through to Year 13. The back end of the new curriculum—the subjects, or learning areas—

was only required to be delivered until the end of Year 10, although achievement objectives for each of the subject/learning areas were provided right through to Year 13.

The reason for this was that the new *NCEA Achievement Standards* for Years 11–13 had not yet been written for the new curriculum. This meant that senior secondary school teachers, at Years 11–13, were expected to implement the underpinning principles, values and competencies of the new curriculum right up to Year 13 while delivering the *existing* NCEA, which was based on the 1993 curriculum and old examination prescriptions, not on the new 2007 curriculum.

It was not until 2011 that new achievement standards (at Level 1 only), based on the new curriculum, were made available to teachers for NCEA. New standards for Level 2 were not available until the 2012 school year, and for Level 3 not until the 2013 school year. This meant that after the new curriculum was officially put in place in 2010, Year 11–13 students were still being taught and assessed on the basis of the previous curriculum and/or old examination prescriptions for up to 3 years afterwards.

The problem was not confined to the senior school. Most secondary schools regarded the junior years (Years 9 and 10) as a preparation for the NCEA years (11–13) and felt that the junior school years needed to provide building blocks for the senior years. Put another way, the washback effects of the NCEA qualification into the junior school prevented effective implementation of the new curriculum into the junior school in most secondary schools because teachers felt it was necessary to prepare juniors for the realities of NCEA.

This unfortunate confusion about what was to be delivered in the senior school, in particular, was further complicated because the amount of guidance provided by the new curriculum for the senior years is limited. According to *NZC*:

> *The New Zealand Curriculum* allows for greater choice and specialisation as students approach the end of their school years and as their ideas about future direction become clearer … Students can specialise within learning areas. (p. 41)

For example, social science students from the junior school can specialise in the senior school by taking a subject such as history, geography or economics at Year 11 (NCEA Level 1). The problem is that the curriculum provides minimal guidance to teachers of these specialised areas. For example, the achievement objectives in history for the new curriculum for Level 1 NCEA are that students should:

- understand how the causes and consequences of past events that are of significance to New Zealanders shape the lives of people and society
- understand how people's perspectives on past events that are of significance to New Zealand differ.

The achievement objectives in economics at Level 1 are that students should:

- understand how, as a result of scarcity, consumers, producers, and government make choices that affect New Zealand society
- understand how the different sectors of the New Zealand economy are interdependent.

The writers of new achievement standards for NCEA history and economics were expected to create a full year's programme of study, with specific outcomes that could be assessed for qualifications, based on these very brief bullet points. Similar problems were apparent in a number of subjects, including geography, music, dance, drama and art, while accounting teachers had an even bigger problem in that accounting does not appear in the curriculum at all.[3]

It is hard to fathom the reason why some popular NCEA subjects were provided with so little guidance. It may be that the curriculum writers were attempting to organise the curriculum into more integrated learning areas. It made sense to ask teachers to think about economics, history and geography as *social sciences* with common themes, ideas and approaches, rather than as compartmentalised and completely separate disciplines.

Furthermore, as a result of the importance being placed at the 'front' of the curriculum, writers of achievement standards for NCEA were asked to focus more on values, principles and competencies than on content. This meant they did not need to include huge amounts of content in the achievement standard, and therefore the amount of

---

3 There is far more guidance available for teachers of core subjects such as English, mathematics, science, physical education and health technology in the document.

guidance required from a curriculum document did not have to be huge. The new curriculum was meant to be *enabling* and allow teachers lots of flexibility to develop their own programmes within these broad achievement objectives.

The problem, though, was that at Years 11, 12 and 13 these subjects had to be assessed nationally for qualifications. So while it may have been completely satisfactory to provide broad, enabling achievement objectives in the junior years of secondary schools and in primary schools, it was extremely problematic when it became necessary to write quite specific achievement standards that had to be assessed nationally, reported in league tables and used as benchmarks for employment and tertiary study.

All this left achievement standard writers in something of a quandary. As they began to write the new achievement standards based on the rather limited guidance from the curriculum, the teachers concerned, and the Ministry staff working with them, were faced with having to re-litigate the original intentions of the curriculum writers. Once they had done this, they had to renegotiate these intentions with their fellow specialist teachers around the country, whom they were required to consult.

To its credit the Ministry did recognise the problem and belatedly tried to fix the mess by writing what were called *Teaching and Learning Guides* to provide more guidance for subject teachers, particularly of those subjects that had received such scant, or no, attention in the curriculum document. Each guide provided a rationale for the subject, unpacked the key concepts and expanded on the learning objectives of the subject (Ministry of Education, 2014a).

There are now *Teaching and Learning Guides* on the Ministry website for most secondary subjects, and they are useful documents. The problem is that most were written *after* the achievement standards were written, and in a sense became an explanation of the standards rather than a basis for writing them in the first place. It would have made much more sense to write the learning guides before the achievement standards were written, so that the writers of the standards were provided with more guidance on the intent and purposes of the subject and the curriculum.

The key competencies

The problems with the implementation of *NZC* in the senior secondary school did not stop here. The key competencies, at the front end of the curriculum, provided another headache for secondary schools, given that they were deemed to be compulsory right through to the end of Year 13.[4] Many primary schools spent time, energy and resources working on these competencies and did some great work in their classrooms as a result. For secondary schools, however, and particularly the senior secondary school, the incorporation of the competencies into the curriculum was problematic because of the assessment requirements of NCEA: teachers, quite naturally, wanted to know whether the competencies were meant to be formally assessed and reported on, and if so, how?

This issue is an irksome one. If, as the curriculum implies, these competencies are crucially important because they focus on the generic ability to learn, not on cramming content, how were schools to measure or report on how 'competent' their students are? The problem was that to attempt to assess both the achievement objectives *and* the competencies on the basis of a particular piece of student work created huge, indeed insurmountable, assessment problems. There are other related problems: which competencies are connected with particular achievement objectives? How accurately and easily can competencies be measured? Some of the competencies such as *relating to others* and *participating* appear so generic that it may be very difficult to make objective and fair judgements.

As a result of these assessment problems it became acceptable to argue that the competencies were presumed to be incorporated in the achievement objectives. For example, success in an achievement objective in English related to formal writing *presumes* success in some related competencies, such as *thinking*.

The Ministry's advice on assessing competencies is vague. It makes

---

4 NZC identifies five key competencies:
- thinking
- using language, symbols and texts
- managing self
- relating to others
- participating and contributing.

little mention of assessment for qualifications, except to say that the competencies are "embedded" in the achievement objectives. In fact, the Ministry does not actually use the term 'assessment' at all in its advice in this matter, preferring instead to suggest that schools need to "monitor" and "document" the competencies:

> Documentation about key competencies should draw attention to how students' capabilities were evident as they participated with others in a specific context. It should be useful to learners themselves, parents/caregivers, and teachers as a tool for reflecting on and thinking about strengthening key competencies in ongoing learning.
>
> *Documentation for monitoring key competencies is not about recording indicators, criteria, marks, grades, or rubrics.* Documentation for monitoring key competencies is more about rich descriptions, examples, accounts, and narratives. (Ministry of Education, 2013b) (Emphasis added.)

This may well be a perfectly acceptable endpoint for teachers in the primary and junior school, but it leaves teachers in the senior secondary school with important unresolved dilemmas. Are they expected to monitor and record competencies in the manner suggested above? And if so, how do they integrate this monitoring with assessing achievement objectives using the NCEA grading system? If competencies are 'embedded', as suggested, how is it possible to monitor them independently? Or is it best, if possible, to monitor competencies and assess achievement standards as two separate processes?

None of this is clear to most secondary teachers. It is this lack of clarity that has meant that, in general, the competencies—supposedly a critical part of the new curriculum—have been side-lined and ignored for years. For many teachers (but not all), particularly in Years 11–13, they are simply not regarded as being as important as the achievement objectives, because it is the achievement objectives, from which achievement standards are derived, that are the key building blocks of the NCEA qualification.

None of this, of course, was a deliberate attempt by the Ministry to confuse secondary teachers; it was much more yet another act of omission. The writers of the curriculum failed to recognise that assessment for qualifications through the NCEA requires a view of assessment that is quite different from that implied (though not very clearly) in the monitoring of competencies.

The eight curriculum levels and reporting on student progress

Achievement objectives at eight levels of difficulty form a central part of *NZC*. The achievement objectives are written in a deliberately broad manner to enable teachers to easily use them in their own teaching contexts. This means that the expected performance of a student at a particular age can easily span over two or even three curriculum levels of the curriculum.

For example, although Level 6 of *NZC* might be most applicable at Year 11, it was deliberately designed so that it could also appropriately be used at Year 10 and Year 12. The logic is perfectly reasonable: children's abilities develop at different rates, and it is not possible, or appropriate, to be too prescriptive in predicting that development. Given this, it is highly likely that students will remain at one particular curriculum level for a whole year, and maybe 2 years. If this is the case, the question then becomes: How is the teacher to describe the progress of that student *during* the year?

From a secondary school perspective, when a social studies teacher teaching a Year 10 class is asked to explain whether a student has made progress during the year, they might be able to report progress with regard to some specific skills, such as drawing graphs or writing essays. The teacher might feel able to suggest that the student's work has improved over the year. However, the teacher would find it hard to measure and report on the progress of the student *against the curriculum level*, because the curriculum level descriptors are expressed so broadly. For example, a student might have remained at the *same* curriculum level for a year, but might have improved in some way that can be described by their teacher. However, there is little in the curriculum document the teacher can refer to in support of such a description.

The most notable attempt to address this problem was developed by Uniservices on contract to the Ministry of Education in 2000 in Auckland and became known as asTTLe (Ministry of Education, 2014b). The asTTLe tool provides a bank of test questions related to the curriculum for students in Years 5 to 10 in reading, mathematics and writing, which teachers can access and customise. Results from a given test can be placed on a common scale, which allows teachers to effectively measure the progress of their students and place these students at a curriculum level and sub-levels within that curriculum level. This means the student could be proficient at the curriculum level, performing at the curriculum level, or performing below the curriculum level. The assessment also provides information about a student's strengths and weaknesses within a particular curriculum level.

We do not need to go into the technicalities of e-asTTLe (as it now known) here, or some of the problems encountered during its implementation, or even some of the technical criticism levelled at it by some teachers. What is important to note is that e-asTTLe attempts to provide teachers with a method of measuring progress *during* the year, something that it is not possible to do with the existing tools provided by those responsible for *NZC*.

With e-asTTLe, a student could progress through the year from being below the curriculum level, to being proficient at the level or even above that level. A very able student might move to the next curriculum level and a less able student could be at the lower level. The important point is that at each level there is enough information to report some gradations of achievement and *progress*.

Unfortunately, the asTTLe tool was not really developed for Years 11 to 13—the NCEA years—nor was it developed for many mainstream NCEA subjects. As a consequence, most secondary teachers were left with a new curriculum that provided little support in terms of measuring and reporting on student progress. The achievement objectives were too broad and—as has already been stated—the competencies too difficult to measure.

All that was left that could be used to measure progress were the NCEA-related achievement standards developed for the senior school. Achievements standards had been written specifically to assess against particular curriculum levels. NCEA Level I was tagged specifically to curriculum Level 6, NCEA Level 2 was tagged to curriculum Level 7, and NCEA Level 3 was tagged to curriculum Level 8.⁵ However, this in itself did not help teachers to measure progress at the senior end of the school because the standards were written at a particular curriculum level.

What did help was the existence of a grading system at each curriculum level. A student could Achieve at the curriculum level, or could achieve with Merit, or achieve with Excellence.⁶ This grading system effectively provided teachers of NCEA with sub-levels within a given curriculum level. Repeated assessments against one standard in a given year, which was becoming increasingly common, enabled students to demonstrate progress over a year (for example, from an Achieved to a Merit or Excellence). For those already performing at the top Excellence level, students could be assessed at the next curriculum level and access the same gradations at that level.

To ensure that teachers were provided with as much support as possible to make these judgements, in 2007 NZQA began to develop exemplars for each standard at each curriculum level and at each grade level. Exemplars are simply annotated examples of student work that explain why a particular piece of work has been awarded a particular grade. The importance of the development of these exemplars cannot be overstated, because they provided teachers with clear guidance about the differences between grades and therefore provided them and students with a clear path for charting progress.

Of course, none of this was particularly helpful for teachers in the junior school, where NCEA was not delivered.

National Standards to Year 8

The lack of specificity in the curriculum levels, as described above, and the problems with reporting progress, particularly in the years in which NCEA is not delivered, may well have been a key driver for the development of the National Standards in literacy and numeracy, currently the

---

5 Readers may be wondering how it was possible to write achievement standards that needed to be very clear about outcomes expected for assessment purposes on the basis of the existing broad and flexible curriculum levels. The answer, as has already been suggested, is that the writers of the standards were required to "interpret" the curriculum levels and create much more specific outcomes for the required achievement standards at each curriculum level. This sort of interpretation was necessary in all subjects, and particularly in the specialist subjects.

6 The student could also fail to meet the requirements of the curriculum level altogether and receive a Not Achieved grade.

subject of so much controversy in primary and intermediate schools.

These literacy and numeracy standards are designed to be specific in their requirements based on the age of the student, *not* a curriculum level. There are no grey areas allowed here. Teachers are required to report, each year, on whether the student is *at* the required standard, *below* the required standard, *well below* the required level or *above* the required standard for their age.

Whatever the problems associated with the National Standards, and there are plenty, they are supposed to provide parents and students with measures of achievement and progress over time—something the national curriculum does not do except in the very broadest terms. In fact, there appears to be only limited reference in the National Standards material on the Ministry website to *NZC*, other than to recognise the problem we have described. For example, in the section on reporting, the Ministry comments:

> A student who has made no shifts on gross measures of progress (such as curriculum levels) can have their actual progress captured in narrative and/or scores from diagnostic assessment that more accurately describes their progress.[7]

The clear implication is that the testing associated with National Standards will be able to report on and measure progress better than any assessment based on the 'gross' curriculum level.

Did NZC achieve its purpose?

NZC had some lofty aims. It is difficult to know how to measure its success. What is clear is that the changes expected in teaching practice were substantial. The purpose here is to evaluate its impact in secondary schools (not primary or intermediate schools). This is not an easy task given the surprising absence of any comprehensive evaluation of the reform almost 5 years after it was due to be fully implemented. Some very early evaluation was completed during and at the end of the implementation process using evidence reported by ERO

---

7 See http://assessment.tki.org.nz/Reporting-to-families-whanau/Guidelines-for-reporting/What-should-be-in-a-report.

and research teams commissioned by the Ministry of Education.[8] An Auckland University study concluded that:

> While there are certainly pockets of significant progress in particular schools, the general pattern is to have made only surface level shifts, or to have addressed only certain aspects of the new curriculum. Many have been thinking about and considering how practices might shift to more strongly reflect the NZC, but fewer have actually applied those practices. (Sinnema, 2010, p. 6)

On the other hand, an ERO report also published in 2010 suggested that:

> 13 percent of the schools were already giving full effect to NZC, and 63 percent had made good progress towards implementation … very few schools had not yet begun to give effect to NZC.

and noted that:

> Apathy and resistance were generally less apparent, and in many schools, curriculum change had gained a momentum that carried staff forward with enthusiasm and commitment. (Education Review Office, 2010, p. 17).

Since 2010 the Ministry has not completed any significant work to produce an objective evaluation of the actual impacts of *NZC* in secondary schools. Have the curriculum's principles been applied? Have the values been embedded? Have the competencies been incorporated? Has teaching and assessment improved? Have the achievement objectives been effectively applied?

The difficulty here—apart from the paucity of research evidence—is that making a judgement about the impact of the new curriculum is difficult given the long gestation period and the fact that it is almost impossible to separate the impact of curriculum change from the very many other changes going on in schools. For example, in secondary schools, has NCEA had more influence than *NZC*? Which drove the other? And what about the impact of a range of other government pol-

---

8 Including a University of Auckland team (the 'MECI' study) and a combined NZCER and University of Waikato team.

icy changes, including professional development programmes, increasing focus on vocational education, changes in funding, and changes in the nature and experience of the teaching force, to name just a few possibilities.

There is little doubt that secondary schools, teachers and principals have supported *NZC*. It would be unfair not to acknowledge that some secondary schools have tried their best to implement the values, competencies, principles and curriculum design. It may be that some progress has been made in encouraging better teaching and assessment based on a more inclusive paradigm, particularly in Years 9 and 10.

Having said this, it is hard not to conclude that it has, as yet, had only limited success, for a number of reasons.

For the front end of the curriculum, we have already argued that the competencies are little more than cosmetic in most secondary schools, and where they are in place it is unusual to find any useful evidence regarding how successfully they have been implemented. Similar arguments could be levelled at the values and principles sections in the curriculum.

For the back end of the curriculum (the achievement objectives), the requirements of NCEA have probably outweighed the requirements of the curriculum, particularly in the senior school. The dominance of NCEA in the senior school is perhaps best illustrated by reviewing the senior course outlines published in just about any New Zealand secondary school, or even listening in on a discussion at a departmental meeting of teachers of NCEA subjects. Almost without exception the courses comprise a simple listing of the *standards* to be offered, with their title and NZQA code number, under the heading of a traditional subject such as economics or English or mathematics. *NZC* is hardly mentioned.

The new NCEA achievement standards written to reflect the new curriculum continue to be delivered in a pretty traditional paradigm. The problem is that the Ministry and NZQA failed to implement *NZC* and NCEA, in a coherent and integrated manner. *NZC* was delivered first, and then, almost as an afterthought, the standards were aligned or rewritten to reflect it. Although the writers of the new achievement standards certainly did their best to align the new standards to the new curriculum, they were hamstrung on a variety of fronts.

- As we have already said, many subjects were provided with very limited guidance from the document itself. Achievement standard writers were left to work it out.
- Where writers did attempt to innovate and reflect the more inclusive view of the curriculum articulated in *NZC*, they often found themselves unsupported by their colleagues in schools, who were naturally keen to protect their subjects and avoid major changes that would increase their workload.
- The achievement standards writers were working with a modular-based assessment system using achievement standards as building blocks. This tended to require that outcomes be focused enough to be assessed consistently as part of a national qualification. The intent of *NZC*, on the other hand, was probably based on the broader outcomes that encouraged linking themes and knowledge across the curriculum. If an attempt had been made to write achievement standards for the senior secondary school that really reflected the intent of the curriculum at the outset, it probably would have required a significant redesign of the assessment demands of NCEA, or a rewrite of *NZC*. And this, of course is the point: somewhere along the line the intent of NCEA as a national qualification, and the intent of *NZC* as a national curriculum, were never integrated properly by the Ministry.

Some readers might be surprised by this conclusion. They might point to some secondary schools that have begun to develop their senior programmes to deliver the new curriculum by using the flexibilities of NCEA, particularly for non-academic students. This is true, but probably a result of a better use of NCEA and more attractive funding rather than of *NZC*.

There have also been some innovative changes to the way subjects have been delivered, reflecting the new curriculum in some schools. However, there is little doubt that in most schools the changes have been minimal because teachers have confined themselves to a fairly traditional view of assessment for qualifications, which is still predicated on a substantial menu of formal paper/pen testing.

The reform process

We have examined the implementation of *NZC*, just as we did the implementation of Tomorrow's Schools and NCEA, to enable us to make some judgements about the success of the reform process itself. We have concluded that as far as the senior secondary school years are concerned, *NZC* has not been as successful as might have been hoped. Readers will recognise some of the issues we will discuss below because they bear a similarity to the issues that bedevilled both Tomorrow's Schools and NCEA.

Poor-quality policy development

As was the case for Tomorrow's Schools, and particularly for NCEA, there was a striking lack of proper policy development, particularly around the integration of *NZC* and NCEA. As we have already argued, secondary school teachers were presented with a curriculum that was difficult to implement because the requirements of assessment for the qualification (NCEA) were simply not congruent with it. As a result, it was (and still is) not the curriculum but the requirements of NCEA that drove the senior secondary school and, because of the wash-back effect, much of the junior curriculum as well.

The fact that the writing of the new achievement standards, which were meant to reflect the new curriculum, did not actually begin until a year after the curriculum was meant to be in place, and was not completed until 3 years after the curriculum was implemented, was bad enough. The situation was made worse because the curriculum document provided so little guidance on a significant number of curriculum subjects. Bizarrely, the teaching guides that did provide some guidance appeared *after* most of the new standards had been written.

The confusion about the key competencies fanned the flames. If they were so important, why was it that the best the Ministry of Education could come up with was to say that they were embedded in the achievement objectives. Furthermore, if they were so important, where was the advice, as the standards were being written, about how they might or might not be assessed?

The structuring of the curriculum into broad levels, which we have commented on above, while perfectly reasonable on the face of it also smacked of poor policy development. Was it the view of the writers of the curriculum that there was no need to provide parents/students with some reasonably specific information about *progress* against the curriculum objectives? How was/is a teacher expected to assess progress?

These were not, and are not, easy issues to resolve, but we know that the lack of thinking and policy development resulted in the e-asTTLe tool being developed, and also probably led to the demand from the public and government for the National Standards. These, of course, are designed to show progress and achievement, but they also have, as we will see, major problems associated with them.

It should not be assumed that the implementation of *NZC* itself was a total disaster. Of all the reforms we have discussed, the implementation of *NZC* was probably the best in terms of preparation and support for teachers, particularly for primary and intermediate schools. The problem for secondary schools was that there was no one in the Ministry taking a holistic *across-school* view of the process. In fact, it is probable that most Ministry officials thought of secondary schools as being somewhat peripheral. The senior secondary school and NCEA were, in their view, the domain of NZQA, and NCEA was at the time receiving quite a lot of negative media coverage.

NZQA officials, meanwhile, were busy during this period trying to 'fix' the qualification. Their focus was not on the curriculum but on beefing up the quality assurance and credibility of NCEA. The opportunity, as we have seen, did present itself to reform the assessment demands of NCEA with the requirements of the new curriculum when the standards were being rewritten to reflect the new curriculum. Unfortunately, this proved far too difficult for both the Ministry and NZQA. Any major changes to the assessment demands of NCEA at the time would certainly not have been acceptable to most teachers on workload grounds alone.

Poor implementation

This is now probably becoming familiar to readers. The amount of change required for the proper implementation of *NZC* was immense and had an impact right through the schooling system, but the amount of time allowed was, as seems usual with such large-scale reforms in New Zealand, far too limited.

A synthesis of research carried out by the Ministry (Schagen, 2011) during the implementation phase highlighted the fact that many teachers felt they did not have enough time for "planning and implementation". Of course, many might argue, with some justification, that teachers will never feel they have enough time to implement major reforms. Regardless of this, for senior secondary schools there was an added and crushing workload associated with the implementation of NCEA. Having set in place the new NCEA with the existing standards from 2002 to 2005, teachers were asked to repeat the exercise for the new curriculum from 2011 to 2013. The time allowed (1 year for each level) for what might have been a significant revision of the curriculum in the senior school was simply inadequate. As a result, the changes made, though useful, did not always address the fundamental changes envisaged by the writers of the new curriculum.

There was at least one good reason to implement the new achievement standards over just 3 years. Not to do so would have meant that the natural progression of the curriculum from one level to the next would have been interrupted. For example, implementing the new curriculum at Level 1 and not implementing it for the next year, at Level 2, would have meant that the Level 1 students (using the new curriculum) would have had to progress on to Level 2 using the previous curriculum, which was not a particularly good progression or fit.

The need for a proper phased implementation over 3 years, however, if accepted as a necessity, should have been matched by substantial logistical and financial resources from both the Ministry and NZQA to support teachers through the process. This support was not generous, and teachers were left to deal with the enormous workloads with limited help. Senior staff at the Ministry continued to regard NCEA as peripheral, and allocated resources accordingly.

Absence of leadership from government agencies

There was a real lack of leadership from the agencies during the implementation process. Technically, the writing of the achievement standards was the responsibility of the Ministry. This was, after all, a curriculum issue. In practical terms the fact that these achievement standards would be assessed through NZQA, for the purposes of awarding national qualifications, meant that NZQA needed to have substantial input. NZQA officials were acutely aware of problems caused during the inception of NCEA by curriculum-focused teachers, together with Ministry of Education officials, writing achievement standards that were almost impossible to assess with any validity.

In order to address this issue, and to co-ordinate the work of both agencies, the Ministry of Education and NZQA did establish cross-agency committees. By and large these committees worked well. Both chief executives were kept abreast of developments and met on a regular basis to ensure that timelines were adhered to and problems were addressed rapidly. However, despite these laudable efforts problems remained, because no one person or agency was entirely responsible for the entire programme.

There were at least two significant consequences of this lack of ownership and leadership:

- no one in a senior enough position at the Ministry was able to ensure the programme was properly resourced. The middle managers responsible for NCEA simply did not get the support they required from those in the Ministry who controlled the purse strings
- perhaps more importantly, no one in a senior enough position was able to ensure that achievement standards, in all learning areas and subjects, were genuinely and properly written to reflect the intent of the new curriculum.

In some cases, such as science and maths, the standards finally written were based on compromises hammered out by teachers and government officials with the prime aim, naturally, of completing the assigned task (getting the standards written) within the tight timelines in place. In this sort of environment no one had the authority to apply a proper quality control process that actually checked whether the standards did indeed reflect at least the intent of the curriculum.[9]

But the leadership issues around the new curriculum went deeper than this, because the original writers of the curriculum were allowed to effectively sideline the senior secondary years in most of their deliberations. Although there is a brief mention of qualifications in the *NZC* document, the focus is on primary and intermediate schools and, to a lesser extent, the junior high school years. As has been noted above, the

---

9 We have already noted how difficult a task this was: see pp. 123–126

lack of any real acknowledgement of the way NCEA and secondary schools actually operate, the paucity of achievement objectives for some specialist subjects, and the confusion around key competencies, in particular, leaves little doubt that no one in the Ministry was leading the process of curriculum review in an integrated and coherent way across the schooling sector as a whole. Ministry officials were obviously not interested in the senior secondary school years, or the NCEA qualification, and presumably thought that NZQA or someone else would deal with these. It is this failure to view and then reform the education system *as a whole* that represents a significant failure in the reform process.

Lack of focus on teaching and teachers

An assumption was made that reform aimed at improving teaching and learning would somehow just happen if schools were 'freed' from the constraints of central government rules and regulations and the delivery of particular content. The new curriculum was deliberately *enabling*. It was designed to allow schools maximum flexibility to develop their own curriculum, suitable for their needs and their context, within some prescribed overarching principles and values.

Even the section in the document that focuses on pedagogy (the teaching and learning) was based on the teaching as inquiry model we have already discussed. Laudable though it is, the model assumes that teachers and schools have the capacity to translate an *approach* to teaching into a realistic and practical methodology that is workable and testable. Similar assumptions, of course, were made about the administrative reforms related to Tomorrow's Schools. By changing the administration of schools, it was assumed that teachers would change their practice for the better.

The new curriculum exhorted school leaders and teachers to be inclusive, to integrate knowledge, and to focus on competencies and values, but in the final analysis the amount of actual professional and financial support offered to secondary school leaders and teachers to help them implement these ideas was inadequate, given the huge changes that were expected. It is true that workshops were held[10] and that documents were produced, and a good effort made, but the sheer scale of the change required *ongoing* and dedicated support over a num-

---
10 Mainly organised by the PPTA

ber of years, which was not forthcoming. We have already noted how the new standards implementation from 2011 to 2013 for the senior school was substantially under funded and under resourced.

In the absence of this ongoing support, teachers tended to continue with their current practice. In the senior school this tendency was probably confirmed as the new standards were being written. Even though the writers were obliged to acknowledge the new curriculum, the teachers around the country who had to be consulted before final decisions were made did not feel such obligation, and were more concerned with limiting the workload that was about to overwhelm them. Rewriting the curriculum and *hoping* that teachers would teach better and embrace its real core purpose, without sustained and substantial pedagogical and financial support, simply did not work.

Concluding comments

It is worth emphasising that, despite criticisms, the new *NZC* is viewed positively by very large numbers of teachers, including secondary teachers. It does encourage them to develop programmes in their schools that have a future focus on learning, on connecting with each other, and on taking ownership. Its principles, values and competencies are inspiring and set aspirational goals for the future. Although there has not been a systematic evaluation of the impact of the curriculum, it is possible that its day is yet to come.

If it is to have the desired impact in the longer term, there will be a need for teachers, government agencies and tertiary institutions, particularly universities,[11] to support and develop assessment processes for NCEA that are more flexible than they currently are, and yet still retain validity and credibility. This requires ongoing work, from both the Ministry and NZQA, in the senior secondary school by way of a substantial professional development programme. The aim must be to use the flexibilities of NCEA to match the potential flexibilities of *NZC*.

However, in this brief review, familiar problems with the reform effort thus far have been exposed: the *NZC* reform process, in echoes

---

11 The impact that universities have on the delivery of schools' curriculum is often underestimated. If universities, for example, continue to demand that students remain focused on traditional disciplines and subjects that are taught in traditional ways, many schools will no doubt have to deliver what is required, regardless of the potential for new approaches that might be offered in a Ministry of Education curriculum document.

of Tomorrow's Schools and NCEA, was flawed because of poor policy development around the integration of *NZC* and the NCEA, poor implementation (particularly with regard to the writing of new achievement standards), an absence of appropriate leadership from the Ministry and NZQA, and, in schools, far too little support for teachers to implement *NZC*— particularly the front end of the curriculum—in the senior secondary school.

Chapter 9: National Standards

Background

The Ministry of Education informs us that the literacy and numeracy standards for Years 1–8 were written to support teachers in implementing *The New Zealand Curriculum* (*NZC*):

> The National Standards will help by setting clear expectations for the reading, writing, and mathematics knowledge and skills students need to achieve at each level of the curriculum ... The New Zealand Curriculum provides direction and opportunity for schools to develop their own school curriculum to meet the learning needs of their students. National Standards will provide schools with valuable evidence to more fully understand those learning needs and to make decisions about curriculum planning, implementation and review. This ongoing curriculum planning and review will ensure achievement in literacy and numeracy and across the curriculum is improved. (Ministry of Education, 2009c, p. 1)

The purpose of the standards is to measure attainment in literacy and numeracy, referenced to the age of the student. Students are assessed against these standards from Years 1–8 and are told whether they are well below, below, at, or above the expected standard. In this way, it is argued, parents can be given unambiguous information about their children's literacy and numeracy skills compared with other children of a similar age.

It has already been made clear in the previous chapter that the writers of *NZC* made each curriculum level deliberately broad because it was felt that linking a particular curriculum level with a specific age was inappropriate. Children learn at different rates, and this is precisely why a particular curriculum level could easily and legitimately be used with children of various ages. Given this, it seems clear that the new literacy and numeracy standards introduced by the National Government are not a good fit with the philosophy of *NZC*. They are clearly motivated by a desire to provide parents and the community with *age-specific* information—something not supported by *NZC*.

The argument put up by the proponents of the National Standards is simple enough: if we can be specific about the particular level of skills in literacy and numeracy at a particular age, and if we can make schools accountable for reporting to parents with regard to these standards, then poor performance of children and/or schools will be quickly identified. Furthermore, poor performance, once identified, will be *remedied* and as a consequence the literacy and numeracy of the population will improve. This improvement will, in turn, enable students to more successfully access the entire curriculum.

The primary/intermediate school teachers union, the New Zealand Educational Institute (NZEI),[1] is appalled and argues as follows:

- It is not possible to accurately calibrate the standards against an age cohort, precisely because students learn at different rates and this is perfectly normal. Therefore, many students will fail to meet the standards and be labelled as failures, without cause.

- Teachers do not need a special set of standards to know which students need extra help. They are perfectly well aware of these students as a result of their normal testing and assessment processes.

- *National* assessment of, and reporting against, these standards will

---

1 The New Zealand Educational Institute (NZEI) is a union and represents mainly primary and intermediate school teachers and principals, as well as supporting staff in schools. The NZEI has been vociferous in its opposition to National Standards since they were first mooted by the National Government (see, for example: www.scribd.com/doc/34557285/NZEI-and-NS).

lead to school league tables, similar to ones that exist for secondary schools, and these league tables will provide unreliable data at best, and force schools to compete with each other. This will lead to a waste of resources and reduced collaboration between schools in communities throughout the country.
- This in turn will lead to 'teaching to the test' and the demise of a rich, holistic and broad curriculum, as has been demonstrated in countries that have tried to implement similar reforms.
- Assessment against the standards will not be consistent among different schools. This moderation problem, similar to that suffered with NCEA, will lead to a loss of confidence in the results of the tests and the teachers who administer them.
- Research overseas suggests that any improvements in literacy and numeracy as a result of introducing national testing are short lived.

The Government has responded by arguing that parents and students have a right to know "where they are at", and anyway, the objective is not to establish league tables but to improve teaching and learning. Where students/schools are below the required standards, they should be identified and assisted so that learning outcomes can be improved.

- There will not be one national test. In fact teachers will select from a range of possible tests, which many of them use anyway. This 'broad church' approach, therefore, avoids the one national test and the resulting teaching-to-the-test concerns that teachers raised.
- Teacher professional judgement will be a critical part of any assessment decision and will be used alongside the test data.
- Teachers will be provided with web-based tools, which will enable them to ensure their judgements are accurate and comparable with other schools.
- Resources will be made available to support schools in understanding the standards and in supporting students to reach them.

The Government has remained insistent that the assessment data need to be made public and that there is no prospect of preventing the media using it in some fashion.

None of this has convinced the NZEI, or school boards, who continue to oppose the entire concept, warning of the dire consequences of publishing assessment data that, in their view, will be used to judge school performance and label students so early in their education as failures.

The Prime Minister admitted in the first year of published results that the data were a little "shonky", while the Minister of Education has pointed to the growing acceptance and success of NCEA as a model for the new standards. The implication, of course, is that the inevitable initial bugs and teething problems (and shonky data) will be sorted out in the future as the system beds in, just as happened with NCEA.

Have the new literacy and numeracy standards achieved the desired objectives?

It is probably too early to make a judgement on this question. On the one hand, most schools have now complied with the requirement to complete the assessments and report the data to the Ministry of Education. The Ministry has provided some support for schools and teachers for the implementation of the new standards, and there is little doubt that schools have refocused their energies on ensuring that literacy and numeracy skills are addressed. On the other hand, although schools are complying with the requirements, it is clear they many do not agree with, or support, the fundamental purpose and philosophy that underpin them.

The most significant problem with the reform lies with the external *moderation* of the assessments that are being carried out. There are growing concerns about this issue, and ironically the problem has been made worse by the decision to avoid the use of a single test and to emphasise the importance of teacher professional judgements. This is what the Ministry says about moderation on its website:

> Moderation is the process of teachers sharing their expectations and understanding of standards with each other in order to improve the consistency of their decisions about student learning.[2]

Some commentators refer to this approach as "social moderation" (Robertson, 2011), because it is about teachers working together in a professional and trusting environment to talk about a particular piece

---

2 http://assessment.tki.org.nz/Moderation/Why-moderate

of student work. Through discussion centred on comparisons of student work, teachers come to build a common and consistent view of what the standard looks like, and therefore are able to grade their students' work validly and reliably. Furthermore, through this discussion, teachers are able to identify problems their students are having and possible problems with their own teaching. Clearly, this form of moderation is a very powerful professional development tool for teachers.

All this is fine, and supports the notion of good, high-trust professional practice, rather similar to the approach adopted around moderation for NCEA when it was first established: trust the teachers to work collaboratively and professionally to ensure their assessment judgements are accurate and defendable. Readers will recall how, early in the development of NCEA, teachers were asked to work together to establish common approaches to the standards, and were asked to send student work to specially appointed part-time moderators, who would provide advice and guidance to support teachers in their deliberations. The emphasis was on helping teachers to *develop understanding* of the standard, as is the case with the current national literacy and numeracy standards.

Readers will also have already noted that the high-stakes nature of NCEA[3] as a qualification resulted in this high-trust model developing major credibility problems for the qualification. How could the public be sure that teachers were being accurate or even honest in their assessment? If NCEA results were going to be made public and schools' performance placed in league tables in the newspapers, surely there needed to be some method of validating the assessments more objectively, rather than simply relying on teacher professionalism and 'social moderation'?

In the end, and probably to save the qualification from total failure, the Ministry and NZQA agreed to employ full-time moderators and collect random samples of students' work. NZQA also agreed to publish agreement rates to assure the public that there was an external and objective monitoring process underpinning what was considered to be

---

3 NCEA is high stakes because students are working to gain a qualification, and competing with others using this qualification, for university places and jobs. Furthermore, the results are made public and used as a basis with which to compare student, teacher and school performance.

a high-stakes assessment process.[4]

The problem for the new literacy and numeracy standards is that they are now considered high-stakes assessment, just like NCEA, despite the protestations of the Ministry, precisely because the results are publicly available and judgements about the performance of schools are being made based on them. However, this high-stakes assessment of the standards is to be moderated in a high-trust model, similar to the model that failed in the early days of NCEA. Assessment judgements are being made about student literacy and numeracy based on the professional judgement of teachers and a range of tests administered by schools, without any significant external monitoring or checking by an independent party. We know from the NCEA experience that this will not work.

The Government and the Ministry find themselves in a bind. On the one hand, they are arguing that they have no wish to create a national test, or even league tables, or increased competition between schools. All that is required, they argue, is that schools report to parents in plain language about whether their child is at, above, below, or well below the expected standard for the age of the child. Schools and teachers are to be provided with professional development and resources to support them to improve literacy and numeracy rates for the most disadvantaged students. Viewed through this lens, there is little need for an NCEA-style external moderation process that provides a checking function.

And yet, by bringing the various tests and professional judgements teachers currently use together (the child is above, at, below or well below the National Standard), to make them comparable, and allowing the results to be published, the Ministry has effectively created a scenario that will inevitably be viewed as a form of national testing. This, in turn, will create the high-stakes environment that will require a much stronger NCEA-style external checking function, which currently does not exist.

Of course to create an NCEA-style moderation process for the literacy and numeracy standards would not only be expensive; it would

---

4 Some would argue that this focus on accountability and checking carried out by NZQA moderators is not moderation at all. It is checking. Interestingly, the NZQA moderators have also managed to fulfil a social moderation function by providing national moderation best practice workshops for teachers and producing various supporting publications.

effectively confirm the view that many teachers currently hold: the National Standards are really just a form of high-stakes national testing, which, in their view, will have significant negative impacts on schools, teachers and students. *Not* to introduce such an NCEA-style moderation system, however, will leave the credibility of the published school results open to question.

The reform process

Only a brief summary of some of the major issues relating to these new National Standards has been presented here because the standards are not used in most secondary schools, which are the focus of this book. However, the parallels with NCEA in terms of the moderation issue are really bothersome. How has the Ministry managed to repeat the same catastrophic error for two major reforms?

Poor-quality policy development

Little educational research was produced to support the standards reform in the primary sector. The research that is available tends to support the opponents of the reform. National testing in England, the US and Australia, it has been contended, encouraged teaching to the test and narrowing of the curriculum, along with league tables, not better teaching and learning.

The Government argument that the New Zealand version of national standards is different in that there is no one national test, as is the case in many overseas jurisdictions, was never clearly explained until quite late in the development process. However, the fact that various tests are used, together with teacher professional judgement, to rank and classify students against what are meant to be national standards, leaves opponents such as the NZEI with ample opportunity to be critical of the proposals by citing overseas evidence of the problems associated with what they contend is *in effect* national testing. The end result, after all, is that students are ranked and classified as if they were sitting a national test.

It has been contended that the reform could not be based on any real research evidence because it is unique to New Zealand. Even if this argument is accepted, a sensible and useful first step (as part of a sensible reform process) would have been to properly *trial* the standards for at least 2 years to ensure they were calibrated properly to the appropriate age cohort, and that moderation could be properly addressed. However, the desire to implement the reform quickly, given the Government's clear election promise to do so, resulted in the standards themselves being written with undue speed and consequently probably without adequate quality controls. Only very limited trials were possible in the time frames available. As a result, there is already evidence emerging that the National Standards are poorly calibrated to curriculum levels and age cohorts and will need to be rewritten. Once again, we see shades of previous rushed implementations, such as the NCEA standards (from 2002), which were introduced under timelines that were too tight and without anything like adequate trialling.

One of the stated intentions of the new standards was that they would provide benchmarks from Years 1–8 to enable students to be properly prepared for the literacy and numeracy demands of NCEA Level 2 at Year 12. This is difficult to believe since no literacy or numeracy standards were written for Years 9, 10 and 11.[5] If the intention was to ensure that students are ready for NCEA Level 2, then logic would dictate that Year 9, 10 and 11 standards should have been written to provide the appropriate benchmarking. The fact that they were not tells us something about the absence of a policy development process at the Ministry.

In fact, the 'preparing students for Level 2 NCEA' justification is nonsense. The imposition of these standards was driven by the Minister and the Ministry for primary and intermediate schools because these years were seen to be the key years for literacy and numeracy development, and a clear political promise had been made by the incoming Government. The benchmarking to NCEA Level 2 was an afterthought—and not a very convincing one at that.[6]

The same muddled thinking is apparent when the development of the standards is defended on the grounds that we need to prepare *all* our students to achieve Level 2 NCEA. Assessing these standards at Years 1–8, it is argued, will somehow ensure that *all* students will

---

5 NCEA Level 1 (Year 11) does have some literacy and numeracy requirements, but they bear no relationship whatsoever to the National Standards.
6 As an aside, we should also note that writing standards at Years 9, 10 and 11 would have involved taking on the secondary teachers union, which, without doubt, would have strongly opposed any such development.

achieve this goal. However, the fact is that around 80 percent of students already achieve NCEA Level 2. In order to get the bottom 20 percent across the line one wonders why it was necessary for *all* students to be subjected to a massive new accountability regime. Surely a more targeted approach would have been more sensible?

There *may* have been a good case for a set of literacy and numeracy standards to be applied to *all* students despite the fact that 80 percent already achieve NCEA Level 2 without them. The problem is that the policy development process at the Ministry did not articulate what that case was.

I have already commented on the moderation of the new standards. The contention here is that the failure to address moderation issues *early* in the development of the standards represents one of the most significant failings of policy development in the reform process. It is worth repeating the argument here.

The new literacy and numeracy standards represent high-stakes assessment because schools and teachers will be compared with each other and they will be held accountable by the Ministry and the public for failures, whether real or perceived. A social moderation process, whereby teachers support each other to improve their understandings of the standards, though highly desirable, will not suffice to ensure that schools and the public view the resulting data and the assessment results as credible. There needs to be a stronger moderation system that *checks* and holds schools accountable for the quality of their assessment. This need was made obvious in the early years of NCEA, when strong moderation systems had to be introduced to save it from total catastrophe.

It should be noted in passing that NZQA was not formally consulted by the Ministry of Education regarding the development of the moderation processes to be used for National Standards. This was despite the fact that moderation had become a huge and very public issue for NCEA. At the time I was Deputy Chief Executive at NZQA, with responsibility for NCEA, and was told by ministry officials that moderation would "not be an issue" for National Standards, and that the minister was not interested in discussing it!

The rush in 2013 to create an online tool[7] that would allow teachers to check their assessments to ensure consistency of assessment is laudable, but once again starkly illustrates the muddled thinking that has been the hallmark of this reform. If the tool is designed to help teachers make consistent (national) assessment judgements, which are then published and for which schools are made accountable, the Ministry has in effect created data that will be seen as the equivalent of a national test.[8] On the other hand, if there is no external checking of assessment decisions and the model remains a high-trust one, the incentive for teachers to manipulate their assessments and make professional judgements that may be somewhat generous is substantial. The end result of all this will be continued "shonky" data on the basis of which schools are judged by the community.

It is worth repeating here that the Minister remains optimistic and points to NCEA as an example of a successful outcome. It took a few years for the NCEA school-based moderation system to settle down, she says, and for teacher judgements to improve. The same, she argues, will happen with the National Standards. This is unlikely to happen until the Minister puts a much stronger NCEA-type moderation system in place. Unfortunately, if she does this, it will not only cost millions but will make it clear that the standards are indeed high-stakes assessments and a form of national testing, which of course is pretty much regarded as a failed approach for primary and intermediate schools.

Leadership from government agencies and school principals

The Government regarded the National Standards as a flagship policy, and to this extent it was always going to be difficult for the Ministry to expose the contradictions and problems associated with the policy that have been described above. However, one is left with some questions about the quality of advice the Minister was given by the Ministry, and the extent to which she was *aware* of these contradictions and problems as it was implemented. For example, was the Minister made aware of problems with moderation? Was a proper trial seriously considered? Was the absence of standards at Years 9, 10 and 11 thought through?

---

7 The Progress and Consistency Tool (PaCT).
8 The absence of such a tool to help teachers is, of course, just as bad, since teacher assessment judgments will not be seen to be consistent across the country.

Was the impact of league tables properly considered?

The Minister could not be expected to have the depth of knowledge to address these questions on her own. This was a job for officials at the Ministry, and was possibly a job that was not done particularly well. (This issue of free and frank advice to the Minister will be discussed more fully in the next chapter).

The other key leadership issue relates to the leadership of primary and intermediate school principals, who were almost universally opposed to the reforms. The Minister and the media took the view that school principals were public servants and were therefore *required* to implement the reforms as enacted in the statute. Principals and teachers did not have to believe in the reform, but they were expected to implement it and make it work.

There is little doubt that some officials at the Ministry, and probably the Minister herself, saw the imposition of these standards as a means *to reduce* the influence of teachers and principals in schools. The Government claimed it had a mandate from the public to introduce the National Standards to 'fix' the education system. Since principals and teachers were clearly unwilling to make the required changes, the Government and the Ministry had no other choice but to impose them.

The real leadership issue here is the extent to which any Government should attempt to put in place a reform that is so strongly opposed by the leaders and practitioners in the sector. Without a certain level of support, or at least acquiescence, from principals of schools and their teachers, the chances of achieving successful long-term and sustained change in teaching and learning is limited.

Focus on teaching and learning

The Ministry has argued that holding schools accountable for the literacy and numeracy capabilities of their students will result in better teaching and learning, just as it was argued that the Tomorrow's Schools administrative reform and the NCEA assessment reform would result in better teaching and learning. It has already been argued that neither of these reforms produced better teaching and learning, largely because not enough support was provided to schools and teachers to make the desired changes.

In the case of literacy and numeracy standards, however, the

Ministry *has* made a reasonable attempt to address this issue head on, and with some success. Schools are to be held accountable for their students' literacy and numeracy capabilities, and they are to report results to the Ministry and establish goals for improving, and the Ministry has provided substantial support for this to happen.

Support for schools, particularly low-decile schools, *has* come, particularly with the appointment of student achievement advisers, who have been able to provide (particularly low-decile) schools with support to improve their performance in literacy and numeracy. The Ministry has also made efforts to provide support, in the form of online resources, and some leadership training to help schools to implement the new standards.

This is encouraging, and a welcome sign that the Ministry and Government have recognised the mistakes of the past. One might begin to hope that the combination of requiring schools to set goals, holding schools accountable for these goals, *and* the provision of dedicated and focused professional support to teachers and schools to meet these goals *might* lead to better teaching and real gains in achievement for students in schools.

The chances are, though, that it won't, because the entire reform itself is currently so fundamentally flawed, and principals and the teachers now so implacably opposed to it.

Concluding comments

The National Standards were introduced by the Government despite opposition from a large number of teachers and principals. The intention was to provide parents and teachers with a clear measure of the capabilities of all students in reading, writing and mathematics against specific standards at Years 1–8.

It is probably too early to make a definite judgement about the success of the reform but it is clear that its development has not been well planned or managed, particularly with regard to moderation. Although schools have, by and large, complied with the requirements for National Standards, and the Ministry of Education has provided good professional development support for teachers and schools, the policy is unlikely to succeed because of the contradictions inherent in its development.

If the National Standards are to be regarded as a tool to support schools and teachers, a "social moderation" process would be perfectly acceptable. However since achievement data is made public on a school-by-school basis, and league tables constructed, there is a need for a much stronger NCEA style moderation process.

Putting such a process into place will not only be expensive, but will turn National Standards into "high stakes" assessments—which the Government has consistently denied wishing to put in place, and which could easily result in high stakes "national testing"—the consequences of which could be dire.

Poor policy development once again will probably result in a Government flagship policy failing to achieve its objectives.

PART 3:
Problems with the Ministry of Education, the PPTA and principals

In Part 2, I examined a number of educational reforms carried out in New Zealand. In most cases I was critical of the reform process that was put in place. We clearly have some systemic problems, including:

- poor policy development prior to the implementation of reforms, often followed by limited or no evaluation of reforms after implementation
- poor, often rushed, implementation of reforms
- a lack of focus on teachers and teaching
- poor leadership from government agencies and principals.

These failings have been shown to have been *repeated* across a variety of large-scale reforms. In this part of the book I will try to explain why this is so, and I will argue that the Ministry of Education, the PPTA and secondary school principals must all accept some responsibility for this sad state of affairs.

Chapter 10: The Ministry of Education

Introduction

Over the years[1] the Ministry of Education has been a moribund, dysfunctional organisation, despite being headed by highly competent and passionate chief executives who have reported to a mixture of competent and not-so-competent Ministers. A major review of the Ministry carried out by the State Services Commission, Treasury and the Office of the Prime Minister in 2011 was not complimentary: in the summary section, titled 'Organisational Management', it classified 12 out of the 17 key performance indicators as "needing development". The indicators included leadership, culture and values, structure/roles and responsibilities, engagement with staff, and risk management (State Services Commission, 2011).

There is nothing amiss with the people in the Ministry. Many arrive committed, prepared to work hard and highly skilled. The problems they have to address, however, are familiar.

---

1 It should be made clear that all the remarks made in this section apply to the Ministry of Education on the basis of its performance prior to 2012.

Poor policy development

Policy development: a generic model

Ideally, policy development for a significant change will start with a policy paper written by policy analysts. The need for such a paper could be generated by officials or by the Minister, and arise out of a political commitment made by the Minister or the need to address some issue or problem. The paper might outline the identified issue or problem, include reference to available research, indicate how success might be measured, identify risks to the government, Minister and stakeholders, and estimate the costs and support required. It will also suggest timelines for implementation and articulate its fit into long-term government or Ministry strategy.

A competent policy analyst needs to research and consult exhaustively and then provide nuanced options to decision makers. Such a process takes time and requires the application of a highly trained and sharp mind. In order to do the job well, policy analysts need to have an in-depth understanding of the content area they are working in. If they don't already have this, they need to be very quick learners. Research skills are critically important. If decision makers are going to be provided with nuanced options, they need to be assured that the identified options and the possible implications and results of the proposed policy are based on evidence and data. Decision makers need to be able to ask detailed questions about policy options and, as far as possible, receive answers based on sound evidence.

For large-scale reforms, a steering group or committee will be established to co-ordinate the policy development and implementation processes. The committee can include people from relevant business units or other government agencies, policy analysts, an external quality assurance person, a project manager, and other key experts. The committee will probably be headed by a senior official. The membership of the committee can change as the process shifts from policy development to implementation.

The senior management of the Ministry, or the Minister, will probably need to be kept abreast of, and even approve the development of, the policy and its implementation. The final Cabinet paper, if one is required, will highlight the benefits, risks, costs implications and various alternative options available for changes. Finally, the Cabinet-approved paper will be handed back to the relevant part of the Ministry for implementation. Staff will be assigned to lead and implement the change, and an internal restructure may be put into place as considered necessary.

This is a brief and fairly generic description of a process. It could be different, depending on the nature of the policy development and the complexities involved. For a major change such as NCEA, for example, there would have been a number of papers written and developed over a number of years. Ideally, these papers would have been co-ordinated to ensure the multiple strands of such large-scale reform remained coherent and focused on the proper issues or problems.

Policy development: the reality

Policy analysts often produce poor policy, based on limited research and/or data, with too few viable options for decision makers. What is worse, policy papers are often written with a predetermined endpoint in mind, based on the particular opinion of the analyst and or the opinion of his/her superiors. Analysts are encouraged, as far as possible, *to please* their superiors (see below for more on this). They are aware that their superiors, in turn, are focused on pleasing their Minister. As a result, there is a strong tendency to avoid rewrites by minimising the available policy options and maximising the benefits of what is perceived to be the desired endpoint. In such a scenario, decision makers and the public are left exposed to huge risks as they embark on a policy change that has not been properly developed or even fully understood by senior managers.

Why has the Ministry so consistently failed to develop policy well? There are a number of factors at play here. First, chief executives often feel they are quite sure about what needs to be done and want it done quickly, often because of political or media pressures. They, in turn, will put pressure on their staff. This is, to some extent, the reality of the politics of policy development. Politicians often also insist on a policy change because they have decided there are strong political imperatives which trump anything else—including a proper policy development process. Ministers, of course, are entitled to be firm in their position if they feel they have a democratic mandate to implement a policy based, for example, on an election promise. National Standards are probably a good example of this. The consequences of rapidly imposed national changes that have not been properly developed, however, as we have seen, can be dire.

Secondly, policy papers are often written by analysts who are not well trained to be able to do the requisite research or to think through the issues carefully. Despite the fact that they are well paid (considerably more than experienced teachers), many are not well versed in the subject area they are asked to work in, and are unable to gather the required content, either because they do not have the skills to do so or because they are not given the time.

It is not just the policy analysts who are the problem here. Many senior managers at the Ministry are not abreast of the educational issues they are dealing with, and are consequently unable to discuss them in depth. This is hardly their fault given they were appointed for their more generic strategic thinking or change management skills, and not educational knowledge and understandings. This absence of bright and experienced educational thinkers in the Ministry is a major concern, particularly if policy analysts are underperforming. Without the in-depth knowledge of the sector, managers are not even able to ask the right questions.

The third problem with policy development relates to the inability of various education agencies to work with each other, as they often must, particularly in the policy development phase of a reform. A very good example of a flawed policy development process across agencies can be found in the early development of NCEA and the confused roles of the Ministry and NZQA in this process. We have already discussed this issue in Chapter 7.

The final problem with policy development, already alluded to previously, is related to the advice the Minister is given. It is likely that at least some senior Ministdeparture of a considerable number of these managersls have found it difficult to provide 'free and frank' advice to their Minister. The notion of free and frank advice means that officials must provide detailed and well-researched policy options and the possible consequences and implications of each option to their Minister. At times this means that officials should firmly discourage a policy option because of the risks it entails. Instead, it seems safer to do the Minister's bidding by accentuating the positives and downplaying the negatives of a policy the Minister seems to be in favour of. In terms of policy development, this means that what actually gets to the Minister has been self-censored by officials.

It appears that some officials do not have the disposition to disagree and argue with a Minister, because to do so may well damage their relationship with that Minister. This may, of course, be the fault of the Minister who is unwilling to listen. Whatever the case, to be the cause of a breakdown in the relationship between the Ministry and the Minister is regarded as probably the greatest sin possible in the public service, and could be career limiting for the official concerned. As far as possible, therefore, the intention of some officials is to cultivate and nurture the relationship with their Minister by supporting a relatively narrow range of policy options that are likely to please and be accepted by that Minister. As a result, what could easily be missing is free and frank advice.

Poor implementation

Policies need to be *implemented*. The problem is that policy is quite capable of morphing during the implementation process, sometimes to the extent that the initial policy intent is thwarted or sidelined. New Zealand has not been good at implementing educational reforms, as we have already noted in this book.

One can understand the problem. Once the shift is made from the realities of Wellington offices to the realities of classrooms, and once people who are required to implement and actually take action are faced with their tasks, they will tend to do only what they *need to*, in their current circumstances, as quickly and painlessly as possible. There are a number of issues here.

Lack of regional presence

The Ministry, as it is currently constructed, has only a limited regional presence. This was the intent of the Tomorrow's Schools reforms. Schools as Crown entities were to be self-governing independent entities with their own boards. Although the Ministry has recently been trying to rebuild its regional base, the basic Tomorrow's Schools structure remains intact.

This presents a significant implementation problem. In studies carried out by McKinsey and Company (Mourshed, Chijioke & Barber, 2010), a "mediating layer" was noted as being a "critical" element of school improvement in every one of the 20 systems studied. The mediating layer (regional offices for our purposes here) was explained by McKinsey and Company as akin to that of an operating system (for a computer) acting as a conduit and interpreter between the user interface (schools) and the central processing unit (the Ministry of Education) (pp. 83–84).

According to the McKinsey and Company study, there are typically three tasks for those operating in this mediating layer:

- providing targeted support for schools
- acting as a buffer between the centre and the schools, while interpreting and communicating improvement objectives in order to manage any resistance to change
- enhancing the collaborative exchange between schools, and helping them to support each other, share learning and standardise practices.

(Mourshed, Chijioke, & Barber, 2010, p. 94)

The sweeping away of regional offices and the inspectorate by the Tomorrow's Schools legislation ironically made it much more difficult to implement reform: ways to target support were dismantled, the buffer to interpret and communicate was removed, and competition between schools replaced collaboration. Precisely the same problems eventuated with other reform efforts from Wellington, particularly NCEA, where one central NZQA office in Wellington was left to deal with every individual secondary school in the country, on its own, when NCEA was introduced from 2002.

Handover problems

It is not just about a mediating layer. We also need to consider how policy makers can sometimes complete their jobs and then hand everything over to the implementers, who must work more closely with schools. This sort of division can occur *within* the Ministry itself as different teams take responsibility for the different tasks, or it can occur *across* agencies. For example, the Ministry handed the implementation of

NCEA (in theory at least) to NZQA. Similar handovers have occurred between the Ministry and the Tertiary Education Commission.

Handovers such as this, if poorly handled, are often a cause of major implementation issues. Policy makers wash their hands of the matter once they have handed over. Implementers are left to interpret what was intended by policy makers, and complain bitterly that those who developed the policy did not consult with them properly, and that the policy is 'ambivalent' or 'confused'. Furthermore, if policy oversight is not maintained throughout the implementation process, the likelihood of the policy morphing into something unintended by policy makers increases dramatically.

There is obviously a need to ensure that policy development and implementation are *integrated* much better than is currently the case. Some suggestions on how this can be done will be made in Part 4.

Ad hoc policy development and implementation

The transition from policy to implementation has too often become an incredibly fraught process, not only because of a lack of regional presence or handover issues, but because timelines for implementation have been too short and supporting resources too scarce. This lack of time and resources for implementation *after* the policy phase has been completed represents a significant—and common—problem.

We have already discussed these issues in Part 2 with regard to the introduction of Tomorrow's Schools, NCEA, the National Standards and the new national curriculum. In all cases, poor policy formulation, poor implementation, and very tight timelines, in particular, forced officials to loop back into *ad hoc* policy decisions to fix the implementation problems that inevitably arose. This is why education reform has so often appeared to many in the sector to be put in place 'on the hoof' in response to a crisis or problem, rather than in a proactive and planned manner.

Lack of trialling

In the case of Tomorrow's Schools there is no evidence of trialling the proposed governance model for schools. In the case of the National Standards, only the newly written standards went through some rudimentary trials and there was no attempt made to properly trial them for a cluster of schools over a reasonable period of time to gauge their possible longer-term impact. This might have avoided the now evident problems with the level of difficulty of some of the standards. It would also have allowed proper consideration to be given to the crucially important issue of how teacher judgements can be moderated.

Standards-based assessment *was* trialled prior to the development of NCEA (and the trials were useful in that they identified real concerns about the use of unit standards for school subjects), but NCEA as a qualification was not, and nor were any of the newly written achievement standards, which were its key components.

The problems with trials is that they cost money, delay implementation beyond an election cycle, and may produce findings that suggest the reform should be abandoned. Those with a stake in the reform— particularly the politicians and officials—would probably find these potential outcomes too worrying to contemplate. And yet it seems incredible that they are prepared, and allowed, to spend millions of dollars on reform efforts that are justified, on the most flimsy of evidence, by the claim that they will achieve what is intended.

Siege mentality

An important effect of these problems is the impact that continued implementation-related problems have on the morale and engagement of Ministry staff. Being repeatedly involved in policy initiatives that appear to disintegrate, and that often result in negative feedback from the sector and the media, is never easy, but becomes very hard to deal with if it is sustained for long periods of time. As a result, staff gradually move into a siege mentality, because they are consistently assailed from all sides with vitriolic criticism. Very soon the idea forms in the minds of large numbers of staff, including highly pressured senior managers, that some people (for example, the teachers' union) are just being unreasonable and need to adjust to the new environment.[2]

This is not the end of the problem, however, because the besieged

---

2 Many Ministry of Education and NZQA staff have taken the view over the years that teachers and their union, the PPTA, are too slow to change and are more interested in protecting their working conditions and reducing their workload rather than addressing key issues of underachievement. While there may well be some truth in this view, holding it as a default position while trying to effect change as a government official is unlikely to produce solutions that have buy in from the sector.

officials become increasingly unwilling to seek out or even pay attention to opinions expressed by what are now seen as their opponents. The resulting them-and-us approach to implementation of reforms almost always leads to poor decision making and dissatisfaction throughout the sector, because potential problems and solutions to a policy or implementation problem are simply not given serious consideration.

A siege mentality was particularly strong at NZQA and the Ministry of Education throughout the NCEA implementation process, and resulted in many managers from both agencies, but particularly NZQA, dismissing—with disdain—continuing and widely held concerns from the sector. It took several major crises, a State Services Commission inquiry, a new board chair, a new chief executive and management team, and a major internal restructure to eventually return NZQA to a more open and genuine public service approach. The Ministry of Education has recently demonstrated a similar mentality, and this is perhaps best illustrated by the development and implementation of the National Standards already referred to above.

Given that one of the fundamentals for successful reform in education is at least some buy in from teachers and principals, it is hardly surprising that we find the sector in almost continuous revolt. The notion of the public *service* listening to the sector, seriously and carefully, and being prepared to engage in genuine dialogue to achieve common goals has unfortunately been hard to detect.

Lack of evaluation

Surprisingly, there is little evidence in the last 30 years of any significant evaluation plans being built into the roll-out of *any* major reforms.[3] For example, there is no evidence of a public evaluation or review of Tomorrow's Schools. Although various researchers, including NZCER,[4] have produced a number of critiques and surveys about its impact, none of these could be regarded, or were intended, as com-

---

3 Evaluation should be integrated into the policy development and implementation phases. In other words, there should be a process and timeline for evaluation *built into* the reform process. This evaluation will need to report on the extent to which the reform achieved its stated objectives.

4 The New Zealand Council for Educational Research (NZCER) is an independent research and development organisation which also produces and markets a range of resources to schools and teachers.

prehensive public and evidence-based evaluations of the respective reforms.

Similarly, there appears to have been little evaluation carried out on NCEA, although, once again, numerous papers have been written by academics about the successes and failures of various aspects of the new qualification.[5] The curriculum review did build in some evaluation related to the *actual implementation* of the new curriculum, but there is no evidence of any evaluation of whether the intended outcomes of the review have been achieved or not. Finally, there is no sign whatsoever of a formal review of the purpose and impact of National Standards.

The general absence of robust evaluation of education reforms is surprising given the huge expenditure and the massive commitment required from the teaching profession to implement them. New Zealanders seem satisfied with mainly anecdotal evaluation evidence at best.[6]

Of course, education is a complex business and involves huge numbers of variables. Evaluation is therefore difficult, but certainly not beyond the capability of competent policy makers and researchers. The absence of proper evaluation is not due to its obvious complexity. It is more related to an unwillingness by politicians and officials to set in place metrics that provide data that might suggest that millions of dollars have been wasted because the initial policy development and implementation of many reforms have been so badly handled.

Leadership issues

Decision making by panic button

The Ministry of Education is an enormous ministry, which has to make difficult and often highly political decisions in the full glare of the media and public scrutiny. Mistakes are mercilessly exposed and accountabilities are keenly felt and exploited, both internally, within the Ministry of Education hierarchies, and externally, in the wider edu-

---

[5] The Doug Martin reports, which were written after the Scholarship debacles of 2004, might be viewed as evaluations by some, but they were really reactive actions taken by government in response to a political crisis.

[6] Data on student achievement exist, such as NCEA results and PISA, which (incidentally) is of questionable value, but we certainly have nothing that allows us to trace a causal link between the reform and the stated objectives of the reform.

cation sector. As a result, senior managers often find them themselves pushed into a command-and-control mode of leadership.

As increasingly frustrated and cynical staff learn that their superiors are unwilling to place a great deal of trust in them, and instead prefer to micro-manage them, their perfectly natural response is to protect themselves from any possible criticism or mistake. They do this by refusing to make substantive decisions without first checking with their boss. In this way, a staff member is able to absolve himself/herself of any potential responsibility or blame by ensuring the decision-making process moves up the chain of command as quickly as possible, which of course satisfies the inclination of nervous senior managers to micro-manage the work of their subordinates.

The organisational culture resulting from these forces is problematic to say the least.

- Senior managers/leaders refuse to delegate and are overloaded with work. As a result, they are forced to postpone and delay decision making, causing milestones to be missed and decision making to be rushed.
- This same refusal to properly delegate creates dissatisfied and cynical staff, who respond by making the situation even worse. They learn to avoid making decisions, thus absolving themselves from blame or responsibility, or ownership of the decision.

This process reverberates *upwards* at every level of decision making, from team leaders, to group managers, through to divisional managers, deputy secretaries and the Secretary, and even the Minister (see below), finally overwhelming those in the most senior positions. Decision making by panic button is often the result, as stressed and overworked managers are forced into making panic-stricken knee-jerk decisions to meet impossible timelines they themselves have created. As a result, very poor decisions are made or, perhaps, not made.

On not making decisions

Not making decisions is also a result of a dysfunctional organisational culture. Where staff feel that their boss is unlikely to buy into a proposal they might be considering, they will tend *not* to put up the proposal at all, particularly if it carries significant political risks. The result is that a policy initiative that should at least be considered by senior management group never makes it through the management structure, simply because staff are focused on pleasing their managers and gaining their approval, rather than being good decision makers themselves. This self-censorship is a result of the same hierarchical, low-trust model of management described above, and which has been prevalent at the Ministry of Education for many years. The end result is the gradual erosion of initiative, creative thinking and risk taking.

Critically, all this has an impact on the advice provided to the Minister by her officials. As the Senior Management Team advise her, they do so based on a process of decision making that has been convoluted, poorly thought through, risk averse and based on often incomplete information.

The focus of the Secretary of Education

Ultimately, of course, this rather unfortunate state of affairs is the responsibility of the chief executive, the Secretary of Education. Unfortunately the current structure and organisation of the ministry work to prevent the Secretary of Education focusing on internal management and organisational problems.

Instead, the role of the Secretary of Education appears to be externally focused. This work is critical: it is important that the Secretary be seen to lead policy development related to student achievement. It is important that the secretary be out there, building relationships with external stakeholders, both nationally and internationally. The Secretary must also work closely with the Minister and other chief executives in the public service.

However, without a functioning and efficient Ministry, externally focused work is not going to be successful. There is a clear need for the Secretary of Education to focus internally—on the functioning of the Ministry itself. Otherwise future attempts at national educational reform, such as the ones we have discussed in Part 2, will continue to fail.

Constant restructuring as a management tool

One manifestation of struggling leadership is a propensity to constantly restructure the organisation. The Ministry of Education, perhaps like many other large organisations, seems to be regularly changing its management and operational structures. This constant grind of restructuring, although sometimes necessary, has had at least three major negative impacts.

- The whole process of asking people to reapply for their jobs, or asking them to move into reconstituted business units, is stressful, time consuming and has a tendency to create losers and winners. Losers tend to nurse their losses and gradually disengage from the organisation. Even winners go through periods of anxiety and stress, during which they are likely to be less productive than they should be.

- As the new structures begin to emerge, there is often massive loss of productivity as staff jostle for power and influence or simply try to protect their jobs or pet projects and programmes. New structures very rarely work efficiently from day one, particularly in reconstituted divisions and business units. Managers will inevitably take time to develop new working team relationships.

- Constant restructuring creates significant confusion about reporting lines and responsibilities, particularly if the restructuring process is not properly controlled by the chief executive. The Ministry of Education appears to have developed a spaghetti-like and overly complex structure, which even those within the organisation find bewildering (Ministry of Education, 2014c). For those outside the organisation, the structure appears chaotic and lacking in any continuity for long-term planning and relationship building.

Whether there has been a real need for all this restructuring is an important question. Although there is nothing wrong with restructuring an organisation to enable it to deliver its services efficiently, one wonders whether the urge to restructure has on occasion really only arisen out of attempts by the second and third tier in the Ministry of Education to *manage* the organisation. In other words, restructuring might be seen as an easy substitute for proper leadership and management. For example, although managers might deny this vehemently, many restructures could be viewed as excuses to fire or pay off unwanted, poorly performing or uncooperative staff.

Even when there are no hidden agendas, senior managers can sometimes be seduced into thinking that restructuring is the *end* of the change process rather than the beginning. The restructuring might involve months of consultation and discussion, followed by staffing changes that could take even more time before they begin to operate efficiently. It is usually at this stage that senior managers tend to turn their minds to other pressing matters, leaving newly appointed staff to work through the inevitable problems and probable confusions that are a normal part of any restructuring. The result is that the expected benefits of the restructuring do not eventuate as planned, or do not eventuate at all, and many staff become increasingly demoralised and cynical about the process, their managers, and the potential for any future benefits.

Finally, it is worth pointing out another less well-known effect of constant restructuring: a failure to follow up and evaluate. Once a team has moved, or disappeared entirely, or been split up, much of the institutional memory of the organisation becomes hard to maintain. As a result, the willingness or ability to review and evaluate reform is diminished. If evaluation processes were part of the reform process, and built in, this should not really be an issue since the project manager would need to ensure the evaluation was carried out as part of their project requirements. However, evaluation of reform, as we have seen in Part 2, too often seems to be an afterthought, an add on, or not done at all.

The 2011 review of the performance of the Ministry of Education carried out by the State Services Commission, Treasury and the Department of the Prime Minister, referred to at the beginning of this chapter, summed up the management/leadership issues at the Ministry as follows:

> There are examples of strong leadership in some groups and parts of groups but this is not evident in a coherent and visible way across the Ministry (p. 39)

Also:

> It's the responsibility of the leadership team to establish a culture that best helps deliver the desired results. We did not observe this to be a conscious continuing priority of the leadership team. (p. 40)

And:

> Better alignment of culture and practice would mean ... staff within the Ministry feeling personal ownership for the results of the Ministry and being empowered to act as necessary to achieve these results or ensure that issues are recognised and dealt with by those who have the capacity to do so (p.10).

(State Services Commission, 2011)

Poor support for teaching and teachers

If teachers are a critically important element in any successful reform, the Ministry of Education has not always shown that it has understood this.

The delivery of professional development to teachers

Prior to the implementation of Tomorrow's Schools, most professional development (PD) was delivered to schools via the Department of Education in Wellington. National subject advisers worked with school inspectors (who were based in the regions) to deliver national courses and to work with individual schools, departments and teachers. Capable teachers were often seconded from their jobs for various periods of time to deliver many of these courses and workshops. For secondary schools, the emphasis of the PD was often on teaching *subjects* and not so much on generic, school-wide issues.

With the advent of Tomorrow's Schools, and amidst fears that all PD would be privatised, the Ministry of Education distributed the PD provision to what became known as the School Support Services. These services were all provided by the universities, which were contracted to provide PD specified by the Ministry of Education. For example, during the implementation of *NZC* from 2007, the Ministry of Education wrote detailed contracts for the School Support Services which specified the required range and type of PD they were to deliver to schools.

There were a number of advantages to this approach to PD.

- It was regionally based, so that schools could usually access a provider physically located in their region who was therefore aware of their specific teaching environment and requirements.

- It allowed the *pre-service* training of teachers, which the universities were already responsible for, to be linked with their *in-service* PD, which was subject to Ministry of Education contracts. The synergy between *pre-* and *in-service* PD was considered to be important.
- The contracts were negotiated annually on a 3-year rolling basis so that the School Support Services university-based providers had some certainty in their planning. In other words, much centrally funded PD was essentially non-contestable.
- The system also allowed for other nationally delivered PD programmes, which were run by a range of other providers, as necessary.

A review of the system commissioned by the Ministry of Education (Sankar & Chauvel, 2011) identified a number of problems with PD delivery at the time, including:

- a lack of detailed *national* information about which schools were or were not accessing PD
- a suspicion, at least, that access was too "demand driven" and not adequately based on a strong strategic view of school, regional and national requirements
- sometimes confusing differences between the contracts offered to the School Support Services and other national providers selected by the Ministry of Education to deliver one-off programmes
- the School Support Services not always consulting with local regional Ministry of Education offices, leaving Ministry of Education staff in the regional offices in the dark, though it was recognised that the regional offices were often not appropriately staffed to take any real part in the PD delivery
- the evaluations of the contracts being too narrow and often requiring deliverables to be checked off without adequate analysis of the deeper, long-term impact of the delivered PD on teachers, departments, schools and, importantly, nationally.

Despite these issues, the review report was clear that the overall centrally funded and centrally driven delivery structure should be maintained, with some important caveats, including:

- the need to identify fewer but more strategic PD initiatives, based on good evidence and data

- ensuring better accountability of providers while still allowing flexibility to account for regional differences
- better, more outcomes-based evaluation of key initiatives at the teacher, school and national level, rather than a reliance on compliance-driven, tick-box deliverables.

Despite these findings, during 2010/11 the Ministry of Education went ahead and effectively dismantled the entire existing PD delivery system by making the process contestable. This meant that all contracts for PD were opened to all-comers, and the previous preferred provider status of the university-based School Support Services was removed (PPTA, 2013b).

The impact on the delivery of PD to teachers has been significant.

- A number of consortia[7] have effectively been handed almost all the PD contracts based on the tender process set in place by the Ministry of Education to select providers.
- Contracts are to be renegotiated and reviewed every 2 years in an open and competitive process.
- Providers are also free to bid for contracts outside the consortia, and do so.
- The emphasis of PD has increasingly shifted, for secondary schools, to generic school improvements projects focused almost entirely on lower-decile schools.
- This has meant that subject- or department-based support has been greatly reduced for most secondary schools.

By 2013 it was clear that the wholesale changes put in place had been very unpopular with principals, teachers and the PPTA.

- Many schools have been forced to work with providers not located in their region, with resulting mismatches between what is required and what is delivered. The range of providers working with each consortium has sometimes lacked institutional knowledge, expertise and credibility.
- Some providers part-way through their contracts have found themselves unable to properly plan for the longer term, given the possibil-

---

7 There are a number of consortia, each made up of different combinations of universities and private providers to bid for particular Ministry of Education contracts.

ity they might not be selected by the Ministry of Education for the next round of contracts from 2015.

- Middle- and higher-decile schools have found very limited PD available to them.
- Low-decile schools, apparently poorly performing, have been identified by Ministry of Education officials and pressured into accepting whole-school PD. Although well intentioned, the result has been a further labelling of low-decile schools as failing schools.
- Some schools have been offered, and have accepted, multiple providers working on different contracts, often causing confusion and work overload for teachers.
- The emphasis on *school improvements* has reduced the ability of teachers from different schools to collaborate—something teachers place considerable importance on.
- Specific subject advice, one of the key requirements for secondary schools, though still available from one university (for the North Island) and one consortium (for the South island) in one shared contract, is very limited.
- The speed of the change has left Ministry of Education regional offices, schools and even the providers confused about their particular roles.

So what does all this mean in the context of the working of the Ministry of Education?

It has already been argued that governments in the past have made the mistake of *assuming* that administrative education reform would have an impact on the classroom, that changes in assessment practice and curriculum would automatically lead to better teaching, and that the implementation of national standards will magically improve literacy and numeracy. The changes to the delivery of PD represent yet another assumption about education reform: that making the provision of PD contestable would *somehow* improve teaching and learning. There was, and is, no basis for this assumption, and it is certainly not something that was suggested by the 2011 Sankar and Chauvel review of PD, which the Ministry of Education itself initiated. All the indications thus far are that for many schools this change has represented a step backwards.[8] In fact, it has caused dismay and uncertainty across much of the sector.

The problem has not just been related to the reform itself, but also to the speed of its implementation, with the general consensus being that the roll-out has been rushed and poorly co-ordinated. This is obvious, given that by 2014 yet another review of the PD model (given these concerns) prior to the 2015 renegotiation of contracts was already underway.

On the positive side, it is worth noting what may be the beginnings of a positive innovation in PD support for teachers with the establishment of the Student Achievement Function.[9] This places expert advisers (experts in teaching and learning) in Ministry of Education regional offices, whose job it is to partner with selected schools who have particular problems with the achievement of Māori and Pasifika students. The adviser works with individual schools to establish what is known as a 'change team', made up of representatives from the school, board of trustees and community. Any of five areas of school operations are targeted.[10] The adviser is tasked with brokering specific PD development for teachers, if required, and generally works with the school for approximately 6 months. Currently, although these advisers work in some secondary schools, their main focus appears to be with primary schools.

Equally importantly, the Ministry of Education has also placed one project lead into each of the four regional offices. It is the job of this person to co-ordinate much of the PD going to schools in the region, based largely on NCEA achievement data and ERO reports. The main focus of these project leads appears to be secondary schools.

The larger role these student achievement advisers and project leads may play in supporting teachers' PD in the future is discussed in Part 4

Support for teachers who need help and guidance

The second problem with the way the Ministry of Education supports

---

8 However, some low-decile schools have benefited from, and have appreciated, the additional resources made available to them because of the decision to target low-achieving schools.

9 We have already noted the reasons behind the introduction of the Student Achievement Function by the Ministry of Education (pp. 77 and 78).

10 The five areas are: cultural and linguistic inclusiveness and responsiveness; powerful connections with parents, family and whānau based on learning; instructional; organisational; and evaluative capability.

teachers is related to teachers who need help and guidance. We will address this issue in more detail later in this section, but an important point needs to be made here: where a teacher is struggling to be a good classroom teacher, there is currently remarkably little help available to school principals to address the issue—assuming they have decided to do so. The Ministry of Education makes it clear that it is up to the school to address the matter, generally without any additional external resources.[11]

As a result, the advice and guidance the principal can deliver to a struggling teacher depends largely on the availability and goodwill of other teachers in the school. Typically, a struggling teacher will be allocated another staff member (often a senior teacher) to work through an observation and support programme, which might last 3 to 6 months. Unfortunately, the senior teacher will be given little in the way of additional support or time to do what is required, but will generally commit to do their best. Although well intentioned, this initial enthusiasm and energy will often gradually dissipate in a matter of weeks as the realities of workload overwhelm both parties.

The Ministry of Education will argue that supporting such teachers is the responsibility of the principal and the board of the school, and of course this is correct under the current model. However, this is simply not good enough. Principals and boards need more support to assist these teachers. Every single non-performing teacher inflicts harm, possibly permanent harm, on literally hundreds of students on a daily and weekly basis.

The important point is this: good classroom practice is critically important and worth investing in if we want to effect real change in schools. Teachers who are not performing, and who could be helped, should be helped with vigour. Such action would represent a highly cost-effective intervention to improve the quality of teaching across the nation. Right now this is not happening, and it seems a significant abdication of responsibility by the Ministry of Education that this situation is allowed to continue

We will return to the matter of an effective PD model, and further support for teachers, in Part 4.

---

11 The Teachers' Council has responsibilities in terms of the registration, certification and competence of teachers, but it can only offer minimal support, given the legal and financial constraints it must work under.

Concluding comments

The Ministry of Education is a large and complex organisation with responsibilities ranging from early childhood education to tertiary education. It is a vast bureaucracy, employing thousands of people with responsibility for thousands of educational institutions.

The education of our children, and the care the state provides, is not only an enormously personal matter for parents everywhere; it is also of huge importance for the future wellbeing of the nation. Although the Ministry of Education is meant to be apolitical, it *is* in the business of politics, because almost everything it does involves making judgements of a political nature.

This chapter has been critical of the Ministry because its management and leadership structures need to be improved. If these internal issues were to be addressed successfully (and we will see how in Part 4), New Zealand would find that some of the recurring problems related to educational reform we have identified will dissipate and the Ministry of Education will be better able to do its job.

Chapter 11: The Post Primary Teachers' Association

Introduction

The PPTA is a powerful trade union with a strong professional perspective, and it has a rate of membership that is the envy of most unions anywhere. It has often been a positive force in New Zealand education. Over the years it has encouraged and led a considerable amount of professional discussion in the teaching profession and the community about issues related to curriculum, assessment and the professional development of teachers. It has also been generally successful in both encouraging governments to focus on real educational issues and in protecting the working conditions and salaries of its members. Unfortunately, it has not done enough to remove mediocre and incompetent teachers from the profession and it has done little to properly address issues of teacher workload.

Teacher competence

The official PPTA position is that it does not support incompetent teachers and that there is an agreed process employers should follow, as documented in the teachers' collective agreement, to remove them.

Where a teacher is causing some concerns, principals, according to the teachers' collective agreement, must put in place "an appropriate assistance and personal guidance programme to assist that employee".

The length and scope of this programme is not specified, but normally it would be at least 10 weeks. If, after this, the principal is still not satisfied, the teacher "is to be given a reasonable opportunity, normally 10 school weeks, to remedy the matter(s) of concern that have been identified" (PPTA, 2014). If after this further 10-week period there is no improvement, the teacher can be dismissed without further ado.

On paper the official PPTA position on incompetent teachers is not unreasonable. It does not appear to be overly difficult to remove incompetent teachers. There is no question that PPTA field officers *often do* work successfully with principals to ensure they are removed or paid out. So what is the problem?

One of the issues is that the threshold to start a formal competency process, in the eyes of many school principals, is rather high. Teachers generally need to have reached a *very* poor level of performance, over many months, before it becomes feasible to even begin putting it in place. A bigger problem is that the process of trying to remove an incompetent teacher in a school situation can become both very divisive and extended. Inevitably some teachers will have supporters, who will accuse the principal of being unreasonable or vindictive. The PPTA often gets called in at this time and will fight to ensure, quite rightly, that the teacher's interests are protected and that the principal is following due process. As a result, given the collegial nature of staffrooms, many principals opt to avoid potential staffroom and union disagreements. A common solution is to move the teacher to a less-demanding or less-exposed role.[1]

Even if the principal does decide to continue the competency process, he/she will know that it lends itself to short-term fixes. The teacher may well be capable of improving their performance over a 10- or 20-week period and thus get a clean bill of health. However, once cleared, there is often a tendency for the teacher to gradually revert to previous problem behaviours. This leaves the principal with the unen-

---

1 For example, a principal might receive multiple complaints about a teacher who is teaching a high-ability group of students. The solution might be to move that teacher to work with a remedial group who are not so demanding and whose parents, likewise, are less likely to complain.

viable task of possibly starting the process again in some way.

Unfortunately, this is only the tip of the iceberg. The processes outlined in the collective agreement are designed to address issues of incompetence only. They do not address the bigger problem of teachers who consistently hover in the only-just-competent area. These are the 'free riders' in the teaching profession: teachers who refuse to work past 3.30 pm unless called to a compulsory meeting, who do nothing, or very little, during their holidays, and who effectively do the very minimum required in their classrooms. These are the (relatively few) teachers who give the profession a bad name and place unnecessary burdens on others.

To put it bluntly: the current collective agreement does not allow principals to easily deal with often deep-seated and long-term issues of negative attitude, laziness and a sense of entitlement exhibited by some teachers, who nevertheless, under formal scrutiny, might be considered competent.

None of this is directly the fault of the PPTA. The PPTA may well argue that the problem is that principals fail to carry out their responsibilities to challenge these incompetent and/or mediocre teachers, and it is principals who fail to follow due process and therefore unfairly penalise their teachers. There is no doubt that there is some truth in this argument. Principals cannot complain about incompetent or mediocre teachers if they are not prepared to make the sometimes very hard decisions required to challenge and possibly remove them. (See Chapter 12 for more about this issue.)

Teacher pay and performance

However, the vexing issue facing school principals and boards in the context of the mediocre free-rider teacher is the salary scale enshrined in the collective agreement, which makes it hard for them to address this problem. Generally speaking, teachers progress up their salary scale on the basis of years of service. Although the principal, in theory, does have the power to prevent a teacher automatically moving up the scale, he/she must do so by challenging the competency of the teacher, and thus bringing the entire competency process into action. The result is that a mediocre (though possibly just-competent) teacher gets their salary increments and progresses to the top of the salary scale *at the same rate* as a high-flying, highly competent teacher. Performance, effectively, does not matter.

Consider the following quite common staffroom scenario.

Teacher A: (bachelor's degree and teacher trained)	
Does the minimum, gets mediocre results, meets few performance objectives, blames others, takes few initiatives. Students find him boring and unhelpful, but he is deemed to meet the required professional standards.	
Starting salary (degree and teachers qualification), 2014 pay scales:	$47,874
Maximum salary (after 8 years)	$72,645
Teacher B: (same bachelor's degree and same teacher training as Teacher A)	
Excels, works hard, meets ambitious performance objectives, takes the initiative, gains excellent results and the students absolutely love her.	
Starting salary (degree and teachers qualification), 2014 pay scales:	$47,874
Salary after 8 years	$72,645

Both teachers—one highly competent and talented, the other mediocre and indifferent—after 8 years of service end up with exactly the same salary. Surely, this is a nonsense!

And it gets worse: even if one were to assume that moving up the scale provides some incentive to maintain and improve performance, once a teacher reaches the top of the scale there remains no financial incentive to maintain or improve performance. Apart from collecting management units (MUs)[2] for management or other responsibilities, a teacher can sit on the same pay (other than cost-of-living adjustments and collective agreement changes) for literally decades, regardless of performance.[3]

This is an effective pay freeze for any teacher who wishes to remain in the classroom to teach and who does not wish to take on additional responsibilities. No matter how good the teacher is, no matter how well he/she meets performance objectives, no matter how superb his/

---

[2] Management units are awarded to teachers permanently or for fixed terms. Each is worth $4,000. Units can be awarded in multiples and are designed to acknowledge management tasks that teachers carry out; for example, being head of department.

[3] So long as the teacher is declared to be competent.

her students' academic results, the teacher will be paid the same as the most mediocre classroom teacher in the staffroom.

This is *the* key issue of teacher performance that needs to be urgently addressed, but to do this successfully requires union co-operation. However, the PPTA asserts that rewarding the performance of particular teachers is a red herring, because *all teachers* need to be outstanding. The way to achieve this, it is argued, is for the government to provide additional funding and support, for example, by cutting class sizes and providing PD. Furthermore, since teaching is a co-operative and collegial profession, paying teachers based on their performance will destroy that collegiality. The problem is not so much about mediocre teachers as lack of resources from government. And anyway, actually measuring the performance of teachers is far too complex a process to be fair to all.

It should be noted that the PPTA *has* been keen to work with governments to create a more robust career structure for teachers. For example, the Ministerial Task Force on Secondary Teacher Remuneration (Bazley, 2003) supported the notion of salary progression based on PD and new qualifications.[4] The PPTA was also very supportive of the successful development of the specialist classroom teacher role in schools (one per school), rewarded with additional remuneration.[5]

This is all very good, but it does not directly address the issue of *classroom performance*. As a professional organisation the PPTA needs to be much more actively involved in raising the mana of the profession by working with the government and boards to establish a more robust process of rewarding the highly competent classroom teacher and genuinely addressing the issue of mediocre teachers. Instead, it continues to insist that all classroom teachers be rewarded in *exactly the same way*, largely regardless of their performance. We will return to what might be done about this in Part 4.

---

4 In the end this notion was not supported by the Government, presumably because of cost.
5 The specialist classroom teacher role provides one teacher per school with some additional time and salary to support the PD of other teachers in the school.

Teacher workload

I have been in classrooms and working with teachers for three decades—as a classroom teacher, Head of Department, Deputy Principal and Principal. I have also worked in the more corporate environment of NZQA at a senior level and been able to observe many wonderful teachers across the country. Given the nature of the job and the demands made by the community on teachers, there is no doubt that teaching is a tough job.

However, I know that many others, in a variety of professions, have equally tough jobs. Teachers, though, always seem to be complaining loudest about their workload. Teachers insist that their profession is different and that the pressures on them are greater than for many other professions. After all, teachers have to deal with groups of 30 children and build relationships with each of them—*at the same time*. Lawyers and doctors have offices and have to deal with only one person at a time. Teachers are also required to be mum, dad, judge and jury, while doctors and lawyers have more defined jobs. There are plenty of these sorts of arguments, which are mainly unconvincing. Doctors and lawyers, for example, face enormous pressures which teachers do not, including dealing with matters of life and death or ensuring that the bottom line of profitability is met, or someone is sent to prison or not.

Regardless of all this, the contention here is that the workload pressures teachers complain about are often self-inflicted. While many other professions such as doctors and lawyers work flexibly, and cope, teachers have tied themselves up in a collective agreement that prevents them and their principals from being able to do anything at all to address the problems they seem to consistently complain about.

Probably the best example of this is the way the school year is organised and teacher workload is distributed throughout this school year. The four school terms punctuated by holidays always follow a similar pattern. Staff arrive fresh from their break. The more enthusiastic ones are bursting to get into class and have lots of plans they want to put into place. Others will arrive on the first day of the term already beginning to count down for the next holiday. By the last week or two of the term a growing number of staff will complain that "this has been an incredibly busy term", and that staff are "stressed and tired" and "can't wait" for their much-deserved holiday.

Most principals will try to avoid extra pressure during the last couple of weeks of term because many secondary schools seem to be operating in crisis mode. To see why, we need to delve a little deeper into how the school year is actually put together.

At the beginning of the year or semester teachers are given a teaching load. They are also provided with some non-contact periods for their preparation and marking time. This teaching load is generally considered to be quite demanding. Teachers have to interact with hundreds of challenging teenagers who are crammed into classrooms and made (too often) to listen and write for hours on end. Teachers are increasingly required to keep detailed records and to assess comprehensively and accurately.

However, as the term progresses, teachers are required to take on *additional tasks* over and above their normal (demanding) teaching load. To take on these extra tasks is not easy. For example, once, twice even three times a year teachers must write examinations, mark them, and then write student reports, and finally front up to parent interviews. Each one of these activities is highly stressful and time consuming, and it is a workload *added* to the already significant workload assigned to the teacher at the start of the year. Other examples of this sort of additional work include carrying out appraisal interviews. These additional tasks are, of course, essential and are placed on the year planner for the school, often towards the end of each term.

As the term races by, the workload ramps up and teachers become overloaded.

Generally all this happens during the 38 weeks of term time, when students are at school. To cope, many dedicated teachers will work evenings and weekends. It is no wonder that teachers get stressed and complain about their workload towards the end of each term. Extra work just gets piled onto their already busy schedules, and no work is taken away.

Of course many jobs have peak times, and this is to be expected. However, in most professions, *at predicted* peak times managers are required to plan so that the peak workload time can be negotiated with minimum stress: stressed and overworked workers make mistakes and are inefficient. A manager might, for example, bring in extra staff or reduce other current demands.

The problem is that in the teaching profession this doesn't really happen. Some schools have tried, for example, by hiring exam supervisors to save staff time on the supervision of examinations, or buying in examinations from commercial suppliers, or even closing the school for an afternoon to allow for parent interviews during the day rather than in the evenings. In general, though, every year, every term, towards the end of the term/year, even though everyone knows the workload is going to peak—to explode—principals do nothing and teachers wait, forever complaining how tough their job is.

And then the term ends, teachers are ecstatic that they have made it to the end, and promptly go on holiday to recover.

Teachers are on 'holiday' for 12 weeks every year. Although many teachers undertake school work during their holidays, such as catching up on marking or preparing new units of work, this sort of frenzied stop–start pattern to the year is a major problem. It happens every year, in almost every school in the country, and has been happening for a long time. It is not good for our students, or for our teachers, and it certainly prevents sensible implementation of new reforms. Major reforms generally represent extra work added to already very busy school terms.

Although they are not paid a fortune, teachers are reasonably well paid, and it is likely that their *total* workload is not entirely out of kilter with that of many other professions. The problem is that too much of the workload is funnelled into just 38 weeks of the year— four school terms.

There are some obvious solutions that involve spreading some predicted and known work throughout the year, including both term time and holiday time. Such a change would have a very significant impact on the perceived workload of teachers and would probably produce teachers who are less stressed and far happier in their work.

However, it will be impossible to consider this sort of approach unless the PPTA and teachers are prepared to think outside the constraints imposed by the teachers' collective agreement. There is an urgent need for some teachers to stop thinking of themselves as victims, which appears to be their current default position, and start thinking about creative solutions. Some specific suggestions as to how this might be achieved will be canvassed in Part 4.

Teachers who spend too much time *not* teaching

Teachers are required to spend too much time not really teaching Many teachers are required to carry out a range of duties such as running sports teams and debating teams, putting on the annual production, and much more. Many teachers will argue that these sorts of *extracurricular* activities are important because they help build positive relationships with students, which are then very helpful inside the classroom. This may well be true.

Telling stressed and busy teachers they could reduce their workload by giving up their cherished sports team or debating team, in many cases, might well be met with howls of outrage from the very same teachers who are complaining bitterly about workload. Telling a drama teacher not to bother with the annual production because it will be too much work might well be met with urgent requests to "please reconsider because all the students and the staff really want to do this, and anyway putting on an annual production can be highly educative, and earn NCEA credits."

Notwithstanding the benefits of this extracurricular activity for teachers and students, the end result is that, as the end of the term draws near, it is these stressed and exhausted teachers who find it hard to fulfil their core teaching responsibilities and become concerned about their workload. There is something of a judgement call to be made here: is all the extra work involved in extracurricular activities really worth it?

Probably not. At some stage we need to consider the trade-offs involved. Do schools focus on sports, for example, or the requirements of good teaching and assessment if, as seems the case, there is not enough time to do both properly?

There is another issue that lurks here, which complicates matters. Many teachers take up extracurricular activities such as sports and drama because they *want* to. They enjoy drama productions, or cricket, and it is these very teachers who are often also the most committed and highly competent teachers in the school. The whingers and the moaners, and the barely competent, head home at 3.30.

Having said this, a decision still needs to be made about how teachers are expected to spend their precious time and energy. The answer is pretty obvious, but making such choices is hard, and requires courage from our leaders and, of course, from the PPTA.

It also requires parents and the community at large to think about what might be more realistic expectations of teachers and schools in this regard. We will return to these issues in Part 4 as we search for more solutions to some of these often intractable problems.

Concluding comments

Quality teaching is a critically important part of delivering quality education. This is why it is important to seriously address the problem of incompetent and mediocre teachers. It may be that principals need to use the existing terms of the collective agreement more courageously to address incompetence, though this will undoubtedly be a challenge, given the divisiveness that is likely to result in many staffrooms.

The time-served model of progressing through the pay scales for teachers, regardless of performance, and supported by the PPTA, must be done away with. Teaching is too important a profession to tolerate free riders and leave high flyers unrewarded. There is a need for teachers to think seriously about how they might better manage their workload, which, though substantial, would be more manageable if the teachers' collective agreement were more flexible. The PPTA's failure to properly address this problem has only made the working conditions of teachers worse.

In this context, schools need to consider how many extracurricular activities they really want their teachers to be involved in, given this work takes them away from core teaching activities.

Chapter 12: Secondary school principals

Strong school leadership is a key part of any successful reform process. Without the active input, support and critique of principals, the chances of a successful reform process are very limited. Unfortunately, principals over the past three decades have not always succeeded in providing this strong leadership, either for the sector or for their own schools.

Two principals' organisations

There are two organisations that claim to represent New Zealand secondary principals: the Secondary Principals' Association of New Zealand (SPANZ) and the Principals' Council (PC) of the PPTA. SPANZ is an independent organisation, which is completely funded by its members. The PC is associated with the PPTA, the teachers' union, and is financially supported by it.

I have been personally connected with, and been a member of, both organisations. In addition I was on the National Executive of the PPTA as a teacher representing Taranaki, and also National President and Executive member of SPANZ.

SPANZ was established in 1988 as a result of some frustration with the PC expressed by a number of more traditional, Auckland-based principals. Can principals, the founders of SPANZ asked, sensibly be represented by the same organisation (the PPTA, the teachers' union) that represents the teachers they employ through their board? Many PC principals see no problem here. Principals, they argue, have no role in bargaining with their teachers. This is properly a job for the Ministry of Education and school boards. As far as the principals' collective agreement, is concerned, this can easily be negotiated with the Ministry of Education through the PC.

This division within the ranks of New Zealand secondary principals is not just about negotiating contracts. There is a deeper issue here, about the role of the principal in a school. One view is that principals are chief executives, with all the duties and responsibilities this title bestows, and therefore cannot possibly be represented by the union that represents their 'employees'. The other view is that principals are, in fact, teachers with a leadership role and therefore *can* be represented by the teachers' union. It is the first view that led to the establishment of SPANZ as an independent principals association, with no formal ties to the PPTA whatsoever.

The establishment of SPANZ means that there are two organisations that represent New Zealand's secondary principals, the leaders of which often express quite different views. Both organisations are now jointly involved in collective bargaining with the Ministry of Education, and both claim to have a professional wing that runs conferences and provides legal, professional and personal support to principals. Most principals choose to belong to one or the other organisation and some even opt to belong to both.

It is not particularly relevant to go into the details of the ongoing rivalries and sometimes open warfare that has been the result of the establishment of SPANZ. The sad fact is that because of these rivalries secondary principals have generally failed to present a unified and well-articulated view on any major reform initiated by government. They have thereby minimised their effectiveness as a potentially very powerful political pressure group. One strong and united organisation during the development and implementation of NCEA, for example, may well have produced very significant gains for schools. As it was, the two organisations took differing views on this, and other reforms, and as a result were often ignored by the Ministry of Education and the Minister.

Principals are overwhelmed by their jobs

A number of secondary principals seem to find themselves overwhelmed by their jobs. They are expected to act in a chief executive role to their boards of trustees, which are independent Crown entities and have a range of responsibilities similar, but not identical, to many commercial boards. Boards and the principals, whom they appoint, have responsibilities in financial management, property management, human resource management, strategic planning and review, and, of course, instructional leadership.[1] As has already been noted, principals do not have any involvement in negotiating the pay and conditions of their teachers,[2] though they often have to deal with the consequences of failed negotiations, such as strikes and working to rule.

Since the core purpose of a school is to provide *quality teaching*, one would have to assume that the core purpose of its principal is to ensure that quality teaching is being delivered, and this requires *instructional leadership*. The best secondary principals in New Zealand are able to focus on this core role as an instructional leader and thus ensure quality teaching is being offered to each and every learner in the school. These principals understand how students learn, and they are up to date with the latest educational research. Some of these principals carry the load themselves, and some are able to delegate this core task to another member of their team. This delegation may well release the principal to concentrate on other critically important but essentially support roles, such as property and financial management, recruitment of fee-paying students, and discipline.

Delegating the core task of instructional leadership is a risk. In the end, what the leader of any organisation chooses to focus on is considered by employees and others to be the critically important part of the business. A principal who does not focus on instructional leadership and elects to take charge of (say) remodelling a teaching block or mar-

---

[1] The term 'instructional leadership' is used here to summarise the role the principal has to maximise the quality of teaching and learning taking place in their school.
[2] Neither do boards: collective bargaining is carried out by the Ministry of Education and the relevant union.

keting the school overseas sends confusing messages to his/her staff. Having said this, there are examples in New Zealand of principals, particularly of large schools, who have successfully delegated instructional leadership to a deputy or even a team. In all these cases, though, the principal repeatedly and clearly articulates the teaching and learning goals of the school as being central to its purpose.

The problem is that too many New Zealand secondary school principals are so overwhelmed by their jobs that they fail to ensure appropriate attention is paid to the core role of instructional leadership. There are a number of reasons for this.

The wrong people are sometimes appointed to be principals

Boards of trustees are currently responsible for appointing principals. While some boards are capable of doing this well, plenty are not, particularly in small, rural, isolated schools. The government does not set any minimum requirements to become a school principal. Too often boards appoint the wrong people to the job, and there are few checks in the system to ensure this does not happen.

There is limited competition for many principal positions

While it may be that there are many high-quality applications for high-decile schools, for many small, medium-sized, lower-decile schools competition for the position is not always very strong. At least part of the reason for this may be that salary rates are not attractive enough given the size of the job. But the problem is not just about the money. Principalship is seen as a very, very tough job in the teaching profession, and not enough quality teachers regard it as a particularly desirable goal for their career.

There is no required career process for principals in training

Principals are often appointed to their position from deputy principal (DP) positions. In most schools the DP runs the school on a daily basis. The DP role is, therefore, often very much an *operational* job, and the incumbent generally has little opportunity to focus on instructional leadership.

Moving from the DP role to the principal role represents a huge change in focus, but generally new principals are expected to prepare themselves for their new roles without a lot of external support. It is true that the Ministry of Education has made an effort in this area over the last few years with the introduction of 'aspiring' and 'new principals' PD programmes. Although these programmes have proved popular, and principals have been appreciative of what has been developed, we should be under no illusion that these initiatives represent a thorough and rigorous training and preparation for the job. They do not.

The aspiring principal programme lasts for 1 year but is largely an online, part-time programme designed to be completed while still working full time. According to the material online, participants will be involved in:

- an online reflective blog journal
- a national hui
- four online modules of work based on the role of the principal
- three personalised inquiry coaching sessions with an experienced facilitator
- peer coaching
- contributing to a professional learning group.
- three regional meetings
- shadowing leaders in another school. (Educational Leaders, 2013)

There is nothing wrong with this. However, there is no requirement for principals to have gone through *any* programme, let alone this one, prior to appointment. More importantly, this sort of part-time, online, low-cost programme cannot replace a (more expensive) full-time programme of study specifically designed to prepare selected individuals for school leadership. Such a programme could lead to a qualification, possibly at master's level.

There is often limited capacity in schools to support principals

As suggested above, really good principals can cope with the extraordinary demands of the job and are able to prioritise and delegate effectively to allow them to focus on the core task of instructional leadership. This presupposes that the principal has the required support structures in place. In small, rural and isolated schools these support structures can be sadly lacking. The principal of a school of 200, for example, will have very limited administrative or professional support. His/her DP or assistant principal will have a substantial teaching load and will probably lack the required administrative financial and property skills.

In hard-to-staff, low-decile schools the lack of applications for principal positions will be compounded by lack of applications for DP and assistant principal positions as well. Lower-decile, smaller schools are also less likely to be able to access funds to employ non-teaching administrative staff. For larger and higher-decile schools, however, the principal does have more options in terms of hiring specialist staff and using existing staff to pick up some of the administrative load.

Principals behave badly in a competitive environment

Many principals take the view that their primary purpose is to maximise the reputation of their school, to boost their school roll, and to protect/nurture their public image. This is not surprising given the competitive environment they are required to work in, and the inclination of boards and the media to judge their competence on the basis of indicators such as school roll, media reports and NCEA results.

Unfortunately, this approach to principalship can lead to significant problems with student welfare and student learning. To be more specific, many principals take the view that their major aim is to advocate for their *school* but not necessarily for their *students*, and certainly not neighbouring schools, or their students, or the wider community.

A regrettable example I was involved in while principal at Rosehill College in Papakura illustrates this issue very well. Papakura was at the time a divided town, with Papakura High School catering largely for low-decile Māori and Pasifika students, and Rosehill College catering for the middle-class, aspiring parents in the community along with a minority of Māori students. When I became principal of the college in 1995 the roll was around 1,250; when I left around 7 years later the roll had reached around 1,850.

This roll growth created many significant advantages for the school and for my reputation, including extra funding, new buildings and excellent marketing. However, there is little doubt that at least part of the roll growth was at the expense of Papakura High School, because of the application of the enrolment rules operating at the time.[3] The impact on Papakura High School was devastating: able students who should have attended Papakura High School were accepted at Rosehill College, and some less able or socially difficult students who should have attended Rosehill High School, given their home addresses, were refused enrolment and forced to attend Papakura High School.

The point is this: as principal of Rosehill College I was unarguably working within the law at the time, in the interests of my college. I was successfully maximising the entry of well-adjusted, high-ability students into my school. This resulted in better exam results, fewer discipline problems and greater recognition from government agencies. The Ministry of Education funded extra buildings, the community viewed the school as the school of choice in the region, and the quality and number of applicants for teaching positions improved considerably. Students at Rosehill College were well served. However, the success of Rosehill College was probably detrimental to the interests of Papakura High School, whose students posed increasingly difficult social and educational problems for the school board and its principal. This increasing level of educational and social dislocation at Papakura High School, in the end, created a real cost to the community of Papakura, and the region as a whole, as increasing numbers of disaffected youth leaving Papakura High School hit the streets.

The two schools were meant to be competing with each other, but the competition was hardly fair and created a situation where one school and its staff were left to deal with massive social and educational issues, while the other school, and its staff, were left to take advantage of their already reasonably privileged position. The whole situation was brought about because the principal of one school was acting, for whatever misguided reasons, in an unethical manner.

There are plenty of other examples of what can only be described as principals behaving badly. Many principals have no compunction about luring élite sports students from low-decile schools with inducements of various types, including quite lucrative scholarships. The idea of schools 'buying' players in this way, like English soccer teams, is faintly ludicrous. It also works against schools and communities that

---

3 The rules have since been changed.

are already disadvantaged, thus aggravating New Zealand's social, economic and educational divide. Attempts have been made to put a stop to this practice, but it still goes on.

The problem is not just *between* schools—it also occurs *within* schools. Principals have been known to banish apparently less-able students to 'alternative' classes within the school to ensure they are not counted in the school's exam statistics. Better that the student misses out (on even a slim chance of exceeding the dismal expectations of their teachers) than the school risks slipping down the NCEA league tables. This sort of behaviour was common in many so-called élite schools at the time of School Certificate and University Bursary exams, and remains so in the current NCEA environment.

The NCEA environment, however, raises more ethical issues related to the programme a student should be placed in. For example, it has been common for schools to run 'alternative' unit standards-based programmes in maths, English, tourism, hospitality, employment skills, etc. Many of the standards offered in these programmes are not particularly challenging, but nevertheless contribute to NCEA. When students leave school they leave with useful skills and a detailed transcript, which documents the standards they have achieved. Many potential employers might well be interested in offering these students employment based on the specified skills.

There is nothing inherently wrong with this approach, if done for the right reasons.

However, placing students on these courses could also be viewed rather more negatively if the reason for placing students on such programmes is to improve school pass rates. Why risk failure by making students go for more challenging standards when the school gets the pass rates up by aiming lower? The problem is that many principals suffer considerable pressure to act in a manner that maximises benefit to the *school* (higher pass rates, for example) rather than the *individual* (who might well benefit from being challenged and encouraged to aim higher).

Teachers can fall into the same trap. Faced with demands from the principal to boost pass rates, they can easily acquiesce in the entire process, perhaps with the very best of intentions. Parents and students themselves can be useful regulators of principals' behaviour in this context. In some schools, parents and students will ask questions about what programmes of study are offered and why. Some parents will challenge the principal on the placement of their children into 'alternative programmes'. However, predictably, these parents are likely to be those from higher socioeconomic backgrounds, while those already disadvantaged by the system will be less likely to challenge the principal and more likely to suffer long-term consequences as a result.

Given that it is Māori and Pasifika students who dominate these alternative programmes, we are left to ponder the negative impact on the community created by the desire of some principals to maximise success for their *school* rather than the individuals who make up that community.

There are other examples. A number of schools have elected to dump NCEA and adopt the Cambridge examinations. While a few are genuinely concerned about some of the inadequacies of NCEA, there is little doubt that the majority see this as nothing more than a *marketing* opportunity. Adopting the Cambridge exam is seen as an instant makeover, which could encourage more academic students to enrol and which in turn could boost the total roll. A discussion about the woefulness of the Cambridge exams is not required here; the point is that once NCEA is dumped by so-called prominent schools, the reputation and credibility of the national system—both nationally and internationally—is brought into question, which affects the morale and confidence of every student and teacher willingly participating in NCEA.

It is not easy to be a school leader in New Zealand. Our total population is smaller than many local authorities in the UK and many school districts in the US. And yet we run a may-all-flowers-bloom education system based on competition for students, led by principals in highly devolved schools. Given we have this system, and given it is unlikely to change, it is up to school principals to work to the highest ethical standards possible, both individually and collectively. Too many (including, I have to admit, me at times) have failed to measure up, instead indulging in self-promoting and unethical behaviour, citing the needs of their school as an excuse.

New Zealand secondary principals themselves, as a collective group, must bear some responsibility for this state of affairs. They have failed miserably to establish or enforce any sort of ethical code of conduct on their members and have been completely unable to provide any useful critique or alternative policy options to address the issues creating the problems. We will return to this issue in Part 4.

Concluding comments

The leadership of secondary school principals is crucial to successful educational reform, but this leadership has not been forthcoming for many years. Instead, principals have too often squabbled among themselves and have behaved badly in some cases. There are also continuing problems with principal recruitment and training that need to be addressed.

As a result of these matters, principals have patently failed to apply their undoubted *leadership* influence to ensure good evidence-based educational reform is implemented and supported. Some suggestions for how these issues might be addressed will be discussed in Part 4.

PART 4:
Future pathways

In this last part of the book I will outline a set of proposals designed to address the problems and concerns that have been raised in Parts 1 to 3. I will start with a brief discussion about the relative importance of socioeconomic status (SES) and schooling in determining educational outcomes, and then suggest how we can:

- make better judgments about the effectiveness of schools and the schooling system, given what we know about the use and misuse of NCEA data and ERO reports
- support teachers better so that they can actually make effective changes in their classrooms, which is the essential part of any worthwhile educational reform
- improve school leadership so that school leaders can work to make educational reform successful
- ensure the educational reform process, including policy development, implementation and evaluation, both in the Ministry of Education and in schools, is made more robust.

Setting out a future pathway for reform in a book that has been highly critical of the reform and policy development process in New Zealand may seem dangerously contradictory. None of the proposals here have been through any sort of policy development process at all!

It is important, therefore, to be clear that although these proposals are intended to address many of the problems that have been raised in earlier parts of this book, they are *proposals* for reform. Politicians and officials will need to take careful note of the reasons behind the failures of the past identified in this book to avoid the very same mistakes being made again.

Chapter 13: Socioeconomic status matters: Address economic and social disparities

We have already established that the impact of socioeconomic factors on student achievement is huge—far bigger than the likely impact of whatever a teacher or school can achieve. As a reminder, Pasi Sahlberg, a former inspector of schools from Finland, argued in the *Washington Post*:

> Research on what explains students' measured performance in school remains mixed. A commonly used conclusion is that 10% to 20% of the variance in measured student achievement belongs to the classroom, i.e., teachers and teaching, and a similar amount is attributable to schools, i.e., school climate, facilities and leadership. In other words, up to two-thirds of what explains student achievement is beyond the control of schools, i.e., family background and motivation to learn. (Sahlberg, 2013)

References to this issue have been made throughout this book, with Marzano suggesting that the impact of what students bring to school is even larger than this (around 80 percent).[1] Educationalists some-

---

[1] See Chapter 3, p. 33.

times underestimate this issue, and politicians and bureaucrats *always* underestimate it. If we really want to make an impact on educational achievement and disparities in New Zealand, we need to look to our government to address the economic and social causes of the disparities. We also need to support teachers when the government absolves itself of its responsibilities by blaming teachers and expecting them to fix the problems caused by years of government neglect and poor decision making.

The current Ministry of Education and ministerial mantra about teachers being *the key* to addressing disparities in educational achievement is very misleading. Of course teachers can make a significant difference (as we have explained earlier in this book), but this does not mean that the socioeconomic disadvantages that some students come to school with in New Zealand can be ignored.

Education reforms that focus on better teaching practice alone, or better student–teacher relationships, or better administration, or better assessment, or even better literacy and numeracy, will not be as effective as they might be without proper attention being given to the socioeconomic factors that are the underlying causes of many of the problems.

Various governments have made attempts to provide this support: social workers have been placed in primary schools, guidance counsellors employed, and free milk provided with corporate support. Early childhood education funding has been a priority, and there have been attempts to co-ordinate service provision in low-decile schools. This is all positive—but not nearly enough. We have a crisis in this country based on social class, and it is conflated with ethnicity. If the gaps in educational achievement are not substantially and properly addressed urgently, we run major risks of social and economic dislocation and further declines in our international PISA ranking.

Governments must make the required changes at the macro level with appropriate economic and social policies. This is critically important, because it will help to prevent problems occurring in the first place. At the micro level, governments need to do better at providing wrap-around services to lower-decile schools and communities. This means that government agencies must work together to further develop school-based networks of support for the community of the schools.

This network of support is likely to build on existing early childhood education provision, adult education, mentoring, food/lunch programmes, social workers, counsellors, and much more.[2]

Money spent in communities to encourage parents and students to participate in education is likely to be far more effective than money spent to employ executive principals,[3] who, despite their leadership skills, will find themselves impotent in the face of these enormous challenges.

None of this, however, provides any excuse for teachers and educators to abdicate their responsibilities. Their job is to focus on educating students, whatever their circumstances. We all know that what we do in schools and classrooms can make a difference, and that achievement gaps *can* be closed. We cannot shirk the obligation to act.

So, we are left with a question: given the issues and problems we have identified in the last three parts of this book, what needs to be done?

---

[2] The idea of schools acting as community support centres is not new, though the PPTA is working to develop the concept of 'Equipping schools to fight poverty through a community hub approach' (see PPTA conference paper, October 2013, retrieved from www.ppta.org.nz).

[3] The National-led government announced in 2014 that it would fund new executive principal positions. The idea is that these 'super principals', while retaining the leadership of their own schools, would be released and funded to support other struggling school principals.

Chapter 14: Find new tools to measure school effectiveness

Publishing league tables

In Finland there are no school inspections, and the results of the one exam the students sit at 18 years of age are made available to the schools and students (so that they can analyse their performance) but they are *not* made public. There are no league tables. The government runs national sample assessments to keep track of the whole system, but these are not made available to the public either. Teachers and schools are held in high regard by the community and the focus is on improving all schools by encouraging them to work together and support each other (Wilby, 2013). According to PISA data, Finland does very well educationally.

In New Zealand, on the other hand, the media, schools and school principals seem to obsess over NCEA results and ERO reports on a regular basis. This despite the fact that comparing NCEA pass rates is not sensible, that analysing ERO reports is problematic, and that placing NCEA results in the media leads people to draw inappropriate conclusions. It also creates unintended consequences, drives unproductive school competition and encourages poor assessment practice.

Finland of course is not New Zealand and has a far more homogeneous population which make any comparisons of the two countries questionable, at least. However, the debate about the publication of assessment data goes much further afield than Finland. In their report for McKinsey and Company on *How the World's Most Improved School Systems Keep Getting Better*, Mourshed, Chijioke, & Barber (2010) point out that the publication of school data is not a common practice among top-performing very diverse Asian education systems. The leaders of these Asian education systems argue that naming and shaming hurts both educators and learning:

> Making results public demotivates staff and results in paralysis. They stop being open to learning and trying new things. Instead they ... focus on protecting themselves and finding ways to make their students look good on tests. (p. 79)

However, according to the McKinsey and Company report, there are considerable variations in practice around the world. In England, for example, literacy and numeracy targets are set, league tables published and schools ranked. Repeated poor performance results in schools being closed down. The justification is that "we are here for the kids ... This is not about protecting the adults in the building."[1]

A middle ground was illustrated by Boston in the US, where targets were established, and results gathered, but not made public. Instead, principals were held accountable.

Given the current expectations of New Zealand parents, politicians and the media, as well as existing Official Information Act legislation, it seems unlikely that we will be able to gain agreement from governments or the media—or even parents—that we should follow the Asian or Finnish examples. Maybe this is something we could aim to achieve in the future.

---

1 Statement by a US "system leader" who is not identified by the authors (p. 78).

Publishing useful and valid achievement data

Meanwhile, we should make sure that the school achievement data we do collect about school effectiveness, whether we make it public or not, are at least more valid than is currently the case. I propose four effectiveness indicators for further debate:

1. determine what value a school adds to its students between their entry and their exit from the school, which would require the development of a credible 'value added measure' (VAM)—admittedly this will be a challenge
2. monitor and publish the retention rates of the school and what happens to students who leave school in relation to NCEA results
3. make judgements about the quality of the teachers in the school
4. monitor the performance of a representative sample of students in key skills, over time, for all schools, nationally and internationally.

1. Value added measures

There are plenty of examples internationally of governments attempting to measure the value a teacher adds to her/his students by teaching them. These attempts to measure 'value added' have often been linked with performance pay for teachers, but there are problems with this. A Massey University paper authored by Ivan Snook and others in 2013 (Snook et al., 2013) provides a powerful reminder to policy makers that measuring the value added for a teacher is almost impossible, given the variables such as student motivation, home background, other teachers' impacts and school resources.

It is not the intention here to promote a value-added measure (VAM) for *individual* teachers. However, it may be feasible to devise a measure that allows us to shed some light on how much value a *school* might add to *a cohort or group* of its students in relation to its NCEA performance. Instead of listing NCEA results in the newspaper alongside the name and decile of the school (which we now know is not a valid way of making any sort of comparison), we need to establish the *difference in achievement* between what a particular group of students arrives at a school with and what that group leaves with. Measuring this value add, regardless of the school decile, would allow the community to make better judgments about the effectiveness of the school.

Entry data

Many New Zealand schools currently use Progressive Achievement Test (PAT) data to assess students' literacy and numeracy skills on entry to Year 9. These tests are extensively trialled and provide good-quality information about key skills. Currently most schools use the data to allocate students to particular streamed ability classes, or to identify students who need special assistance. These test results[2] could also be used as a base for entry achievement data that provide an achievement profile of the Year 9 cohort at entry for a particular school. Such a profile would inevitably reflect the socioeconomic characteristics[3] of the intake at Year 9.

These achievement data are not *subject* based, but focus more on generic skills. Given that they are *test* data they will be subject to all the caveats we have already discussed about testing. However, they will provide some information about the capabilities of students in a specific range of generic skills on entry to the school.

PAT data may not be the only way of establishing an entry profile for a given cohort, and other possibilities should be investigated, including properly moderated National Standards data. The point here is that there is a need to establish a reasonably sensible way of benchmarking a particular cohort of students as they enter secondary school.

Exit data

The most relevant exit data for a secondary school are NCEA results. However, the publication of raw NCEA results, as we have explained in Chapter 5, will certainly not give us the information we are seeking. Schools currently offer a range of courses and standards that vary hugely in terms of their level of difficulty and relative pass rates.

For the purposes of creating a useful exit measure, school NCEA results need to be 'adjusted' to take account of the level of difficulty of standards that students in the school use. This sounds a bit like the old scaling, but the intention here is not to create artificial pass marks,

---

2 Results from other proven national assessments might be available. For example, an alternative entry data profile might be provided by the asTTle tests referred to in Chapter 8, or even National Standards assessments once they are regarded as valid and reliable.

3 Clearly low-decile schools will probably have a lower achievement profile at Year 9 compared with high-decile schools because of the SES disadvantages students in lower-decile schools start with.

but to report results so that they are reasonably meaningful *when compared*—standard to standard, and subject to subject.

For example, suppose a group of students who pass standard A, for which there is a national pass rate of 70 percent, need to be compared with another group who pass standard B, for which there is only a 50 percent pass rate. Standard A is easier than standard B, and this fact needs to be taken account in calculating a VAM. The same sort of procedure will need to be carried out for Merit and Excellence grades, since these are easier to gain in some standards and subjects than in others. One obvious example is that Merit and Excellence grades from externally assessed standards are much more difficult to gain than those from internally assessed standards. Relative performance, therefore, can only be properly compared if adjustments are made for the level of difficulty of each standard at the Achieved, Merit and Excellence grades.

The task of producing such an adjusted profile of results will be highly technical, and it will not be easy for members of the public to understand. In fact, this 'black box' processing of data would be just as difficult for the public to understand as the technical work carried out by the OECD with PISA data.[4] It may also be subject to challenge regarding its accuracy, just as PISA data are. Nevertheless, the aim would be to produce an adjusted *exit achievement profile* based on NCEA performance for a group of students in a school. It would only be necessary to collect these exit data once every year, probably at Level 2 NCEA given that Level 2 NCEA has been set as a major exit benchmark by the Government.

It is important to emphasise that the data would need to be *aggregated* data for the cohort or group of students in the school, so there would be no question of individual teachers being measured for their performance.

The value added

If a PAT (or similar) achievement profile at Year 9 is put alongside *an adjusted* NCEA results profile at NCEA Level 2, it would create a

---

[4] OECD PISA findings have been considered perfectly acceptable and valid by politicians, the media, school principals and the public, despite the fact that country rankings are based on a highly technical statistical process that for most people is totally incomprehensible.

useful VAM for the school as a whole. Such a measure would provide some indication of how much impact the school and teachers have had on student achievement across the entire school. For example, a group of students who arrive at School A in Year 9 with a *very low* entry achievement profile and leave at Level 2 NCEA with a moderately good adjusted NCEA Level 2 profile will have had more value added than a second different group who arrive at School B with a *very good* entry profile and leave with the same, moderately good, adjusted NCEA Level 2 profile as School A.

This proposal will be controversial. It will need to be thoroughly researched and trialled before any thought is given to implementing it. There are many questions that will need to be answered, such as:

- Exactly how would an achievement profile for a cohort of at NCEA Level 2 students be compared with the Year 9 profile for the same group of students?
- If entry data are likely to be derived from what is essentially a generic skills test and the NCEA data are more subject based, would the resulting value add be comparing like with like?
- Would teachers begin to game the system? For example, would there be an incentive to depress entry data scores in order to show bigger value adds with exit data?
- Would any resulting league tables be understood by the public and schools?
- If the league tables are made public, what impact would this have on poorly performing schools, and how might they be supported?
- How valid would the data be for very small schools?

Given the assumption that the New Zealand public wishes to compare schools, and wishes them to compete, it is important that the school-to-school comparisons that *are* made are based on valid and credible information. The VAM outlined in this section is one possible approach, which focuses on school-wide factors and avoids problems associated with measuring the performance of individual teachers.

It has the added advantage that there would be no need to change anything to do with the delivery of NCEA in schools, or the range of assessment activities teachers could use. Students would continue to receive their NCEA grades and NCEA certificates as they currently do, and NZQA would continue to monitor the quality of assessment taking place in all schools, just as it currently does.

2. Retention and participation rates

The extent to which students stay at school is an important element of school effectiveness, but a complex one. Retention rates can be calculated by working out the number of students attending the school at Year 9 and the number of those students at school at some point in the future, say at the end of Year 12.

However, retention rates can be confusing if a school has high numbers leaving *and* arriving. A simple calculation based on students present might indicate a high retention rate, but this rate could be masking the fact that *different* students are moving in and out of the school. This is why retention rates are better calculated by tracking what happens to the actual students who start school at Year 9.

Low-decile schools will tend to have low retention rates as students drop out of schools early. Students may be less engaged in their schooling, or may simply be encouraged by their families to leave and find paid employment. High-decile schools will tend to have higher retention rates. Given all of the above, it is clear that using retention rates on their own as a measure of a school's effectiveness is problematic.

The calculation of NCEA pass rates, however, is closely related to retention rates, although this is not widely understood. The pass rate depends very much on the denominator used. Stay with this: it is not a difficult thing to understand, and it is important. NZQA has published a number of options for calculating NCEA pass rates, as follows.

Participation based

This pass rate is based on the number of students for whom it was at least technically possible to gain an NCEA certificate—known as a *participation rate*. So, for example, because 80 credits are required for an NCEA Level 1 pass, the only students who are used as the denominator in this calculation are those who have "entered" at least 80 credits. Students who have been withdrawn, or left school, or who have simply not "entered" 80 credits are excluded from the calculation.

This is a perfectly acceptable calculation and was introduced to avoid penalising schools that have students who have special remedial needs (and therefore do not attempt NCEA), or who have entered for alternative qualifications, or who have large numbers leaving prior to attempting NCEA. Before the introduction of this participation rate, the only other option for the denominator was the actual number of students on the school roll on 1 July each year. This is referred to as the *roll-based* denominator.

Roll-based rate

This pass rate provides a rate based on a denominator of the number of students on the school roll on 1 July of the year in question, even if they have since left the school or if they have no intention of attempting NCEA at all, such as students doing Cambridge exams or special remedial needs students for whom NCEA might be inappropriate.

Participation-based pass rates compared with roll-based pass rates

These two methods of calculating pass rates can produce some quite different results, each telling a different story. Here is a simple example for just one school.

Hypothetical example of pass rate comparison	
Shortis High school NCEA pass rates (Level 1):	
Roll at 1 July: Students entered for 80 credits or more:	200 150
NCEA certificates gained (80 credits):	100
The participation-based pass rate is: The roll-based pass rate is:	66% *(100/150)* 50% *(100/200)*

The pass rates are both perfectly valid in terms of the way they have been calculated. The question that needs to be asked is: what happened to those 50 students—the difference between the roll as at 1 July (200) and the number of students who actually entered for 80 credits (150)? Have they left the school? If so, where have they gone and what are they doing? If they are at school, what are they being offered by way of education, and is it appropriate?

Some schools might try hard to keep students at school and offer non-credit programmes through training providers rather than see students on the streets and without support. But why are these students not being offered an opportunity to gain NCEA? Is it a genuine desire on the part of the school to ensure they do not just fail, or is it a way of boosting pass rates and avoiding providing challenging programmes for all students? And how can someone wanting to compare schools work all this out?

The obvious thing to do here is to ensure that schools publish their NCEA pass rates using *both denominators*: the roll-based and the participation-based, and be required to explain the difference. The report could be reasonably straightforward and succinct, and included as part of an annual audit process to the Ministry of Education. In the case above, the question will be: what happened to those 50 students?

Once again, readers may be asking questions about the complexity of this approach to making judgments about a school's effectiveness. There could be a range of alternative approaches to the problem. For example: schools could be required to report their Level 2 NCEA pass rates as a percentage of that same group of students when they entered the school at Year 9. So if 150 students entered the school in Year 9, how many of *that group* gained NCEA Level 2? And of those that did not, what happened to them?[5]

Finally, we should note that the Ministry of Education has already developed a dashboard approach to school comparison called School Smart (Ministry of Education, 2010). This is not available to the public but does provide a great deal of information about schools' achievement, attendance and retention rates. Unfortunately the data are subject to the same problems of comparison we have already alluded to. Presumably this is why they have not been made available to the public.

3. Quality teaching

Whatever view we have about NCEA results, or value added measures, or retention and participation rates, most people would agree that the

---

5 Such an approach might penalise low-decile schools, which have high rates of turnover, and favour high-decile schools, which tend to hold their students at school for longer. However, proper explanations of what happened to these students would certainly provide information about the effectiveness of the school in question.

effectiveness of a school has got a lot to do with the quality of the teaching going on in that school. But how do we find out about this?

The fall-back position for most researchers, as we have seen, is to look at the results—the test scores of the students. Good results/test scores are assumed to mean quality teaching is taking place. In Chapter 4 this reliance on test scores was questioned. It is not that test scores should be ignored, but we really need to understand that test scores do not measure everything, and may not measure teacher quality very effectively at all on their own.

In response I suggested (see Chapter 4) that a focus on quality *teaching*, as opposed to test scores, may provide another way of looking at effectiveness. We might be able to draw conclusions about the quality of a teacher by examining the teaching strategies that are used in his or her classroom. This sort of approach is certainly not as objective as using test scores, and of course also has its problems, as has already been argued, because it oversimplifies and encourages a mechanistic tool box approach to teaching, which most experienced teachers will reject out of hand.

In response, I suggested that the focus should not be on the teaching strategy but the teacher himself or herself. Effective teachers can be identified by examining their approach or 'states of mind', or, in John Hattie's, words "mind frames". Effective schools have lots of teachers with the right "mind frames". Most parents know this perfectly well already.

However, this sort of approach will not go down well with those who are interested in outputs and objective evidence and proof. They will ask how we might even begin to collect and report any meaningful data about teacher quality as defined here. This is only partly a reasonable argument. We know that test results, even the value added measure discussed above, are limited. At best they measure a *slice* of something that happens in the classroom. The same can be argued about attempting to make judgements about the quality of teaching, or teachers' mind frames. Such judgements may not capture everything that happens in the classroom, but they might well capture a slice of it.

For example, an effective teacher may not always be aiming to produce better test results if the assessments required by the school are not relevant to his or her learning and teaching intentions during a particular lesson. The learning that happens in a classroom discussion about ethics, for example, may not even been assessed at all.

The contention here, therefore, is that the effectiveness of teaching and teachers in a school can be observed, and judgements made, *independently* of test or assessment results.

How would this information be gathered and reported? Teachers cannot simply *tell us* they are effective; effectiveness must be demonstrated and reported, particularly if we want to compare one school with another. External reviews of schools carried out by the ERO already comment on the quality of teaching. Given the other effectiveness indicators we have already proposed in this section, it may be that evaluating the *quality of teachers* and teaching could become the *sole* purpose of an ERO visit. Experienced and well-trained evaluators are perfectly capable of making such judgements. The basis of the judgement would be related to *both* the strategies being used in the classroom and the mind frames demonstrated by the teachers.

This judgement would need to be based on classroom observations over a period of time. This would require some of the current ERO methodologies based on planned 3-yearly visits to be changed. For example, some classroom visits might need to be unannounced drop-in visits by ERO staff. Evaluators would need to examine students' work and assessments and lesson plans more thoroughly than is the case at present. In addition to this, student surveys designed to gauge the level of students' engagement in learning could be administered, and parents and caregivers questioned.

There are undoubtedly complexities involved in this proposal. What would it mean, for example, if the quality of teaching and teachers is reported to be very good but the value added is low? Such a situation, I expect, would trigger informative discussions between the school and ERO.[6]

Probably the biggest criticism will be that such judgements will be more subjective than supposedly more objective achievement data. However, it has already been demonstrated that existing achievement data are hardly reliable. The proposed VAM will provide a more robust judgment—but not a perfect one by any means. It will certainly not pro-

---

6 It may be that a school cannot expect to add as much value to a very high performing intake as another school ,with a different intake, whose performance may be particularly low

vide an overall picture of the quality of teaching and teachers because it cannot reflect the richness of teaching going on in the classroom.

This judgment may well be subjective, but if made by experienced and skilled evaluators it could form part of any overall judgement of the effectiveness or quality of a school.

4. Quality checks over time

National quality checks

It is important that data from all three measures above be used to benchmark the development of the whole secondary sector by way of a triennial report. This national checking could be augmented by a *sampling process*, which would allow for key skills or competencies to be assessed through a combination of formal tests and observations of groups of students over time, using standardised methods of testing and assessment. Results would be used only for the purposes of national checking, and not as any basis for comparing schools or teachers.

New Zealand has a good history of national monitoring through the NEMP[7] (University of Otago, 2013) project originally run out of the University of Otago from 1995 to 2010, and then through the National Monitoring Study of Student Achievement run in collaboration with NZCER and the Ministry of Education. The purpose of NEMP was to monitor student achievement precisely in key curriculum areas from Years 4–8, over time, using a sampling method, rather than requiring all students to sit national tests.

Such a sampling approach expanded to include students through to Year 13 would serve as a useful method of gauging the overall performance of the education system over time, and would identify strengths, weaknesses and potential areas for further investigation and investment.

International quality checks

There are a number of international quality checks New Zealand participates in on a regular basis, the most important of which is PISA. It is clear that New Zealand should continue to participate in these international tests, albeit with a degree of caution as to the conclusions to be drawn from such tests.

---

7 National Education Monitoring Project.

Concluding comments

We have a choice. We could agree that we do not wish our schools to *compete* with each other and that we do not wish to *compare* our schools with each other. In this case we would reject the current obsession with league tables and, like Finland, focus on strengthening the entire system so that all schools are viewed positively. We would agree to some national and international sampling to monitor the whole system, but not individual schools.

Alternatively, we could decide that it is important to maintain a competitive school environment. In this case, we would need to come up with a more robust way of measuring effectiveness (for comparing schools) than we currently have. If, as is likely, we are not prepared to copy Finland—at least not yet—we need to work further on a value add measure (VAM), and we need to analyse roll-based and participation-based NCEA pass rates better than we currently do. Finally, we need to focus on the quality of teaching and teachers as a perfectly acceptable measure of school effectiveness, quite independently of test scores.

None of these proposals are easy to implement, and each will need detailed further policy analysis and proper trialling. These measures, or other alternative measures designed to meet the same ends, might, coupled with comprehensive national sampling and continued international testing, provide the New Zealand Government and community with better information about the quality of our education system and of the schools operating in it than at present.

Chapter 15: Focus on teacher support and professional development

Introduction

As has already been suggested, it is difficult, in the current New Zealand environment, to conceive of a situation in which school achievement data are not made public. Given this, it is critically important that the focus of the Ministry of Education not be on blaming and shaming underperforming schools. Instead, the focus should be on providing support and encouragement to improve.

We know that simply holding underperforming schools *accountable* for their performance is not generally a successful strategy, because it is these very schools that are least capable of helping themselves. Schools need to be given support to meet their accountabilities.[1] It is in the classroom that we must seek change if we are to have any chance of success, and although this may be obvious, it is clear from observations made in Part 2 of this book that this has not always been the focus of reform.

---

1 The Ministry of Education has begun to recognise this fact and has been doing more to support these schools since 2012 through a range of targeted strategies, particularly in support of Māori and Pasifika students in low-decile schools.

Changing the practice of teachers in the classroom is not an easy thing to do, and requires multiple interventions, careful planning, appropriate professional development, teacher buy in, as well as accountability. It is here that any future successful educational reform must focus, specifically, deliberately and consistently, over long periods of time, despite the often contradictory requirements of our political electoral cycle. It is important that the Minister of Education, of whatever political party, and the chief executive of the Ministry of Education be seen to openly and honestly champion ways to improve classroom practice and do nothing that could have a negative impact on improving classroom practice. It is our teachers to whom we must turn if we are to succeed.

Unfortunately, teaching in New Zealand is not generally regarded as a job for high flyers. At the risk of being pilloried by many outstanding teachers, teaching *tends* to attract the second or third tier of graduates. School principals do not sweep through the universities offering substantial scholarships and incentives for the outstanding graduates in the cohort. This approach seems restricted to only one or two government departments and some commercial concerns.

So what is it that we need to do in New Zealand to recruit and retain the top tier for the teaching profession? The answer, of course, is complex because the attractiveness of teaching (like any other job) depends on many variables. Some specific interventions that may achieve what is required are outlined in the rest of this chapter.

Attracting the top tier to teaching

All secondary teachers should have, or be working towards, at least a master's degree in their specialist subject(s)

A deep and genuine understanding of their discipline is a critical part of the job of any secondary teacher. A teacher needs to understand the intricacies of their subject matter in order to teach it, so that students can comprehend its interconnectedness and perhaps experience its wonder and relationship to their lives. A teacher who does not have the required depth of content knowledge is not likely to teach well.

There could well be a number of ways for prospective teachers to achieve a master's degree, which will require further investigation and thought. For some it might just be a matter of gaining the degree in their chosen discipline. For others it might be possible to construct, or build on, an existing master's programme that combines both subject content and pedagogical studies.[2]

There will be those who will disagree with this proposal. The job of the modern secondary teacher, they might argue, is not to disseminate content and knowledge, it is more about communication and building relationships—in fact, the more specialist the teacher is in their subject area, the *worse* they will be as a teacher. But this is not an either/or argument. It is not a matter of a teacher having in-depth knowledge of the discipline *or* having the ability to communicate and build relationships. It is a matter of the best teachers having *both* in-depth knowledge *and* the ability to communicate and build relationships. Teachers cannot teach in a vacuum. Their ability to communicate and build positive relationships and to truly enthuse their students with the wonder of their subjects must, in the end, be enhanced by a strong and deep knowledge base.

Requiring a master's degree as an entry requirement for teaching may initially reduce the potential field of applicants. Some might be put off by the extra time and resourcing required to gain the master's qualification. However, the *quality* of applicants is likely to substantially improve. The additional time and resourcing required could be partially compensated for by reducing the time required for teacher training, as we will discuss below.

Putting in place a higher entry threshold for teaching will:

- improve the prestige and attractiveness of the profession by signalling that it is one that requires highly intelligent and able graduates of the type that currently try to enter, for example, the medical profession
- improve the overall quality of applicants by sifting out candidates who do not possess strong academic and thinking skills, which will be of enormous benefit in the classroom.

There will be transition issues. While existing teachers will need to be allowed to work their way out of the system, it may well be that the master's requirement is introduced gradually alongside the school-based

---

2 Pedagogical studies: learning about teaching and learning.

training proposals that are discussed below. Clearly if this proposal is to be seriously considered for implementation a great deal of preparatory work and trialling will need to be completed to ensure it achieves what is expected. If it is put in place alongside the current requirements for teacher training, it may me that some additional financial incentives over and above those that already exist for master's-level entry need to be put in place.[3]

Focus more on teacher training on the job

The critical part of the current 1-year teacher training system which works well is the practicum. Teachers are placed in a number of schools for periods of 6 weeks or so (sometimes longer, sometimes shorter). Trainees work with their supervisor (the training provider) and are allocated a school-based mentor in each of the schools they work in.

The part of the current system that does not work so well is that based with the training provider. This generally consists of theory work in a lecture hall or in tutorials, which encourages students to think about pedagogy, learning, psychology and behaviour management.

All this is absolutely essential. The problem is that it is not always easy for students to *intertwine* theory with practice, which is of course what they must do. The emphasis in teaching training should be placed more on practice that is *guided* by theory. The proposal here is to flip the current model and adopt some of the key features (with some significant variations) of new approaches to training teachers already being tried and evaluated in the US, the UK—and in New Zealand.[4]

Master's graduates should be screened on application regarding their suitability for teaching. This screening process should be thorough and demanding. Recruiters will be looking for the sort of people who are likely to have very good interpersonal skills and who have the right mind frames. One would expect that the screening would draw information from multiple sources, such as tutors/teachers, work mates and interactions with recruiting staff. The process might take several months or more.

The successful candidates would then be employed directly into

---

[3] New teachers with a master's degree already start their teaching career on a higher salary step than those with only a bachelor's degree.

[4] See Teachfirstnz.org for details of the scheme currently operating in New Zealand.

specially selected and quality-assured 'teaching schools'[5] for an initial 2-year training period. They would be paid on the current 1st-year teachers' pay scale. During this time they would gradually build to a half-time teaching load by the end of their 1st year, and a three-quarter-time teaching load by the end of their second year. They should move to a full load at the start of their 3rd year.

The programme would provide trainees or *interns*[6] with practical teaching experience, in partnership with an accredited and trained *school-based* mentor (an experienced teacher). This training would be supported by periods of entirely pedagogy-based training provided by an external accredited provider, probably a university. Schools would need to provide release time for this externally based training.

Trainees would be closely monitored, both in terms of their content knowledge and their mind frames. Those failing to meet the required high standards could be given additional time to reach the standard, but would mostly be counselled out of the programme and out of teaching. Retaining a poor trainee teacher in the profession would be viewed with as much seriousness as retaining a poor trainee doctor in a hospital.

The school-based teacher mentors would need to be provided with adequate time to carry out their duties, which would include classroom observations and advice.

They would need to be properly selected and trained as accredited mentors. They would also be suitably remunerated and supervised by the national provider.[7] Not all schools would have the capacity to become teaching schools, but those that did would need to be properly resourced. Funding could be shifted from the current training providers over time.

The national providers would need to be limited in number, and probably university based. They would need to carefully manage their training programme with schools to ensure the theoretical content is presented in the context of the very practical requirements of the trainees in their schools.

---

5 Teaching schools would be normal mainstream schools with added teaching-teachers functions.

6 The term 'intern' is used deliberately to invite comparisons with the medical and other professions.

7 A model of this type, in which experienced teachers can engage in meaningful and deep conversations about good practice with trainees/novices, will probably be of *mutual* benefit.

This is not such a radical proposal. Versions of it have been tried throughout the world and it is currently operating in New Zealand in a small way for 20 bright graduates (per intake) who may wish to try out teaching, particularly in low-decile schools, for 2 years.[8] What is being suggested here is that this model could easily be grown and developed, with a master's degree as a compulsory entry requirement for people who want a career in teaching.

Provide more effective ongoing professional development

Teachers need ongoing professional development (PD) and support, as do those in all other professions. Teachers need to keep up to date with changes in their subjects, with new ideas related to pedagogy, and—possibly just as importantly—they need to refresh their passion.

The future focus of teacher PD should avoid all assumptions. No one should *assume* that freeing up schools from bureaucracy or making them more accountable to their communities, or creating new qualifications based on standards, or putting National Standards into place, will make a great of difference to what teachers do in the privacy of their classrooms. Nor, as we have already argued, should it be assumed that making PD contestable will make any real difference.[9] What is required is direct and thoughtful interventions that support teachers in their schools and their classrooms in matters where they can see the relevance.

Subject-based professional development

For secondary teachers, a significant amount of PD needs to be delivered through their specialist subjects. The Ministry of Education needs to accept that secondary teachers are subject specialists and that they are immersed in their subjects. The best way of encouraging them to change their practice is to allow them to work with an expert who is a specialist in the subject they teach. This is what will enliven and enthuse a secondary teacher. Unfortunately, the current approach to PD, much to the dismay of many teachers, places much more emphasis on generic training about teaching and learning than it does on sub-

---

8   See Teachfirstnz.org for details of the scheme currently operating in New Zealand.
9   See pp. 172–173.

ject-specific (for secondary schools) training.[10]

NZQA has appointed around 30 full-time, subject-based moderators, but their role has been limited to supporting subject teachers in their *assessment practice*, to improve the credibility of school-based assessment for NCEA (Years 11–13). As such, they have little involvement, or time, to address the curriculum and teaching issues facing secondary school teachers from Year 9 right through to Year 13.

What is required is a larger group of expert subject teachers than currently exists, across all subjects, in enough numbers to provide comprehensive national coverage. These teachers would be seconded from their positions and their task would be to work with subject teachers in every school in the country. They might work in individual schools, but would also be expected to bring together teachers of a particular subject in a region for ongoing training. Most secondary teachers are particularly keen on working together, across schools, to advance the teaching of their subject.

Consideration should be given to appointing groups of subject experts who *combine* the PD and NZQA moderation roles. The current separation of NZQA moderators from teaching and learning PD is not sensible and is potentially dangerous.[11] Seconded subject experts should be employed and funded though university-based providers on 3-year rolling contracts. The current contestable model needs to be dispensed with as soon as possible. This will have the enormous advantage that subject advisers will be able to work with university-based *pre-service* trainers and other subject experts based at the university. As a result, these seconded teachers would benefit from training based on current research on key generic *and* subject-specific messages relating to teaching and learning.

Universities would need to employ these subject specialists. They would be accessed through the existing Ministry of Education lead

---

10 There are still some subject advisers employed by the larger consortia. However, the coverage across subjects and across the country is limited, particularly for classroom teachers. Teachers have tried to help themselves through their own subject associations and conferences, and this has been a very positive development, but it is not enough. Most subject associations rely on volunteers and are simply too small to make a significant national impact.

11 NZQA moderators must advise teachers about the outcomes of assessment. In order to provide this advice, the moderators must have an understanding of, and provide advice related to, effective teaching and learning. Separating the assessment/moderation from the teaching and learning PD, as is currently technically the case, has the potential for teachers to receive contradictory advice.

PD advisers and Student Achievement Function advisers (see below) in Ministry of Education regional offices.

It is important to be clear here: the dominant philosophy of the current PD model is to deliver generic messages about good teaching through a variety of non-subject specialists (facilitators, consultants, etc.) and then expect specialist teachers to translate this into action in their classrooms. Something of a familiar unwarranted assumption is made that teachers will *somehow* be able to do this, or even that they will see the need. Unfortunately, the message is easily lost in translation.

The proposal here is that the message be couched in the language of the specific subject. The core generic messages should be articulated and demonstrated in *subject-based PD*. This is real, it is immediate, it is not fuzzy, it cannot be dismissed as theory, and it is very much focused on helping teachers to deliver their subject-based lessons.

Generic professional development

The big problem with only providing *subject-specific* PD, as suggested above, is that it does not necessarily do enough to address school-wide PD needs, particularly in failing schools. It is therefore important to maintain a programme of PD based on school-wide improvement. Such programmes could be focused on failing schools as well as areas that are deemed to be a national focus for all schools by ERO, or the Minister, or the Ministry of Education itself.

PD offered on these generic programmes should be accessed through the development of existing regionally based Ministry of Education project lead advisers and Student Achievement Function advisers (see below). The PD itself, however, would be provided largely by regionally based university providers employed on 3-year rolling contracts.

Co-ordination of professional development

The proposals above involving both subject-specific and generic PD sourced from regionally based universities will need to be carefully co-ordinated and managed for individual schools. For example, it will be important to ensure that subject specialists are working *together* if there is more than one in a school, and that their key messages are congruent with the more generic work occurring in the school.

It has already been noted that each of the four Ministry of Education regional offices already employ one PD lead adviser. Their job is to co-ordinate most of the PD to schools in their region through a team of regional advisers.[12] Student Achievement Function advisers, whose task it is to work with low- and middle-decile schools and broker PD as required, *also* work in regional offices but they report directly to the Ministry of Education Head Office in Wellington.

These positions clearly overlap and should be combined and rebranded as PD co-ordinators (in each regional office) and PD advisers (the experts who will work with schools and university-based experts).

The objective here must be to increase the numbers and expand the roles of these rebranded PD advisers. It would be the task of each PD adviser to ensure that the PD provision for each and every school the adviser is responsible for is underpinned by a coherent PD plan, which is properly supported by current best practice research. Much of this support will come from the local university, but the advisers will also be expected to work in schools with principals and teachers to develop *in-school* PD programmes and to access other PD support as necessary. They will also be responsible for ensuring that failing schools and failing subject departments are identified and appropriate action taken— regardless of whether the school principal or teachers from the school make an initial approach.

Contracts would need to be negotiated with university providers based on identified strategic needs, as determined by the Ministry of Education in Wellington, after consulting with principals, teachers and other key stakeholders. Once negotiated, regional PD budgets based on student numbers in each region, weighted to favour low-decile schools, should be distributed to the PD co-ordinator in each regional office, who would then purchase the required services from the university providers on 3-year rolling contracts.

Current specialist teachers

The Ministry of Education already funds schools to appoint secondary school 'classroom specialist teachers', whose job it is to mentor other teachers in generic pedagogy and teaching skills. Although this is laudable, it is the wrong approach because it places these teachers in a next-

---

12 They do not currently appear to oversee the limited *subject-based* PD available to schools, which is provided to schools directly by contracted providers though a Ministry of Education contract

to-hopeless position because they do not provide *subject-specific* advice.

The teaching of literacy in secondary schools is a good example of the problem. Many schools have run school-wide PD on literacy, arguing that *all* teachers are teachers of literacy. And yet, again and again, maths and science teachers, for example, find themselves struggling to adapt generic approaches to their unique teaching and learning programmes.

Lead and expert teachers

Similar problems will, without doubt, arise as a result of the 2014 announcements on providing resources to appoint lead and expert teachers to provide (probably) non subject-specific PD for teachers in schools.[13] Although details are sketchy at the time of writing, it is likely that the 'expert' teachers will not only be asked to work within their own school but also in other schools. The welcome that these parachute-in teachers are likely to get from the various subject silos in other schools does not bear thinking about.

Unfortunately, it is abundantly clear already that the chances of success of the new scheme are low. The government announcement of the new initiative was accompanied by a statement that the details are yet to be worked out, which implies that very little policy work has been done, other than perhaps an overseas visit to PISA 'success' countries such as Singapore.[14]

Training teachers to deliver to Māori and Pasifika students

It has been made clear throughout this book that it is our Māori and Pasifika students, on average, who do not do as well in the system as one would expect. If we are serious about addressing issues of disparity, and if we know that Māori and Pasifika students are often not well served, do teachers need special training to meet their needs?

Some of the debate around this issue has already been alluded to, but it is useful to summarise it here. On the one hand, there are

---

13 Lead teachers will act as role models for teachers within their own and other schools, while expert teachers will work with executive principals in their own and other schools.

14 It is doubtful whether any serious thought has been given to whether what Singapore does to support its teachers can be translated to New Zealand. For example, Singapore has a highly centralised education system, just one national teacher training provider, and a very strong performance-based system of pay. What is successful in Singapore will not necessarily work here in New Zealand.

some (e.g. Rata, 2011) who argue that the issue of Māori and Pacific underachievement is very much related to SES and not to ethnicity. In other words, Māori and Pasifika students do not do well at school because they are handicapped by poverty, deprivation and social class. The way to address these issues is to solve the social and economic problems facing Māori and Pasifika students, just as one would aim to solve the same problems for Pākehā and Asian students in the same socioeconomic trap. Ethnicity, in this context, is not the issue. The fact that Māori and Pasifika students are over-represented in this deprived group is largely due to economic and social exploitation, and neglect by governments.

There are others (e.g., Bishop, O'Sullivan & Berryman, 2010) who argue that although SES is important, the bigger factor is one of culture and context. This argument suggests that Māori students are failing in our schools because teachers are not able to *connect* with them as Māori. Instead, teachers fall into the trap of "deficit thinking". Deficit thinking occurs when teachers work from the premise that Māori students cannot be expected to do well at school because they have, for example, poor attendance, family issues and poor motivation to learn. As a result of this thinking, teachers lower their expectations and as a consequence create the very conditions required to disadvantage Māori students in their schools. According to this view, if teachers could begin to understand more about the lives of their students and what their students value, and if teachers were prepared to engage in meaningful conversations with these students, then the students would respond, and do well in the new, more supportive school environment.

The Kotahitanga programme of PD for teachers implemented in secondary schools from 2001 (see Bishop, Berryman & Wearmouth, 2014), which focuses on these relationship issues by placing facilitators into classrooms, has proved reasonably successful in improving student outcomes according to supporters, but its impact has been questioned by some (e.g. Openshaw, 2007).

There is plenty of debate here, for which there is no space in this book. The key question is: what kind of PD do teachers need in order to address the needs of their Māori and Pasifika students? The contention in this book has been that SES is a major issue, and that students' achievement is hugely affected by their background. Since many Māori and Pasifika students come from deprived homes, it is this SES issue that needs to be addressed, but this is not something that teachers can do much about in their classrooms.[15]

What *is* required from teachers is that they be good *teachers* of their subjects. The best way for them to do this is by being prepared to understand the needs of their children and being fully aware of the world their children live in, whatever their ethnicity. To this extent, the subject-based teacher PD suggested above is the right one. A mathematics teacher for example would be involved in PD about delivering the mathematics curriculum to the students she has in front of her. A basic requirement for being a good teacher of mathematics for rural Māori students, for example, necessarily involves a process of developing teaching strategies that work for the particular students in the classroom. Such a process must, by definition, take account of the nature, dispositions, culture and ethnicity of the students in question.

Provide replenishment and exit provisions

Many (but by no means all) teachers who have been in the classroom for a long time are *captured* by it, especially as they age. The result can often be good, solid, even passionate teachers who have become wholly *institutionalised*. As a consequence, these teachers come to believe that their way is the only way. It is these teachers who often offer the strongest resistance to any significant changes to the ways their schools or their classrooms routinely operate.

Such teachers would benefit from being *required* to opt out for a while to gain work experience, study or explore alternative careers. The need for this sort of replenishment has been partially recognised by the Ministry of Education, because there is a wide variety of sabbaticals and study leave options available for secondary teachers already. They include the opportunity to study for almost a full year on full pay, as well as for shorter periods of time (TeachNZ, 2013). The provision is generous, and both the Ministry of Education and the PPTA should be congratulated on achieving some really good outcomes for teachers

---

15 However, at least some action can be taken in schools and in communities by providing wrap-around support, including counsellors, social workers, mentors, breakfasts, goal setting and parent education programmes. Many schools are already doing this well. This, however, does not have anything to do with teacher PD and is much more about schools *becoming part of their communities* and ensuring that shortcomings in the community are compensated for by the school. To do this successfully, schools need financial support from their communities and government agencies.

seeking study leave options.

The problem is that the very teachers who *most* need such replenishment are often the ones *least* likely to volunteer to take up the option. There is, therefore, a need to require all teachers to take time out for study or work, on full pay, probably once every 7 to 10 years. The period of leave might be as short as one term, but would serve to encourage teachers to review not only their subject content but their passion as well.[16] Another (fiscally neutral) option might be to allow teachers to be paid 80 percent of their salary for 4 years and take the 5th year as a sabbatical on the same pay.[17]

Alongside replenishment, we need to accept that some teachers need to be encouraged to leave the profession permanently. These people may well be those who have spent a lifetime teaching and giving sterling service, but unfortunately have simply run out of steam. Or, as we have indicated earlier, they may well be people who hover around the competence bar and do not add a lot of value. For the first group there is a need to work out a depart-with-dignity package. It really is not justifiable to expose our children to teachers who are not up to it. Poor teachers in a school should be regarded as a *crisis* to be handled quickly to prevent major future damage, just as we do in cases of medical emergency. Action needs to be taken for the good of the student (patient) but also, in the teaching context, for the wellbeing of the entire community. A dignified exit package may cost money but will pay huge dividends in the long term.

For the second group, as we have already noted, there are currently provisions for dealing with incompetent teachers in the collective agreement. The problem seems to be that principals are unwilling to use them. Sometimes this is because they are unwilling to deal with the inevitable backlash from other staff and their union. Sometimes, especially in low-decile schools, principals have to consider the very real possibility that they might not be able to find a replacement teacher.

---

16 There would need to be some rules built around this leave to make it affordable. For example, it may be that the replenishment leave is only available to teachers after 10 years of continuous service.

17 One argument put up against the 4/5 pay for 5 years' work concept is that it implies that teachers can live on 4/5 of their pay, thus (presumably) undermining demands for higher pay rates. This sort of illogical approach has prevented the implementation of this proposal for years. Teachers could not be required to take this sort of leave, of course, and would be perfectly capable of managing their own finances depending on their particular circumstances.

Dealing with incompetent teachers is a responsibility that principals must carry out better than they currently do. Leaving these teachers in the classroom not only inflicts long-term damage on students but severely damages the status and standing of the entire profession. The Ministry of Education needs to become more active in providing principals with more support in this area, particularly access to robust legal advice. Principals' associations also need to do better in supporting their members to raise the bar by removing non-performing teachers from the classroom.

Reconstitute the Teachers' Council to deal effectively with incompetent teachers

A review of the council is underway as this book is being written. One would hope that the review group will ensure that the new council is set up to operate as an independent, non-government body with full responsibility for the registration, conduct and competence of teachers. Funding should come from both teachers and government.

Such a body would need to be vigilant and active in ensuring that teachers throughout the country are competent, and that incompetence is addressed urgently, either through boards of trustees or directly through the newly constituted council. The new council should take responsibility for receiving and addressing complaints from the public about teacher competence and conduct, in consultation with school boards.[18] The council should have the power to direct boards in matters of registration, competence and conduct.

The new council would be 'owned' by teachers. Its board would need to be elected by teachers and approved by the Minister. This would imply that teachers would themselves need to take responsibility for maintaining the reputation and wellbeing of the profession.

Use the holidays and terms better

Schools are still focused on the traditional school day and term and

---

18 Currently, for all intents and purposes the only avenue of complaint a parent has about the *competence* of a teacher is to the school board and principal. If a complaint about competence is lodged with the Teachers' Council, it will be referred back to the board of trustees unless there is an actual or perceived conflict of interest, the teacher is no longer employed by the employer who filed the report, or there are exceptional circumstances. See http://www.teacherscouncil.govt.nz/content/conduct-competence/the-competence-process

make very limited use of the school holidays. Some of the resulting problems of workload and stress have been discussed in Chapter 11. How might holiday time be better used by teachers? The current teachers' collective agreement does actually allow principals to call back teachers for 5 administration days and 5 PD days each year during their holidays. However, a careful reading of the wording explains why these clauses are not widely used by principals:

> 5.4.1 The employer may require teachers to participate in professional development opportunities at times when the school is not open for instruction provided that no teacher shall be required to attend for more than five days or equivalent per annum and provided also that the needs of the individual teacher are taken into account and that the teacher's own initiatives in undertaking professional development during time when the school is not open for instruction are considered.
>
> 5.4.2 The employer may require teachers to attend school or elsewhere when the school is not open for instruction for up to five days or equivalent per annum for all or any of the following purposes—school administration, preparation and coordination, departmental or related activities and community, parent and whanau contact and liaison. The employer will endeavour to arrange matters at the school in such a way that any requirement under this section is not unreasonable and that teachers' individual needs are taken into account. Teachers' own initiatives in undertaking work for the above purposes shall be counted when applying this clause. (PPTA, 2013c)

Many teachers, *individually or collectively*, already give up their time when the school is not open to carry out administration and PD tasks. For example, teachers attend conferences, study, and meet with parents in the evenings. According to the collective agreement, all this time could, within reason, be counted against any requirement by the principal for teachers to attend school during school holidays.

Principals are therefore faced with a no-win situation. Any attempt to *require* all their teachers to come to work during their school holidays is likely to buy a fight with the union, which could argue that some or even all of the teachers have already contributed their time. Of course this sort of argument is appalling, because it casts teachers as wage earners and clock watchers on an hourly rate rather than as salaried professionals.

Teachers need 4 weeks of leave, maybe 5—not 12. A careful allocation of holiday jobs for teachers to do, on site, while no students are present, would go a monumental way to addressing their workload concerns and would probably reduce the overall levels of stress in most staffrooms. The collective contract needs to be rewritten to ensure that terms for teachers are not the same as terms for students. Teachers need to be on site during at least some of their so-called holidays. During this time, when *all teachers* are on site, some or all of the following tasks could be completed:

- setting and marking exams and other assessments
- writing student reports
- carrying out appraisal interviews
- holding school and department planning meetings
- updating unit plans and schemes
- attending school PD sessions
- attending parent interviews.

Many teachers will recognise all these tasks as being ones that *add* to their normal school time workload. It has already been noted that it is precisely these tasks that cause many teachers' stress levels to skyrocket as each term draws to an end. By deliberately shifting this work out of term time, the workload for the year would become much more evenly spread, and therefore much more manageable.[19]

The list could probably be extended or edited by any teacher, but the point is clear: *all teachers*—not just some—need to agree to be on site, for a specified time, when students are on holiday. Just to have *some teachers* on site and others working from home and still others doing nothing at all is not a sensible way forward. It is important to be clear here: the total amount of work done by most conscientious teachers would not increase under this scenario. It would mean, though, that

---

19 Some teachers will be concerned about when their national and regional conferences could take place under this scenario, but this is just a matter of planning ahead to use the remaining 8 weeks' holiday time available in the year.

the work would be spread more evenly throughout the year. As a result, workload during the term would dramatically decrease, stress levels would drop, and teachers would be freer to focus on actually teaching. One might go further and argue that the quality of work, both of teaching and administration, would improve under these arrangements simply because teachers will have more time and be less stressed.

The proposal above will probably be opposed by some teachers, who will see it as a way of increasing their workload. Workload is a perennial problem, not just in teaching, although teachers often see themselves as somehow special in this regard. The fact of the matter is that it *is* an issue—teachers *are* overworked for parts of the year. However, neither their union nor the government has seriously considered ways of addressing the issue, preferring instead to engage in a never-ending argument about resourcing—or lack of it.

Pay teachers more

New Zealand beginning teachers are paid just below the OECD average, and well below Australian, German, Canadian, English and Finnish teachers. At the maximum level of the pay scale, New Zealander teachers are still below the OECD average, and once again below their Australian, German, Canadian and Finnish counterparts[20] (OECD, 2013).

Compared with other professionals *within* New Zealand, teachers appear to be relatively poorly paid. For example, a New Zealand teacher can expect to earn around NZ$72,000 after about 8 or 9 years' experience (2014 rates). His or her counterparts in law could draw more like $90,000 and up to $140,000 (New Zealand Law Society, 2012).

If we are serious about getting the best possible people to teach in our schools, and about pursuing a high-quality education brand, there is a strong case for New Zealand to do a lot better. It would not be

---

20 A beginning teacher in New Zealand will earn US$28,251. The equivalent figures are $34,746 (Australia), $57,357 (Germany), $35,534 (Canada), $30,289 (England) and $34,008 (Finland). The average OECD salary for beginning teachers is $US31,348. The top-of-the-scale maximum salary for a teacher in New Zealand is US$42,726. The equivalent figures are $49,144 (Australia), $79,088 (Germany), $56,569 (Canada), $44,269 (England) and $45,900 (Finland). The OECD average salary for the maximum point on the salary scale is US$50,199. All figures are comparable, in equivalent US dollars, converted using PPPs for private consumption (see *Educational at a Glance 2013: OECD Indicators*, p. 388). Note that all figures are for upper secondary teachers, and the number of years it may take to reach the maximum point of the scale varies between countries.

impossible or unreasonable to increase teacher salaries, particularly for experienced teachers, to around $100,000 per annum. As a small country with a good education brand already, such a decision could have an enormous impact on teacher morale, recruitment and retention, and consequently on achievement rates.

There are a couple of issues in this context regarding *how* teachers are paid that should be discussed.

Progressing up the pay scale

Teachers generally progress automatically up the pay grades based on their years of service.[21] The PPTA would possibly dispute this statement and argue that teachers are required to be annually attested as competent against specified performance standards, documented in the collective contract, before they can move to their next step on the salary scale.

This is certainly true, but, as has already been noted, principals find themselves in something of a bind. Not to progress someone up the scale effectively means they are not considered competent, and therefore a formal review process must be started. Saying that someone is incompetent is not the same as saying they have not done enough to gain a pay rise, but this is precisely what principals are asked to do. As a consequence, almost all teachers progress up the salary scale, regardless of their performance, based on their years of service. The situation needs to be rectified so that principals can withhold salary increments from teachers whose performance they are not satisfied with, even though they might be considered 'competent'.

Doing this will not be easy, but it may be that teachers need to satisfy principals that they have met, or done their best to meet, *performance objectives* they have agreed with their appraiser. Currently, teachers progress up the scale simply by meeting the requirements of the professional standards[22] documented in the collective agreement. The proposal here is that they also need to meet performance objectives, which will be established at the beginning of each year. Performance objectives could be specified by the appraiser and negotiated with the

---

21 This is a time-served model, which is not uncommon, particularly in the public sector.
22 The professional standards document what is effectively the generic job description of all secondary teachers.

teacher, or, preferably, set by the teacher and approved by the appraiser based on their own self-review process. What is being proposed is a form of *performance pay*. Payment for time served is a silly way of paying teachers, because it assumes they are all the same—and they are not. My experience as a teacher and principal suggests that many teachers understand this perfectly and would welcome a new approach which does not reward poor performers who are often responsible for both bringing the reputation of the profession into disrepute and forcing their colleagues to carry a heavier load.

Rewarding teachers at the top of the pay scale

Exactly the same process could be applied to teachers once they have reached the top of their pay scale (see the example on p. 181) so that teachers such as the high-flying Teacher B could be better acknowledged. Schools already have a structure in place that could enable this to happen quite easily, involving the use of what are known as management units (MUs).

MUs (each worth $4,000) are used by principals to reward teachers who take on additional *management* responsibilities. For example, the head of a very large mathematics department might be allocated an additional three or four MUs to run the department. The allocation of MUs is at the principal's discretion, though the principal is required to follow due employment process. Some MUs are *permanent* and come with the management job, so cannot be taken away from the head of department (HoD) without a formal competence process. Some, though, can be fixed term, and so can be moved from one teacher to another depending on the needs of the school.

Under the current system, teachers cannot technically be allocated an MU for being a good/excellent teacher. These are deemed *management* units and must be used to acknowledge additional *management* responsibilities taken on by the teacher. However, it would be a relatively easy matter to create additional (let us call them) excellence units (EUs), which could be allocated to schools in the same way as the current MUs are allocated,[23] in order to reward exceptional performance. Principals would probably allocate one or two such units (worth the same as an MU) per year to a small group of teachers who have been

---

23 MUs are allocated to a school based on the size of the school roll.

deemed to have performed exceptionally well. This could be paid by way of an end-of-year bonus.

This merit-based approach to supporting experienced teachers will be good for the profession, will contribute to raising the quality of teaching (though this is not a magic panacea), and if handled professionally by principals will be welcomed by all teachers who value quality. The number of EUs available would depend on how much additional funding government is prepared to put into schools. It probably does not need to be a huge sum of money. Spending money to reward excellent teachers in schools, as suggested here, is probably a better option than creating executive principals and expert/lead teacher positions, which are unlikely to be seen as a straightforward reward for excellent performance.[24]

There will, of course, be concerns expressed by some regarding this proposal. However, nothing too grand is being suggested. It is unlikely that it will spell the end of collaboration and team work in the staffroom, as the PPTA darkly predicts. The need for collaboration and team work is not unique to teaching, and teachers, as a professional group, like others are certainly capable of accepting that rewarding excellent performance and maintaining team work/collaboration are not mutually exclusive.

Teacher pay and decile

We need our very best teachers to teach in lower-decile schools if we are to make good on the Ministry of Education aim of lifting achievement for all students, but particularly those in lower-decile schools. This is not happening at the moment. In fact, there is a suspicion that promotion for some teachers and principals means seeking positions that enable them to move from a low- to a higher-decile school. It has already been suggested that many lower-decile schools find it difficult to attract experienced and capable teachers. It appears that teachers do need something of an incentive to apply for positions in these school.

One option might be to pay these teachers more than their colleagues in high-decile schools. There is some precedent for this: principals of

---

[24] If the reported $150 million per annum ongoing costs allocated to executive and change principals, lead teachers and expert teachers were distributed as excellence units at $4,000 each, this would create 37,500 such units, which could be distributed to high-performing teachers in all schools throughout New Zealand.

low-decile schools are already paid more than their colleagues in higher-decile schools. Staffing incentive allowances and high-priority teacher supply allowances already exist for teachers in the teachers' collective agreement, which allow for small extra payments to teachers in selected schools.[25] However, these payments are manifestly inadequate and do not adequately target low-decile schools. There is a need for teachers in low-decile schools to be *substantially* rewarded for their work, and in so doing create more competition for positions in these schools.

If we figure private schools (which pay their teachers significantly more than teachers in state schools) into this picture, it appears that we currently do the opposite of what is required. We pay the teachers who teach advantaged, easy-to-teach students more than, or the same as, those who teach disadvantaged and generally more challenging students.

Concluding comments

In order for any reform to work it is necessary to have quality teachers. In New Zealand we have good teachers, but teaching is not the highly sought-after and well-respected profession it should be. We can improve the quality of the teaching workforce by raising entry requirements and providing more of an intern approach to teacher training. In addition, ensuring that ongoing training is of a high quality, rewarding good teachers, paying teachers in low-decile schools more than those who teach in high-decile schools, and allowing teachers to depart the profession with dignity will all contribute to improving the quality of teaching and teachers in New Zealand

Teachers also need to address their 'victimhood mentality' regarding workload and start thinking, through their union, about how they can use their paid time more effectively, particularly their so-called holiday time. Finally, teachers need to take control of their profession and ensure the right people are registered, and that incompetence and misconduct are dealt with without delay.

---

25 Up to $2,500 per annum for teachers in around 22 high-priority schools, which are designated by the Ministry of Education to be in need of support for recruitment and retention of staff. A staffing incentive allowance also allows for payment of $1,000 per annum for schools that qualify.

Chapter 16: Improve the selection and training of school leaders

Introduction

Teachers, like everyone else, need to be led properly. It is relatively rare to have sustained improvements in achievement without strong leadership. Leadership in schools is often assumed to come from the principals, and often does. However, it is important to note that many deputy principals, heads of department, deans and subject teachers have been able to exert strong leadership in schools with very positive effects—sometimes despite the activities of the principal.

Whatever the source, teachers need to be provided with leadership, because without it they can join the "dark side" of collegiality (Schmoker, 1999). This form of collegiality is surprisingly common in New Zealand secondary schools. Dark side teachers come together in meetings, or in department based groups, to insist on decision making processes which are not always based on the needs of the entire school or its students.

As Michael Fullan suggests, these teachers attach their loyalties and identities:

to particular groups of their colleagues … with whom they work most closely, spend more time, socialise most often in the staffroom … the existence of such groups … reflects and reinforces very different group outlooks on learning, teaching styles discipline and curriculum. (Fullan, 1996, p. 53)

In this world, teachers argue that they need to *agree* to any changes to the way the school operates that are being considered by the principal, or even the government. The problem with this is that teachers can *together* become a major barrier to change, regardless of how beneficial or achievable that change might actually be for the school community as a whole. For example, a proposal to set higher NCEA achievement targets for the school could easily be stymied by groups of teachers instantly dismissing any possibility of improvement on the basis of the particular perceptions, beliefs and "mind frames" their group has about the students they are required to teach. Worse still, sometimes an entire staff could "collegially" come to such a conclusion, without any evidence or research to support their view.

Over the years unfortunately I have witnessed many examples of this sort of "group think" in schools, particularly involving more experienced and older teachers and staffrooms. The problem can be especially significant in schools where there has been a failure in leadership where school principals refuse to see themselves as managers and leaders, preferring to regard themselves as a sort of 'lead teacher'. These principals are often guilty of abdicating their leadership responsibilities by *buying into* the group think of their teachers. They end up leading their schools on the basis of democratic staffroom votes at Monday-night staff meetings.

Of course it is important that teachers be consulted about significant change. Without teacher buy-in at some level we know that no change will be effective in the classroom. However, as leaders, principals must create a change- and innovation-based culture in their school to ensure that dark side collegiality "group think" is challenged (with evidence and data) when it occurs, and that teachers, no matter how old and experienced, are encouraged to think outside their particular experience. The job of the principal—indeed of any leader—is to inspire his or her staff to seek better ways of doing things while encouraging collegiality and teamwork. Given all this, it is obviously particularly important that boards select and retain the right people to be principals.

Principal appointments and performance management

Principals are currently appointed and their performance managed by boards of trustees. These boards have the authority to appoint anyone who is a teacher to the position of principal of a school. Boards also have considerable freedom regarding the performance management of their principals. There are few national requirements other than that principals, once appointed, meet the professional standards set out in their contract. In addition, boards need to have a performance management process in place.

The theory of local democracy implied here is fine. Local people on locally elected boards appoint and manage their own school leaders so that local aspirations and needs can be addressed. The problem is that boards are not always capable of making good appointments or of managing their principals effectively, particularly in cases where performance is already poor. This is hardly shocking. Many boards, some responsible for huge corporate enterprises, have made mistakes and appointed the wrong people and managed them poorly. The problem with schools is that we have established a governance system that actually makes it particularly difficult for boards to be successful: too many of the people on school boards, particularly in small, isolated and rural areas, simply do not have the background skills or dispositions to properly appoint or manage principals.

This sounds like an incredibly arrogant statement to make. Small and isolated New Zealand has its fair share of highly capable people who live and work in their communities and know them well. Why should they not be able to select and manage their own principal? They select their own local leaders and MPs through the political process after all. The problem is that, in New Zealand, there are simply *too many* schools and not enough people with the capabilities required, particularly in rural and isolated areas, to govern and run them. I am not suggesting that people who sit on school boards need to be accountants or property managers or educationalists. That level of technical expertise is not required. However, boards of trustees do have a governance responsibility which *does* require high-level skills, such as an ability and willingness to be strategic, to look at the big picture, to be able to make decisions based on evidence, and to be able to address performance issues. The fact is that too many New Zealand schools cannot find the right people to do the job, largely because there are far too many schools—many very small—competing for a relatively small group of willing and able people.

The same issues apply to principals. Principalship is a highly demanding job and the number of people who have the capacity to do this job is limited. We have too many schools and not enough high-quality principals. If we are to stay with a board of trustees system, which seems likely in the current political environment, we need to ensure that boards have the *capacity* to do what is required of them, and that every one of our schools is able to recruit a quality principal. This issue will be discussed in more detail below as part of a more general discussion about school size and organisation.

Principals' appointment, training and support

Appointment by boards of trustees

As we noted earlier, the Ministry of Education has made a real effort to provide national support and training for aspiring principals, but this is not enough. New Zealand should establish a single national principals' leadership centre. This could easily be based on the centre of educational leadership already operating in Auckland and would replace several such institutions currently spread around the country. The advantage of establishing such a centre is that it could act as the focus of leadership research and training for all principals throughout New Zealand, and through simple economies of scale provides a comprehensive programme of support to aspiring, new and experienced principals. Such a programme would build on the current aspiring, first-time and experienced principals' programmes. It would also provide compulsory and comprehensive training to principals *prior* to them taking up their positions.

All principals regardless of their experience would be expected to attend coaching and training sessions at the centre, and would also be provided with a mentor/coach.

A formal principals' competency attestation at novice and experienced level should also be a requirement. These would be based on existing professional standards and would need to be rigorously implemented. The experienced principals' attestation would need to be renewed every 3 years by way of an external assessment carried out by the centre. Principals would need to demonstrate competence at the expected level.

Such an assessment would be independent of the board appraisal process, but failure to gain the renewal would result in an initial withdrawal of principal registration and would set in place a supervision process funded by the Ministry of Education. Continued failure to meet the requirements would result in permanent withdrawal of registration, and thus termination of employment as a principal.

Another important function of the proposed principals' leadership centre would be to encourage succession planning in New Zealand schools, which is sadly lacking across the sector. The devolved nature of the system and the autonomy granted to boards to make appointments mean that few people are required to think of preparing principals so that they can do their jobs. The concept of a strategic workforce planning for principalship across the country does not seem to exist. Rectifying this might mean identifying potential principals early in their careers and providing proper and intensive training.

The 2014 Key Government announcement regarding executive principals and change principals is of interest in this context. At the time of writing it appears that executive principals will spend part of their week at their own school, and some part working with a group of other principals, presumably to support them as they make the required changes in their schools. Once again, although the idea seems attractive, it is important to ask some questions: Will a parachute-in type of arrangement work for New Zealand schools, which are highly devolved? How will the competitive model schools are currently required to work under integrate with this more collaborative approach? Will the executive principals offer mentoring and advice, or will they have powers of decision making? Will the executive principals be trained?

There is a sense of déjà vu here, which is very worrying. It is clear there has been minimal policy development, and that an assumption has been made that simply appointing executive principals will result in improved principalship, as if by magic.

New Zealand principals know each other. They have strong views about their own schools and how their schools differ from other schools. The idea that an executive principal will be able to parachute in and tell/advise another principal how best to run their school is almost laughable. But there is at least one other major problem: we know that school leadership is very *context based*. Expecting that a successful principal of a school in Auckland, for example, can offer useful advice to another principal in a small provincial town or even a few kilometres away in another part of Auckland, as if all the issues are entirely generic, is simply not tenable.

Sadly, the executive principal initiative appears to be yet another policy disaster waiting to happen, put in place by Ministers and officials intent on quick-fix political solutions to long-term and difficult problems. A properly developed programme of principal support and development based around a national principals' leadership centre, working with Ministry of Education regional offices, ERO and NZQA, is certainly less newsworthy than the appointment of executive principals, but would probably be much more effective in providing ongoing and relevant support for all principals.

Principals' job descriptions

We know that principals need to play a significant role in any school-based change process. We also know that a leadership focus on teaching and learning in a school is the key to improving students' outcomes, which is the major purpose of schooling. Given this, it would seem sensible that school principals—the chief executives of schools—should focus their energies on the business of improving teaching and learning.

However, we have noted already (see Chapter 12) that this is often a problem for all but the most exceptional principals. Principals have a huge range of related important, but ultimately peripheral, matters to attend to, such as property management, finance and a range of compliance requirements. The result is that many principals find themselves far too busy to attend to the core business of working with their teachers to improve learning. Some principals delegate responsibilities (particularly in larger schools), but others cannot do this because they do not have the staffing capacity. This capacity issue, a recurring theme, is particularly acute in small, rural and low-decile schools.

This issue of the principal's workload needs to be addressed. There will be those who argue that the problems principals face are no different from those of any leader of an organisation with a similar number of employees. The ability to delegate, sort out what is important and what is not, and be strategic is what leadership is about, after all, regardless of the nature of the organisation being led. This is not an entirely convincing argument: schools are actually unique places of work. Principalship is a tough and complex job. A medium-sized school of 700 students is probably more complex, and much tougher to run, than a medium-sized business of 200–250 employees.

There are at least two reasons for this. First, schools are community organisations that are 'owned' by a whole range of people, including students, their families, the extended community and teachers. These people are not just customers who purchase a consumer product (and who can switch to an alternative if they wish). Nor are they shareholders, who are often passive and only interested in making a profit. People involved in schools are stakeholders in a fundamental and intensely personal human endeavour that affects them very deeply. The community, for example, gives school the privilege of being *in loco parentis* all day for 38 weeks a year,[1] and many teachers have a deep sense of vocation and professional independence, which makes them fiercely passionate about what they do and how they do it.

Secondly, schools bring together large numbers of people in one place for long periods of time and expect them to interact on a daily basis in such a way that learning can occur. Nothing tangible is produced in this process as such, and it is very difficult to measure what has been achieved at the end of the day. With regard to teachers, schools bring together large groups of smart, often argumentative and even ego-driven people in one place and expect them to work together co-operatively. With regard to students, schools bring together large numbers of young people who are going through a process of personal development that is highly unpredictable, emotional and unsettling for all concerned.

---

1   In other words, schools are expected to take on the role of parents while students are in attendance.

Given this complexity, there is a case for reducing the workload of principals by requiring the Ministry of Education to take more responsibility for running schools than has been allowed under the current board of trustee model. The Ministry has already begun this process (in 2013) by offering school boards the option of handing back some responsibilities for property management. Such a move is to be applauded. There is a strong case for centralising, on a regional basis, some of the property functions principals are currently required to fulfil. Some principals won't like this suggestion because they will argue that they know what is best for their own schools, and of course they are correct. But at some point trade-offs need to be made to address the issue of the workload carried by principals so that they can focus their attention on their core responsibilities of improving learning and teaching.

There may also be a case for reviewing some of the compliance requirements currently placed on principals. Principals often complain about being constantly bombarded by agencies for a variety of administrative, staffing and other information, often without a great deal of co-ordination by those involved. For smaller schools there is a strong case for additional funding to employ administration and human resources staff as required. Larger schools already generally seem to be able to access the required funds without too much difficulty.

All of this may help, but there is an underlying problem here that relates to the size of our schools and the way we organise them. Principals of smaller schools often find themselves responsible for a similar range of administrative work as principals of larger schools. Strategic plans need to be written, property plans developed, financial systems put in place and monitored, curriculum documents written, and so on. We need to review our current school organisational structures if we are to address these problems effectively. Some options are canvassed later in this chapter.

Principals' organisations

For a small country such as New Zealand, to have two organisations representing just over 400 secondary principals is nonsense. One secondary principal professional association must be established, which takes a lead in properly representing principals to the public, the Ministry of Education and, of course, their employers, the boards of trustees.

The new association should take a stronger line in policing the ethical behaviour of principals. This would probably involve principals working together to rewrite the code of conduct and ethics documents that already exist. Principals should be able to provide support for each other, operate their own conferences and, if necessary, discipline members for behaviour that is regarded as unethical. This might include behaviour that involves poaching students, inflating NCEA pass rates and acting unprofessionally in other ways.

There is no reason why the new association could not provide advice and resources to boards of trustees in matters relating to the appointment and performance management of principals, and to the Ministry of Education in all school-related matters. The new association would also meet with the Minister of Education on a regular basis[2] to ensure the Minister is provided with evidence-based advice. This could include ensuring that any new reform is properly researched and developed, and that implementation issues are taken very seriously and resourced appropriately. It would also be important that the new association insist that reforms be properly evaluated as to their long-term effectiveness.

Concluding comments

Principalship is not easy. Running a school is a complex and demanding job—more so than many people understand. Principals are not just lead teachers. They are chief executives. It is important that they consult with their staff and that their staff are prepared to buy in, but they also need to challenge the dark side of collegiality, which is rife in many staffrooms.

Given that school leadership is critical to any reform effort, it is vitally important that we select, train and performance manage our principals very well indeed. Boards of trustees are sometimes not capable of doing this, and we need to think about how we might address this problem (see the next chapter).

Principals need better training and support. There needs to be a novice and experienced attestation requirement for all principals, which is enforced by a national principals' leadership centre. Such a centre would co-ordinate and lead support for all principals, in consul-

---

2 Both principals groups meet with the Minister already. However, the meetings tend to be politically driven and can often offer opposing advice.

tation with government educational agencies.

Principals need to manage their workload to ensure they focus on the important matters of teaching and learning. To this extent, there is a case for a review of their job descriptions. This review could well lead to a greater role for regional offices in matters such as property management.

Finally, it is time that principals were represented by one organisation, in order to address the many educational, professional and ethical dilemmas they face as a profession. One strong voice for principals could make a big difference in ensuring that future reform is properly planned, implemented and evaluated.

Chapter 17: Ensure that reform is well planned, implemented, evaluated and supported

Improving the quality of policy advice

Any policy can be politically driven, but it is critically important that the longer-term implications/impacts of policy changes are carefully worked through by capable policy analysts and officials and presented to decision makers in writing, with alternative options if necessary. This sort of written advice from public servants is critically important, not least because it is subject to the Official Information Act.

Politicians may decide to remain committed to their election pledge or political positions, or the advice from their own office, think tanks, consultants and media advisers. However, they are more likely to be constrained and encouraged to consider alternative approaches to problems if they are presented with strong advice and potential alternative approaches by their officials. This will particularly be the case if the advice is discoverable and potentially public. There is nothing more damning for a politician than to be shown to have acted against advice that is ultimately proven to be correct in the wake of a messy policy failure.

The tension between public servants and elected governments is built into the structure of democratic governments all over the world. It is not a new problem, or an easy one to solve. However, it is time our officials reminded themselves that they are public servants, and that they are *independent of the Minister* and should give free and frank advice. Technically, at least, Ministers cannot remove chief executives not to their liking.[1]

If we are serious about improving policy development, it is imperative that chief executives resist knee-jerk responses to political pressure. Unless they are prepared to ensure the policy development process is completed properly, the end result will be disastrous, as already noted in Part 2. Politicians must refrain from assuming they can implement policy without a rigorous and detailed policy analysis process. In so doing, they must understand that the process will require expertise, trials, evaluations of the trials—*and lots of time.*

Ironically, Ministers are acutely aware that a robust policy advice process which provides a critique of their own proposals could be very useful if it allows them to avoid later unwelcome public and media criticism. When Ministers go out of their way to appoint special advisory groups, to advise them and develop policy options, as has been the case in recent years, it could well be a sign that they are seeking the robust advice they are not getting from their officials.

Improving implementation and evaluation

The Government should reduce the number of education agencies from five[2] to two, and expand the role of regional offices.

The first new agency

The first new agency would have responsibility for all aspects of early childhood education, primary, secondary and tertiary provision. This would mean that much of the work currently done by NZQA and the Tertiary Education Commission, both of them implementation

---

1 At the same time, it must be noted that public servants are ultimately required to carry out instructions from the duly elected Government of the day.
2 The Ministry of Education, NZQA, ERO, the New Zealand Teachers' Council and Careers New Zealand. Te Kura (the Correspondence School) is technically also a sister agency but is not included in this analysis. A potential third agency carrying out the teacher registration competence and conduct functions suggested in Chapter 15 could be established also, though ideally this would be controlled by teachers themselves.

agencies, would be folded back into the new Ministry of Education. The new Ministry would be larger than it currently is, but would be organised into smaller sub-units, as will be explained below.

One big advantage of this change would be that the policy development and implementation phases of a reform would be brought *together*, within the same organisation, thus avoiding hand-over problems. Policy development and implementation are not separate processes. Policy makers must include implementers in the development process, and implementers must consult closely with policy makers in the development phase: each phase inevitably informs the other.[3]

It would also be crucial in this process to re-establish a strong regional mediating layer and substantially expand the role of regional offices, which will need to stay well connected with Wellington. The regional offices would fulfil the essential role of providing targeted support for schools, acting as a buffer (interpreting, communicating, managing resistance), and enhancing school collaboration, as suggested by McKinsey and Company (Mourshed, Chijioke, & Barber, 2010).[4]

The proposed new, larger Ministry of Education would need to organise itself to reflect how the sector is organised: into four groups, based on early childhood education, primary education, secondary education and tertiary education. Each group would have a chief executive, and all the chief executives, together with other key staff, would form the senior management team, led by the Secretary of Education. Each group thus established would be charged with meeting overall student achievement (and other) objectives, through the stronger regional structures put in place. Chief executives would need to be granted considerable latitude to lead and manage their group. The staff in each group would be expected to build expertise, knowledge and ownership of policy and implementation at the national and regional levels.

It would be the task of the Secretary of Education to ensure that each group works within common policy frameworks, and that the performance of each is closely monitored. There would need to be careful co-ordination across all groups; for example, the transition of students

---

3   Simply moving people into the same organisation would offer no guarantees of a better hand-over between policy and implementation. The new organisation would need to be properly structured and managed.

4   See p. 163.

between primary schools to secondary schools, and from secondary schools into tertiary organisations, would need to be managed properly.

Each group would employ specialist *high-quality* policy analysts and implementers with detailed knowledge of the sector (e.g. secondary education), who would ensure that policy development and implementation processes informed each other and that a substantive evaluation process was put in place for all reforms.[5]

The second new agency

The second new agency should be built around the current ERO and NZQA audit and review functions. This agency must be an independent statutory body, with the ability to work outside the influence of the Minister. The function of this agency would be to review and report on the quality of teaching in individual schools and non-university tertiary institutions. The agency would be expected, through its audit/review process, to identify and highlight weaknesses in the education system and to make recommendations to government to address these weaknesses.

In so doing, it should also be charged with carrying out robust and significant evaluations of major educational reforms, in conjunction with the Ministry of Education. These evaluations would be established and put in place as part of the initial implementation of the reform so that benchmark data and evaluation methodologies can be agreed.

To ensure that evaluation metrics are built into future reforms, it is vitally important that Ministers and chief executives clearly understand and state the *purpose* of the reform and its expected impacts. It is only when the purpose is clear that an evaluation process can be developed. If a reform is fuzzy in its intention, this will become obvious as the evaluation process is developed. Without clear purposes it will be

---

5 The current prevailing view from senior officials in the Ministry of Education is that there is a need for people who have strategic thinking abilities and people skills, and who understand change management, rather than people who have a detailed understanding of schooling and education. There is some justification in this orthodox view, especially at the most senior levels of leadership. People can learn or be told about the workings of secondary schools, but they cannot so easily be taught the high-level soft skills of people/change management and strategic thinking. Unfortunately, in reality this approach does not work well: policy makers and implementers who are not immersed in, and do not have a detailed understanding of the sector they are changing, can easily miss the point and not even understand what the right questions to ask are. Although these officials might consult and set up advisory groups to help them, there is often no real substitute for *deep knowledge* of education and schooling. The people who have this knowledge not only have more credibility with a suspicious workforce, they also know intuitively what the right questions to ask are.

difficult to establish a proper evaluation. In such circumstances, further policy development and clarification of purposes *before* the reform is implemented would become necessary.

The current ERO has begun this sort of work already, with a range of reports on national matters of educational interest. However, these reports have not really focused on the evaluation of large-scale reform. Rather, they have made some judgements about how parts of the existing education system are working. For example, in 2013 the ERO reports ranged from *Use of Equity Funding in PI Early Childhood Centres* to *Mathematics in Years 4–8* (Education Review Office, n.d).

This new agency would also be charged with reviewing the effectiveness of the new Ministry of Education, in consultation with the State Services Commission. Currently, reviewing the performance of all ministries has been solely the responsibility of the State Services Commission. However, given this agency will be responsible for evaluating reforms to the system, it would seem sensible for it also to be responsible for reviewing the agency responsible for putting the reforms into place.

Though relatively small, the proposed new agency would wield significant influence in the sector because of its independence and its ability to critique government, the Ministry of Education and the reform process.

The government must change the way schools are structured and reduce their number

Problems do not exist in the central public services alone. Educational reforms have often been stymied at the school level. Small secondary schools (those with fewer than 700 students), particularly in isolated and/or disadvantaged areas, find it difficult to provide a broad curriculum, are less likely to be able to recruit capable board members, principals and teachers, and as a consequence are less likely to be able to implement and sustain educational reforms. Some of the problems they have had in implementing the new curriculum, for example, and in providing resources for developing better NCEA vocational pathways for senior students, have arisen because of their small size.

Size is not the only issue. The impact of the qualifications delivery which secondary schools are responsible for, including NCEA and

Chapter 17: Ensure that reform is well planned, implemented, evaluated and supported

vocational pathways, often gets in the way of the delivery of *The New Zealand Curriculum* in the junior years and has an unnecessary washback effect. This can cause teachers to become too narrow and qualifications focused too early.

In order to address these issues, junior colleges, catering for students from Years 7–10, should be established by closing down intermediate schools and reorganising secondary schools (see below). These colleges would be relatively large and independent of the constraints of the NCEA or external qualifications. They would be built around an integrated approach to knowledge and competencies, based on learning areas/subjects that would reflect the philosophy of the current curriculum. The new junior colleges would be required to have a major focus on literacy and numeracy, but would offer and support a wider range of subject options (within learning areas) than many smaller secondary schools can offer at the moment.

The junior colleges might be required to report against National Standards, which would need to be developed for Years 9 and 10 and build on the current standards, which do not go beyond Year 8.[6]

Ideally, none of these assessment data would be made public. However, schools would be encouraged to collect and validate data themselves, in consultation with Ministry of Education regional offices. A sampling approach to achievement data across learning areas based on the NEMP[7] could be put in place to monitor performance on a national basis. The Ministry of Education, working with its regional offices, would take responsibility for ensuring that changes/reforms that may need to be made as a result of an analysis of data from both the Year 8/9 literacy and numeracy standards and the sampling across learning areas are properly developed, implemented and reviewed.

Full-immersion, Māori-medium junior colleges should also be established where feasible.

Senior colleges, catering for students from Year 11 to Year 13, should

---

6 The use of existing National Standards and the development of new ones would need to be predicated on the assumption that proper moderation processes are put in place. Junior colleges could use this national literacy and numeracy data to report their value add, based on the profile of the intake at Year 7 compared with the profile at exit in Year 10. Schools could also be required to report against the requirements of *The New Zealand Curriculum*, including the competencies.

7 National Education Monitoring Project, now reorganised and referred to as NMSSA (National Monitoring Study of Student Achievement).

be established to complement the new junior colleges.[8] Senior colleges would be created by amalgamating the remaining smaller secondary schools as the new junior colleges are established. These colleges would deliver both academic and vocationally based qualifications. A great advantage of these senior colleges would be that they could, because of their relatively large size, offer a wide range of both academic and vocational programmes, in association with tertiary providers—something that existing smaller secondary schools cannot do. It will be likely that in urban areas where there is more than one senior college, each could specialise in particular subjects or pathways, including full-immersion, Māori-medium programmes.

Senior colleges would need to work closely with tertiary institutions if they exist in their area. Current 'vocational' programmes in the senior secondary school, such as Gateway and Youth Guarantees, would continue. Where there are no local tertiary institutions, the colleges would be encouraged to develop specialist tertiary provisions brokered by Ministry of Education regional offices, in consultation with interested remote tertiary providers.

It is important to be clear here: implementing these proposals will *reduce* the total number of schools and *increase* the size of many of the remaining schools. Some international research suggests that small schools are not necessarily a bad thing: in fact, small schools (around 400 to 600) can work better than large schools. According to this research, students in smaller schools may feel they *belong* and are known by their teachers, and as a result may emerge from the experience with better achievement and a more positive attitude. The problem with small schools in New Zealand (where there is very limited research about this issue), however, is that they have to operate as Crown entities in our highly devolved and competitive environment. Their ability, particularly in disadvantaged areas (as has already been suggested), to find capable boards of trustees is limited, as is their ability to access quality principals, staff and resources.

Reducing the total number of schools will mean there will be better opportunities to elect more capable boards and principals and resource

---

8 A small number of junior and senior colleges already exist in New Zealand and could provide a good model for the rest of the country; for example, Albany Senior High School and Albany Junior High School.

Chapter 17: Ensure that reform is well planned, implemented, evaluated and supported

them adequately. The Ministry of Education and other agencies will also have the opportunity to focus their support on fewer schools through a reinvigorated regional structure.

Another very important advantage of such an approach, with fewer schools, is that it could encourage better mixing of students across socioeconomic groups. This could be very critical in addressing the school apartheid that currently operates in New Zealand, which sees huge numbers of Māori and Pasifika students banished to lower-decile schools.[9]

The difficulties involved in carrying out changes to the organisation of government education agencies and schools suggested above are likely to be huge. Making the change will require immense political courage, meticulous policy analysis and very careful planning. It will certainly need to be a gradual process, which will require substantial consultation and trialling. Of course, trials could produce other innovative solutions to some of the problems that have been identified in this book. For example, it may be that in some areas it is simply not possible, given the distances involved, to set up junior and senior colleges. This may encourage stakeholders to consider establishing just one board and one management structure for several schools in an area. Such boards might cater for students from early childhood education right through to Year 13 and attract more and better-quality teachers. Another option currently finding favour with politicians is establishing (larger) secondary schools that cater for Years 7–13 (rather than Years 9–13).

Readers will note that that no suggestion has been made to do away with the current Tomorrow's Schools model, despite its obvious problems. In my opinion it is far too late to do this and it is certainly not necessary to return to the top-down centralised system of old. Many New Zealand schools, it is clear, have relished and taken advantage of the flexibility it has to offer. However, by building a stronger regional structure for the Ministry of Education, by reorganising schooling provision and by reducing and reorganising government education agencies it is possible to make it work better.

---

[9] I accept that such a change would be major and require substantial investment in better transport links, especially in low-population and isolated areas. However, this may well be a vital investment in the long-term social and economic fabric of the nation.

The school decile system

There has been some debate over the years about the use of the decile system in New Zealand. The potential misuse of the system has been already been discussed in this book (see Chapter 5). Some commentators and principals argue that it should be done away with because it labels schools and provides excuses for teachers to justify poor performance. The ERO decision not to publish decile ratings in their reports was essentially a political ploy to make this point.

But all this is mainly nonsense. The argument that teachers can overcome socioeconomic factors, as reflected in the decile rating of a school, is not without its attractions. It can be done, to some extent, as has already been explained. However, the fact remains that the correlation between school decile and school performance is very high. That there is a connection between deprivation and poor educational achievement is clear and unchallengeable. It would be a brave person who would argue that there is no causal link. As has already been argued in this book, if we want to address issues of underachievement in New Zealand, we need to address the issues of increasing disparity in income and wealth. This is what creates the educational problem that teachers are required to address.

Doing away with the decile system would provide an opportunity to deny this link. It would allow government and government officials to continue to expect teachers in schools that are dealing with enormous problems to fix these problems with a lesson plan, despite the fact that the problems have been created by misguided and wretched economic and social policies over many decades.

The system could be tweaked to ensure it is not so badly misused. For example, it may be that we do not need 10 deciles but only five categories, especially given the development of larger junior and senior colleges as suggested above. Alternatively it may even be that we do not assign a number. Instead, schools could be profiled with a full and detailed description of the main characteristics of their intake.

However, some form of decile rating or profile is important so that the community can understand what teachers are dealing with and, more importantly, appropriate funding is provided. It is probably true to say that the public does not fully understand how the decile system works and that the system does have a labelling effect. However, if we are to provide additional funding for schools that have particularly significant problems to address, we will need some way of allocating this funding. Whatever system we use, will, in the end, become and provide the label.

Bulk funding of teachers' salaries and resourcing

If the basic building blocks of self-managing and self-governing schools are to stay in place, as has been suggested above, it makes little sense *not* to bulk fund secondary schools, particularly if the proposed junior/senior college organisational model is adopted. For readers who are not familiar with this issue, here is a brief explanation.

Boards are currently provided with an *operational grant* with which to run the school. This money cannot be used to pay entitlement teaching staff because these teaching staff are paid directly by the Ministry of Education. Schools are given a staffing entitlement based largely on their roll number and decile rating. Although schools now do have a little flexibility here, in that they can bank staffing,[10] they cannot use their government operational grant to pay teachers. Likewise, since they are not actually given the dollars to pay teachers, they cannot use teacher salary funds to pay for operational matters such as computers, maintenance and ancillary non-teaching staff.

Bulk funding, which was famously and notoriously tried in schools in the early 1990s, allows for the cashing up of staff salaries and the combining of this money with the operational grant. This combined grant therefore provides the school with one bulk grant to use at its discretion. Boards would then have the flexibility, not currently available, to *choose* to pay fewer staff and use the money to buy more computers, or vice versa.

How bulk funding is delivered is a highly contentious issue, since teachers are paid at different rates depending on their years of service. At what rate are salaries to be cashed up?[11] What is to prevent the

---

10 Schools can "bank" staffing allowing them to overuse or underuse their staffing allocation, within limits, over a specified period of time, so long as the end result balances.

11 The issue here is simple enough. If a school has say 10 teachers on different rates of pay because some are more experienced than others, at what rate does the government "cash up" these salaries in the bulk grant to be delivered to the school? There are variety of options, some of which were tried in the 1990s, which we do not need to delve into here. Whatever formula is chosen for the cash up, it will tend to result in what has become known as "winner" and "loser" schools.

government simply reducing the grant in tough times, thus effectively cutting staffing? What impact, if any, would this have on the collective contract for teachers?

These are all legitimate and sensible questions and could probably be worked through if the negotiating parties (the government, Ministry of Education and the unions) felt they could trust each other. However, the massive negative response to bulk funding from the PPTA in the 1990s showed clearly that there was no basis for trust at the time. Possibly there still isn't.

Nevertheless, I want to make clear that there is nothing intrinsically wrong with bulk funding. Rosehill College adopted bulk funding when I was principal in the 1990s. Although the first 6 months was not easy, given the loss of goodwill I encountered from the staff, the fact of the matter is that I was able to better manage the school because I had access to *all* the funds that were available. Within a year, most staff, and the community of the college, could clearly see the benefits.[12]

Fears expressed by the PPTA that it is a Trojan horse for the privatisation of schools and that it creates winner/loser schools are illogical. If any Government wishes to cut staffing or wishes to attack the collective contract, it is unlikely they will use bulk funding as the hidden route. They will simply do it. For example, the current Government has gone ahead with charter schools, public private partnership (PPP) schools and National Standards despite vehement opposition from the teacher unions and relatively weak support from the New Zealand public.

The winner/loser school argument is difficult to comprehend. Whatever funding mechanism we use, including the current one, favours some schools at the expense of others. There is no funding formula that does not do this. If schools were to be bulk funded, there would need to be a way of calculating how much money the government will hand over. A staffing formula will need to be agreed and, yes, inevitably this formula may well create some winner and loser schools. It will be up to principals to work within the funding they have. Presumably this is no different from any chief executive running any enterprise of any kind.

---

12 It is true that Rosehill College was a so-called "winner school" under the prevailing funding formula, but I am totally convinced that the benefit was in the flexibility made possible to use available dollars, and not the total number of dollars available.

The benefit of bulk funding is that it provides schools with the flexibility to spend their money in a way that meets their needs. If we are to retain the philosophy of Tomorrow's Schools, then bulk funding is a necessary part of that philosophy.

This is a particularly important issue for the proposed new senior colleges, which may well want to use their staffing in a variety of non-traditional ways. Some senior colleges, for example, may opt for a lecture approach, with a combination of teachers and teacher assistants (not teachers) to follow up with tutorials. Junior colleges may also want to explore IT learning resources and delivery, as opposed to teacher-fronted classroom resourcing. The variations are endless, and schools need to be provided with a funding mechanism that will work for them. The current funding model is inflexible and actually inhibits innovation.

Concluding comments

It is important that policy is properly developed. This means we need highly skilled policy analysts and officials capable of giving full, free and frank advice. Once policy has been developed, it is vital that the implementation is properly managed by a regional or mediating layer. As part of this implementation process, it is important that all major reform is trialled before a full roll-out. Evaluation processes should be built into the reform process at the outset, which should include the collection of benchmark data.

The Ministry of Education and other educational agencies are not currently structured to be able to do what is required. In order to carry out its functions properly, the present government educational agencies should be reduced to just two. A new, enlarged, Ministry of Education should be responsible for policy and implementation nationally and regionally, organised on the basis of four groups—early childhood education, primary, secondary, and tertiary, each with a chief executive and each staffed with experts who understand the sector they are working in. This will ensure there is a clear focus on policy, implementation and evaluation in each sector, and that reporting and accountability lines are crystal clear. The regional presence of the new Ministry of Education should be increased substantially to provide the required mediating layer to ensure reform is successful.

The other newly created agency, independent of the Minister, should be responsible for audit and review of the schools and non-university tertiary institutions, as well as of the Ministry of Education (along with the State Services Commission). This agency should also have responsibility for ensuring that evaluation of all reform is carried out and the results of that evaluation are acted upon.

The school sector should be reorganised, gradually, so that junior and senior colleges are established. This will ensure fewer schools, better-quality boards and greater mixing of students across socioeconomic groups. It should encourage better implementation of the curriculum and increased choices for students.

The decile system could be made more useful and less blunt in a variety of ways, but it should be retained because it signals the importance of socioeconomic status in determining student learning outcomes. Governments must not be allowed to place all the fixing at the feet of long-suffering teachers. The reintroduction of bulk funding would provide these new schools with the flexibility they will need to maximise the opportunities that will be created for them

End note

A number of proposals have been made in this book. They have been developed to address the deep-seated problems faced by our educators, which were examined in Parts 1 to 3. However, it is important that we do not fall into the same traps that have been the subject of this book. Therefore, if adopted, all of the proposals should be put through a stringent policy formulation process, and they should also be trialled and evaluated properly. If some are shown to be problematic, they should be dispensed with and replaced.

Many of the proposals will be politically challenging. Establishing a value add measure (VAM), closing and reorganising schools, changing how we select, train and pay teachers and principals, redesigning how teachers access their professional development, taking the current Ministry of Education and other education agencies apart and rebuilding them, reinventing a mediating layer, reintroducing bulk funding, and altering the teachers' collective agreement will not be for the faint hearted.

This cannot be a piecemeal process. We need a package of carefully designed measures that are sustained over more than one electoral cycle—probably more like three—if we are to be successful in not only closing the disparity of achievement in New Zealand but in transforming our education system from being good to being outstanding and world beating.

No reform will be successful without a reasonable level of teacher buy in. It is important that teachers be encouraged and challenged to see the possibilities here, and to engage in constructive problem solving, even if this means a period of tension and disagreement. The key message to our teachers should be that they are hugely valued and critically important, and will be treated as such by government.

Index

A
academic subjects 89–91
accountability systems 73–4, 76–8, 146–7, 257
achievement
  disparity within schools 29–31
  and teaching quality 33–5, 210–3
Achievement 2001 94
achievement data 202–10, 214, 251
achievement data *see also* National Certificate of Educational Achievement (NCEA)
achievement standards 94–5, 100, 104, 112–3, 113, 137–9
  and 2007 curriculum 123, 124–6, 133–4
Achievement-based Assessment (ABA) 93, 118
Administering for Excellence (Picot Report) 74
age-specific assessment *see* National Standards
Asian students 12, 21–22
assessment 88–91, 101, 128–9, 205–6
  internal (school-based) 90–1, 92, 95, 99–100, 101, 102, 104, 111
  norm-based 89–91
  resources 95, 99, 113–4, 116–7, 151, 221
  standards-based 89, 91–3, 93, 94–5, 107, 108, 163
assessment *see also* National Standards
Association of Effective Schools 38
asTTLe tests 128–9, 205
  e-asTTLe 136
Auckland University research 27, 132
Auditor General 106

B
Benson-Pope, David 103
Best Evidence Synthesis (BES) research programme 46
Black, Paul 110
boards of trustees 74, 77–8, 80, 85, 121–2, 252
  as employers 175, 190, 228, 238–9, 243–4
  and funding 255
Bourdieu, Pierre 24–6, 27, 28
bulk funding 255–7
Business Roundtable 108

C
Cambridge International examination 115, 195, 209
Careers New Zealand 247
Coleman, James 38, 39
Columbia University 34
Committee of Inquiry into Curriculum Assessment and Qualifications 93, 108
community education forums 75, 83
Creech, Wyatt 94
cultural capital 24–8

D

deciles 15–23, 208, 254–5
  and ERO visits 63, 63–6, 64
  and ethnicity 21, 21–2
  and NCEA 10–11, 11, 58
  perceptions 80–1, 115
  and student population 20
  within-decile comparisons 56–8, 69
deciles *see also* low-decile schools

E

Easton, Brian 9, 30
Economist, The 34–5
education agencies, proposed 247–50
education reform 36–7, 71–2, 155, 164–5
Education Review Office (ERO) 43–5, 61–6, 78, 212, 249, 250
  frequency of visits by decile 63–4
  methodology 67–9
Education, Department of 74, 85, 170
Education, Minister of 151–2, 158–60, 167, 244, 246–7
  and Ministry 159–60
Education, Ministry of 74, 77, 163–4, 165–7, 168–9, 248–50
  devolution of 76, 160–1
  and National Standards 145–50
  and NCEA 99–100, 115–7, 137, 138
  policy development 156–63, 162–3
  regional offices 161, 174, 222–3, 248
  research 46–7, 85, 110, 132, 137
  reviewed 156, 169–70
  School Smart 210
Education, Secretary of 120, 167, 248
effective school movement 38–40
employment contracts 75, 188, 230, 232

ERO *see* Education Review Office
ethics 60, 193–5, 244
ethnicity 9–10, 12, 21, 21–22, 225–6
European/Pākehā students 12, 12–13, 21–22
examinations *see also* National Certificate of Educational Achievement
examinations, external 96, 97, 105, 106
  international 115, 195, 209
  rationale 88–90
  scaling 60, 88, 103
excellence units (EUs) 233–4

F

Finland 199, 202–3
Friedman, John 34–5
Fullan, Michael 236
funding 18–19
  bulk 255–7

G

Gateway 252
Goldstein, Harvey 7, 8

H

Harvard University 34–5
Hattie, John 50–3, 211
How the World's Most Improved School Systems Keep Getting Better 203

I

intermediate schools 251
International Baccalaureate 115
international students 19, 21, 21–22
Irwin Report 108

J
junior colleges 251

K
kōhanga reo 27
Kotahitanga programme 225
Kreiner, Svend 6, 8

L
Lange, David 73–4, 83
leadership 115–7, 137–9, 151–2,
    165–6, 169, 187
  principals and 85–6, 114–5, 196,
    236–7, 239–41
    instructional 41, 189–90
  league tables 143–4, 148, 152, 192,
    202–3, 207, 214
    international 1, 5, 8, 48
  literacy and numeracy *see* National
    Standards 153
Lough Report 85
low-decile schools 37, 65, 79–81, 153,
    172–3
  and ERO 66–7
  proposals 253
  staffing 192, 227–8, 234–5

M
MacLeans College 19
Maharey, Steve 103
Mallard, Trevor 112
management units (MUs) 180, 233–4
Māori students 26–7, 81, 192–3,
    224–6, 253
  achievement data 4, 9, 12, 12–3,
    37
  and deciles 21, 21–22
  strategies 61–2, 73–4, 174, 251–2
Marshall, Russell 93

Martin, Doug 163
Marzano, R 32–4, 47, 199
Massey University research 9, 204
McKinsey and Company report 161,
    203, 248
MECI study 132
Middle Eastern, Latin American and
    African (MELA) students 21–22
Ministerial Task Force on Secondary
    Teacher Remuneration 181
Ministry of Education *see* Education,
    Ministry of
Morrison, Hugh 5
Mourshed report *see* McKinsey

N
NAME grading (NCEA) 98, 102, 106
National Administration Guidelines
    (NAGs) 76, 77
National Certificate of Educational
    Achievement (NCEA) 88–94,
    98–9
  achievement data 10–13, 11, 12,
    56–8, 59–60, 59–61, 68–70,
    204–10, 209
  grading system 94, 98, 102–3
    endorsements 104
  implementation 99–103, 112–4,
    164
  moderation process 96–7, 146
  policy development 107–112
  reviewed 103–5, 114, 165
  school accreditation 96
National Education Guidelines
    (NEGs) 76
National Education Monitoring
    Project (NEMP) 213, 251
National Monitoring Study of Student
    Achievement (NMSSA) 213, 251

National Qualifications Framework
(NQF) 91–4, 108
National Standards 130–1, 142–8
  implementation of 148–53, 162–3, 165
  potential 205, 251
New Zealand
  international comparisons 28
New Zealand Council for Education
    Research (NZCER) 85, 106, 114, 132, 164, 213
New Zealand Curriculum (NZC) 10, 49, 120–2, 131–4, 251
  competencies and levels 126–30
  implementation of 135–41
  and National Standards 130–1, 142–3
  and NCEA 100, 104, 122–5
New Zealand Educational Institute
    (NZEI) 143–4
New Zealand Qualifications Authority
    (NZQA) 75, 106, 164, 247, 249
  Managing National Assessment
    (MNA) 97
  and Ministry of Education 137–8
  and NCEA 103–5, 111, 114–8, 136
    exemplars 130
    moderation system 96–7, 102, 146–7, 221–2
  Secondary Education Group
    (SEG) 116
New Zealand Qualifications Authority
    (NZQA) *see also* National
    Qualifications Framework
New Zealand Register of Quality
    Assured Qualifications (The
    Register) 92
New Zealand Teachers' Council 175, 228, 247
New Zealand Treasury 28, 29, 85, 156, 169

O

Ofqual 5
Organisation for Economic Co-
    operation and Development
    (OECD) 105
  PISA 4–9, 12, 13, 43, 206, 213
    data 3–4, 28–9, 30, 37, 202, 231

P

Pakuranga College 19
Papakura High School 18, 192–3
Parent Advocacy Council 75, 83
Pasifika students 174, 195, 224–6, 253
  achievement data 4, 12, 12–13
  and deciles 21, 21–2, 81
performance pay *see* teacher salaries
Picot Report 74–6, 82, 83
policy development 248, 249–50, 257–8
  advisers 246–7
  analysts 157–9, 249
  implementation 160, 247–50
Post Primary Teachers' Association
    (PPTA) 74, 93, 139, 163, 172, 177, 201, 256
  Principals' Council (PC) 114, 187–8
  Qualifications Framework
    Inquiry 108
  and teacher performance 178–9, 181, 186, 232, 234
Prime Minister, Office of 156, 169
principals 85–6, 190–2, 241–5

appointments 75, 240–1
    performance 238–9
    ethics 192–5, 244
    and leadership 114–5, 178–9, 188–9, 196, 236–7, 239–41
    and National Standards 152
Principals' Council (PC) 114, 187–8
principals' organisations see also Principal's Council, Secondary Principals Association 243–4
professional development (PD) 170–4, 220–4, 229
    Māori/Pasifika 224–6
    for principals 191
    subject-based 220–1, 222, 226
Profiles of Expected Performance (PEPs) 105
programme manipulation 194, 210
Progress and Consistency Tool (PaCT) 151
Progressive Achievement Test (PAT) 68, 205, 206

Q

Qualifications Framework Inquiry *(Te Tiro Hou)* 108
Queen's University, Belfast 5

R

Rasch Model 7
Rata, Elizabeth 27
Recognising Achievement 111
Record of Achievement (ROA) 103
Record of Learning (RoL) 94, 99, 101
regional qualifications 60
Register of Quality Assured Qualifications, New Zealand 92
remedial needs students 209
Rockoff, Jonah 34–5

Rosehill College 19, 192–3, 256

S

Sahlberg, Pasi 199
Sankar and Chauvel review 171–2, 173
scaling 60, 88, 103
Schleicher, A 7
Scholarship exam 103
School Certificate 60, 88, 91
school effectiveness movement 38–42
school funding 18, 75
school holidays
    and teacher workload 228–31
school roll by decile and ethnicity 2012 21
School Smart 210
School Support Services 170–2
schools 30–5, 43–6, 61–3, 67–70, 74
    comparisons between 56–8
    competitiveness 192–5
    NCEA accreditation 96–7
    restructuring proposals 250–3
    underperforming 215, 222
schools, see also low-decile schools
Scottish Qualification Framework 108
Secondary Education Group (SEG) 116
Secondary Principals' Association of New Zealand (SPANZ) 16, 112, 114–5, 187–8
senior colleges proposal 251–2
Sewell, Karen 77, 120
Singapore 224
Sixth Form Certificate 88, 91, 93, 95
Smith, Lockwood 91
Snook, Ivan 204
socioeconomic status (SES) 4, 13–4, 25, 30, 32, 199–201, 225–6, 253

and achievement 9, 10, 27–32, 28, 33, 36–7
and decile 16–18, 65, 254
SPANZ *see* Secondary Principals' Association of New Zealand
standards-based assessment *see* assessment
State Services Commission 103, 116, 156, 169–70, 250, 258
Stoop, Graham 66
student achievement 33–7, 79–82, 199, 213
  advisers 153
Student Achievement Function 77, 78, 174–5, 222–3
student achievement *see also* achievement data
student assessment *see* assessment; National Standards
student numbers 20, 21
student retention rates 208–10
students, international 19, 21, 21–22
students, remedial needs 209

T

Taranaki Maths Certificate 60
Te Tiro Hou Qualifications Framework Inquiry 108
teacher
  competence 177–9, 226–8, 227–8
  payscales 179–81, 181, 231–3, 234–5
    performance-based 76, 179–81, 204, 232–5, 233–4, 233–5
  qualifications 216–8
  workload 102, 175, 182–4, 228–31
Teacher Registration Board 75
teacher support 86, 139–40, 170–5, 174–5

subject-based 221, 226
teacher training 171, 218–20, 221–2
teachers 32–5, 48–52, 118–9
  and extracurricular activities 185–6
  and leadership 236–8
  Ministry tasks 94–5, 112–3
  specialist 181, 223–4
Teachers' Council 175, 228, 247
teaching 47–8, 51–2, 185–6
  inquiry model 49–50
teaching and learning 117–9, 139–40, 153
Teaching and Learning Guides 125
teaching quality 46–7, 52–4, 186, 210–3, 212, 226, 235
teaching schools 219–20
Tertiary Education Commission 162, 247
tertiary institutions 221–2, 252
TIMSS tests 6
Tomorrow's Schools 73–6, 78–9, 82–6, 87, 117, 162, 164–5, 253, 256
Treasury *see* New Zealand Treasury
Trends in Mathematical and Science Study (TIMSS) tests 6

U

Uniservices 129
unit standards 92–3, 94, 100–1, 104, 110, 194
United States Office of Education 38
University Bursary exam 60, 88, 91
University Entrance 93
University of Bristol 7
University of Copenhagen 6
University of Otago 213
University of Waikato 132

V

value added measure (VAM) 204–7, 211–3, 259
Visible Learning 50–3
vocational pathways *see also* unit standards 57, 90–1, 99, 109, 250, 252

W

Wylie, C 77, 79, 84

Y

Youth Guarantees 252

Z

zoning 75, 83

References

Alcorn, N., & Thrupp, M. (2011). A little knowledge being a dangerous thing?: Decile-based aproaches to developing NCEA league tables. *New Zealand Annual Review of Education*, 20, 67–68.

Alton-Lee, A. (2003). *Quality Teaching for Diverse Students in Schooling: Best Evidence Synthesis Iteration (BES)*, pp. vi–xi. Wellington: Ministry of Education.

Association of Effective schools. (2013, December). Retrieved from Association of Effective schools Inc: www.mes.org/esr.html

Bazley, M. (2003). *Ministerial taskforce on secondary teacher remumeration*. Retrieved from ppta.org.nz.

Bishop, R., Berryman, M. & Wearmouth, J. (2014). *Te Kotahitanga: Towards effective education reform for indigenous and other minoritised students*. Wellington: NZCER Press.

Bishop, R., O'Sullivan, D. & Berryman, M. (2010). *Scaling Up Education Reform*. Wellington: NZCER Press.

Black, P. (2001). *Report to the QDG of the Ministry of Education, NZ, for the development of the National Certificate of Educational Achievement*. Wellington: Ministry of Education.

Controller and Auditor General. (2012). *New Zealand Qualifications Authority: Assuring the consistency and quality of internal assessment for NCEA*. Wellington: Controller and Auditor General NZ.

Department of Education. (1986). *Learning and Achieving*. Wellington: Author.

Easton, B. (2013a). *Ethnicity, Gender, Socioeconomic Status and Educational Achievement: An Exploration*. Wellington: PPTA. Retrieved from www.eastonbh.ac.nz/2013/07/ethnicity-gender-socioeconomic-status-and-educational-achievement-an-exploration/

Easton, B. (2013b). *Economic Inequality in New Zealand: a User's Guide: Key Points*. Retrieved from www.eastonbh.ac.nz/2013/12/economic-inequality-in-new-zealand-a-users-guide-key-points/

Education Review Office. (2010). *Preparing to Give Effect to the New Zealand Curriculum*. Retrieved from www.ero.govt.nz/National-Reports/Preparing-to-Give-Effect-to-the-New-Zealand-Curriculum-June-2010/Findings/School-leaders-preparations-for-giving-effect-to-The-New-Zealand-Curriculum

Education Review Office. (2011). *Evaluation at a Glance: What ERO Knows About Effective Schools.* Wellington: Author.

Education Review Office. (2012). *Burnside High School review.* Wellington: ERO.

Education Review Office. (2013). *Criteria for Timing Decisions.* Retrieved from www.ero.govt.nz/Review-Process/Criteria-for-Timing-Decisions

Education Review Office. (2014). *ERO's Framework for School Reviews.* Retrieved from www.ero.govt.nz/Review-Process/Frameworks-and-Evaluation-Indicators-for-ERO-Reviews/Framework-for-School-Reviews/ERO-s-Conceptual-Framework-for-School-Reviews#1

Education Review Office. (n.d). *2013 National Reports.* Retrieved from www.ero.govt.nz/National-Reports/(year)/2013

Educational Leaders. (2013). *Educational Leaders.* Retrieved from www.educationalleaders.govt.nz/Leadership-development/Leadership-programmes/NAPP-2013

Fullan, M. A. (1996). *What's worth fighting for in your school?* New York: Teachers College Press.

Hattie, J. (2012). Visible Learning for Teachers: Maximizing Impact. In J. Hattie, *Visible Learning for Teachers: Maximizing Impact.* London: Routledge.

Hipkins, R. (2012). *NCEA: One Decade On.* Wellington: New Zealand Council for Educational Research.

Hughes, P. (2013). *Criticisms of maths skills don't add up.* Retrieved from www.nzherald.co.nz/nz/news/article.cfm?c_id=1&objectid=10873571

Johnston, M. (2013). Dr. (B. Haque, Interviewer)

Lee, H., & Lee, G. (2001). *The National Certificate of Educational Achievement (NCEA): "Fragile:Handle with Care".* New Zealand Annual Review of Education,10, 5–38.

Martin, D. (2005). *Report on the Performance of the New Zealand Qualifications Authority in the Delivery of Secondary School Qualifications.* Wellington: State Services Commission.

Marzano, R. (2000). *A New Era of School Reform: Going Where The Research Takes Us.* Aurora, CO: McREL.

Marzano, R. (2003). *What works in schools: Translating research into action.* Alexandria, VA: Association for Supervision and Curriculum Development.

Ministry of Education. (2007a). *Teaching as inquiry*. Retrieved from tki: nzcurriculum.tki.org.nz.

Ministry of Education. (2007b). *The New Zealand Curriculum*. Retrieved from TKI: http://nzcurriculum.tki.org.nz/Curriculum-documents/The-New-Zealand-Curriculum/Foreword.

Ministry of Education. (2007c). *Requirements for Boards of Trustees*. Retrieved from New Zealand Curriculum Online: http://nzcurriculum.tki.org.nz/curriculum-documents/Thee-New-Zealand/Requirements-for Baords-of-Trustees.

Ministry of Education. (2009a). *How the decile is calculated*. Retrieved from www.minedu.govt.nz/NZEducation/EducationPolicies/Schools/SchoolOperations/Resourcing/OperationalFunding/Deciles/HowTheDecileIsCalculated.aspx

Ministry of Education. (2009b). *National Standards and the NZC*. Retrieved from TKI: http://nzcurriculum.tki.org.nz/National-Standards/Key-information/Fact-sheets/National-Standards-and-the-NZC.

Ministry of Education. (2010). *Welcome to the Board of Trustees section: Accessing data about your school*. Retrieved from www.minedu.govt.nz/Boards/ManagingResources/AccessingSchoolData.aspx

Ministry of Education. (2011). *Implementation of the New Zealand Curriculum: Synthesis of Research & Evaluation*. Retrieved from www.educationcounts.govt.nz/publications/curriculum/implementation-of-the-new-zealand-curriculum-synthesis-of-research-and-evaluation/2.-schools-readiness-to-use-the-new-zealand-curriculum-to-develop-a-school-curriculum

Ministry of Education. (2013a). *The National Education Guidelines* . Retrieved from www.minedu.govt.nz/theMinistry/EducationInNewZealand/EducationLegislation/TheNationalEducationGuidelinesNEGs.aspx

Ministry of Education. (2013b). *Key Competencies.* Retrieved from http://keycompetencies.tki.org.nz/Monitoring

Ministry of Education. (2014a). *Senior secondary teaching and learning Guides*. Retrieved from http://seniorssecondary.tki.org,nz

Ministry of Education. (2014b). *Welcome to e-asTTle*. Retrieved from http://e-asttle.tki.org.nz/

Ministry of Education. (2014c). *Meet the Ministry of Education's leadership team*. Retrieved from www.minedu.govt.nz/theMinistry/AboutUs/

LeadershipTeam/LeadershipTeam.aspx

Morrison, D. H. (2013). *TES: Why the PISA league tables could be faulty.* Retrieved from http://paceni.wordpress.com/tag/dr-hugh-morrison-queens-university-belfast/

Mourshed, M., Chijioke, C., & Barber (2010). *How the World's most improved school systems keep getting better.* McKinsey and Company. Retrieved from http://www.mckinsey.com/client_service/social_sector/latest_thinking/worlds_most_improved_schools

New Zealand Law Society. (2012). *New Zealand Law society/Momentum Legal Salary survey.* Retrieved from http://my.lawsociety.org.nz

Nusche, D., Laveaulf, D., MacBeath, J., & Santiago, P. (2011). *OECD Reviews of Assessment and Evaluation.* Paris: OECD.

NZCER. (2013). *Impact of Education Reforms.* Retrieved from www.nzcer.org.nz/research/impact-education-reforms

NZQA. (2014). *Annual Report on NCEA and New Zealand Scholarship Data and Statistics.* Wellington: Author.

OECD. (2009). *Programme for International Student Assessment (PISA): About PISA.* Retrieved from www.oecd.org/pisa/aboutpisa/

OECD. (2010). *Pisa at A Glance: Overcoming Social background.* OECD Publishing.

OECD. (2011). *OECD Review of Evaluation and Assessmentin Education.* Retrieved from www.oecd.org/newzealand/49681441.pdf

OECD. (2012). *PISA 2012 Results: Excellence through Equity: Giving Every Student the Chance to Suceed. (Vol 11).* OECD Publishing. Retrieved from www.oecd.org/pisa/keyfindings/pisa-2012-results-volume-II.pdf

OECD. (2013). *Education at a Glance 2013: OECD indicators.* Paris: OECD Publishing.

Openshaw, R. (2007). *Evaluation of Te Kotahitanga—Phase 3.* Palmerston North: Massey University.

PPTA (2009). *Tomorrow's Schools—Yesterday's Mistake?* Wellington: Author.

PPTA (2013a). NZ Schools: The decile system. *Issues and organising seminar.* Wellington: PPTA.

PPTA. (2013b). Professional Learning and Development. *Annual Conference.* Wellington: PPTA.

PPTA. (2013c, December). *Secondary Teachers Collective contract.* Retrieved from ppta.org.nz/index.php/collective-agreements

PPTA. (2014). *Terms of Employment.* Retrieved from ppta.org.nz/collective-agreements/stca/89-part-three

Rata, E. (2011). The Unintended Outcomes of Institutionalising Ethnicity: The case of Maori Education in New Zealand. *Presentation to Department of Education, Cambridge University.* Cambridge, UK.

Robertson, R. H. (2011). *Moderation and Teacher Learning.* Wellington: New Zealand Council for Educational Reesearch.

Sahlberg, P. (2013, May 15). *The Answer sheet: What if Finland's great teachers taught in U.S. schools?* Retrieved from www.washingtonpost.com/blogs/answer-sheet/wp/2013/05/15/what-if-finlands-great-teachers-taught-in-u-s-schools-not-what-you-think/

Sankar, M., & Chauvel, F. (2011). *Provision of School Support Services-an evaluation.* Wellington: MartinJenkins & Associates.

Sargent, P. (2012). *Secondary Reviews.* Wellington: ERO.

Schagen, D. S. (2011). *Implementation of the New Zealand Curriculum: Synthesis of Research & Evaluation.* Retrieved from www.educationcounts.govt.nz/publications/curriculum/implementation-of-the-new-zealand-curriculum-synthesis-of-research-and-evaluation/1.-introduction

Schleicher, A. (2013). *tes connect:Attacks on Pisa are entirely unjustified.* Retrieved from www.tes.co.uk/article.aspx?storycode=6345213

Schmoker, M. (1999). *Results:The Key to Continuous School Improvement.* Alexandria VA: ASCD.

Secondary Principals Association of New Zealand. (2013). *About Us.* Retrieved from www.spanz.school.nz/Site/About_Us_2.ashx

Sewell, K. (2010, August 5). *Letter to all schools.* Retrieved from www.minedu.govt.nz/theMinistry/EducationInitiatives/StrengtheningStudentAchievement/LetterToSchools.aspx

Sinnema, C. (2010). *Monitoring and evaluating curriculum implementation: Final report to the Ministry of Education.* Auckland: The University of Auckland.

Snook, I., O'Neill, J., Church, J., & Rawlins, P. (2013). *The Assessment of Teacher Quality: An investigation into current issues in evaluating and rewarding teachers.* Palmerston North: Massey University.

State Services Commission. (2011). *Performance Improvement Frameworks Reports and Related Announcements.* Retrieved from www.ssc.govt.nz

Stewart, W. (2011, March 11). Ofqual says Pisa rankings should be viewed critically. *Times Educational Supplement.* Retrieved from https://www.tes.co.uk/article.aspx?storycode=6072565

Stewart, W. (2013, July 26). *Is Pisa fundamentally flawed?* Retrieved from www.tes.co.uk/article.aspx?storycode=6344672

Stoop, G. (2012, September 19). Decile ratings say nothing about school quality. *New Zealand Herald.* Retrieved from http://www.nzherald.co.nz/nz/news/article.cfm?c_id=1&objectid=10834904

Sullivan, A. (2002). Bourdieu and Education: How useful is Bordieu's theory for researchers? *The Netherlands Journal of Social Sciences*, 1–5.

Teach First NZ. (2013). *Our Programme.* Retrieved from www.teachfirstnz.org/programme/faqs

Teach NZ. (2013). *Teacher Study Awards.* Retrieved from www.teachnz.govt.nz/teacher-awards/directory/secondary-teachers/

Teddy, S. (2014). *Data request Decile funding; email exchange.* Wellington: Ministry of Education.

The Economist. (2013, October 12). *Knowledge for earnings' sake. Retrieved from http://www.economist.com/news/finance-and-economics/21587784-good-teachers-have-surprisingly-big-impact-their-pupils-future*

The New Zealand Treasury. (2012). *Treasury's Advice on Lifting Student Achievement in New Zealand: Evidence Brief.* Wellington: The Treasury.

Tzanakis, M. (2011). Bourdieu's Social Reproduction Thesis and the Role of Cultural Capital in Educational Attainment: A Critical Review of Key Empirical Studies. *Educate*, 76–90.

University of Otago. (2007). *About NEMP: An introduction to NEMP.* Retrieved from nemp.otago.ac.nz/_about.htm

Wilby, P. (2010, December 10). *Education's World Cup? Not exactly ... We'd do well to take our slice of the Pisa with a large pinch of salt.* Retrieved from www.tes.co.uk/article.aspx?storycode=6065654

Wylie, C. (2007). *What can New Zealand Learn from Edmonton?* Wellington: New Zealand Council for Educational Research.

Wylie, C. (2009). *Tomorrow's Schools after 20 years: can a system of self managing schools live up to its inital aims?* Wellington: Victoria University Press.

Wylie, C. (2012). *Vital Connections: Why we need more than self-managing schools.* Wellington: NZCER Press.

Further reading

Australian Curriculum and Reporting Authority (ACARA). (2013). *My School*. Retrieved from www.myschool.edu.au/

Careers NZ. (2013). *Who earns What*. Retrieved from www.careers.govt.nz/jobs-database/whats-happening-in-the-job-market/who-earns-what/

Crooks, T. (2005). *NCEA external assessment less consistent than internal*. Wellington: Royal Society of New Zealand.

Dalton, P., & Marcenaro-Guitierrez, O. (2011). LSE: British Politics and Society. If you pay peanuts, do you get monkeys? Paying teachers 10 per cent more results in 5-10 per cent higher pupil performance. Retrieved from http://blogs.lse.ac.uk/politicsandpolicy/pupil-performance/

Education Gazette. (2012, March 19). Receiving Support from the Student Achievement Function.Retrieved from http://www.edgazette.govt.nz/Articles/Article.aspx?ArticleId=8560

First Time Principals Programme. (2013, December). *First time Principals Programme*. Retrieved from www.firstprincipals.ac.nz/

Hattie, J. (2009). *Guest Lecture*. Retrieved www.treasury.govt.nz/publications/media-speeches/guestlectures/pdfs/tgls-hattie.pdf

Loveless, T. (2013). *Tom Loveless: Shanghai PISA Test Scores Almost Meaningless;Hukou a Factor*. Retrieved from www.brookings.edu/blogs/brookings-now/posts/2013/12/loveless-shangai-pisa-scores-almost-hukou-a-factor

Mail Online. (2012, September 14th). *Numbers failing doubles*. Retrieved from www.dailymail.co.uk/news/article-2203506/Numbers-failing-schools-doubles-Ofsted-crackdown-Four-told-improve-Gove-raises-bar.html

May, S., Cowles, S., & Lamy, M. (2012). *PISA 2012 NZ summary report*. Wellington: New Zealand Ministry of Education.

Ministry of Education. (2013). *The New Zealand Curriculum: The school curriculum: Design and Review*. Retrieved from nzcurriculum.tki.org.nz/Curriculum-documents/The-New-Zealand-Curriculum/The-school-curriculum-Design-and-review

Ministry of Education. (2013). *Strengthening Student achievement*. Retrieved from www.minedu.govt.nz/theMinistry/EducationInitiatives/StrengtheningStudentAchievement/

ProfessionalLearningAndDevelopment.aspx

Ministry of Education. (2013). *The National Administration Guidelines (NAGS)*. Retrieved from Ministry of Education: http://www.minedu.govt.nz/theMinistry/EducationInNewZealand/EducationLegislation/TheNationalAdministrationGuidelinesNAGs.aspx

Ministry of Education. (n.d). *Assessment on line:The New Zealand Curriculum Exemplars*. Retrieved from TKI: http://assessment.tki.org.nz/Assessment-tools-resources/The-New-Zealand-Curriculum-Exemplars

New Zealand Teachers' Council. (2013). *Competence Process*. Retrieved from www.teacherscouncil.govt.nz/content/conduct-competence/the-competence-process#process-step-1NZEI news 2010/20. (2014, June).

NZEI News. (2010). *National standardschecklist: Are they ready to implement?* Retrieved from Scribd: http://www.scribd.com/doc/34557285/NZEI-and-NS

Ofsted. (2013). *The framework for school inspection*. Retrieved from www.ofsted.gov.uk/resources/framework-for-school-inspection

Ofsted. (2014). *School Data Dashboard*. Retrieved from www.ofsted.gov.uk/resources/statistics/school-data-dashboard

Shepherd, J. (2010,). *Datablog: World education rankings: which country does best at reading, maths and science?* Retrieved from www.theguardian.com/news/datablog/2010/dec/07/world-education-rankings-maths-science-reading

Statistics New Zealand. (2013). *New Zealand in the OECD: Education*. Retrieved from www.stats.govt.nz/browse_for_stats/government_finance/central_government/nz-in-the-oecd/education.aspx

Thrupp, M. (2008, April). Secondary teaching, social contexts and the lingering politics of blame. *PPTA Professional Conference*. Auckland.

Thrupp, M. (2012). *Continuing pressures on secondary principals around school reputation*. Retrieved from nzspc.org.nz/nzspc-resources/20-what-s-worth-fighting-for-in-education-nzspc-conference-presentations

Wilby, P. (2013). *Finland's Education Ambassador spreads the word*. Retrieved from www.theguardian.com/education/2013/jul/01/education-michael-gove-finland-gcse

www.ingramcontent.com/pod-product-compliance
Lightning Source LLC
Chambersburg PA
CBHW081328230426
43667CB00018B/2869